THE LOBBYISTS

By James Deakin

PUBLIC AFFAIRS PRESS, WASHINGTON, D. C.

To My Parents

Published by Public Affairs Press
419 New Jersey Avenue, S.E., Washington 3, D. C.

Printed in the United States of America
Library of Congress Catalog Card No. 66-25663

INTRODUCTION

It must seem to anyone who has observed the workings of government in Washington over many years that what emerges in the form of news and commentary is like the exposed tip of the iceberg. What lies hidden under the murky waters of obfuscation and secrecy bulks far larger in volume and perhaps even in importance than the tip on which attention is focused. In no area is this so evident as in the complex and ever-increasing tangle of lobbying and the lobbyist. As government grows bigger and more directly involved in the economy, the question of who gets what, through the medium of the lobbyist as broker, is of paramount importance.

James Deakin is a reporter in the *St. Louis Post-Dispatch* tradition. In his 12 years in Washington, he has, in that tradition, worked hard to explore areas of the news too often obscured beneath the gaudy surface of the capital. He was one of the reporters instrumental in bringing the Sherman Adams-Bernard Goldfine story to light, with its sorry pattern of government favors doled out for petty rewards.

This book is in part the fruit of his persistent digging into the haystack of the lobbying industry. But it is more than that. It is a comprehensive inquiry into the practice of lobbying as it has come into being over the years. It is also, therefore, an anatomy of the relationship between the private and public sectors of our national life and the way in which the two interlock. That this makes for fascinating reading goes without saying.

It is by no means a muckraking book. On the contrary, it is a fair-minded study of a phenomenon that is certainly not all good and is surely not all bad. Not the least interesting part of the book is the history of the lobbies as they flourished in Mark Twain's gilded age after the Civil War. Sam Ward, brother of Julia Ward Howe, was a highly successful lobbyist in that era, the archetype of today's rich and flamboyant practitioner.

A flamboyant practitioner of today who figures in these pages

iii

is Charles Patrick Clark. His approach is more spectacular than that of the discreet lawyer-lobbyists with their big and usually undisclosed retainers from America's giant corporations. But he has been none the less successful in helping to obtain for his client, the government of Franco Spain, large sums in grants and loans from the federal treasury. As the author shows, Clark enlivens a craft that tends, as the stakes go up, to prefer discretion if not secrecy.

One of the great lobbying battles told in detail here was that waged by the American Telephone and Telegraph Corporation to gain control over the Telstar communications satellite, into which the goverment had put several hundred million dollars in research. The arena was the United States Senate. The combatants for A.T. AND T. were highly paid lawyers who trained their guns on wavering Senators. While the victory of America's largest corporation was never in doubt, the resistance of a handful of Senators kept the struggle in the public eye for a time. Putting this and other similar struggles between big business and government in proper focus is one of the significant contributions of the book.

The author recognizes the constructive role that lobbyists — not only lobbyists for causes they believe to be in the public good but lobbyists for private interests as well — often play. Even conscientious members of Congress are overwhelmed by a multitude of claims. They are asked to pass on issues involving the most complex matters, as science and technology play a more and more far-reaching part in our national life. The lobbyist in his beneficent role can help the lawmaker to sort out fact from fiction and guide him through the maze of proposed legislation that may affect the lives of millions of citizens.

How to separate the beneficent from the rapacious is a little matter that Congress has never seriously considered. The chapter on remedies deserves the sober consideration of those concerned with the subverting of the political process by the power of money. The author shows that present laws intended to regulate the practice of lobbying and stop the more flagrant abuses are farcical. They are so loosely drawn that they could hardly be enforced even if there was a determined effort to enforce them.

In short, this might well serve as a handbook for the conscientious Congressman who wants to do his duty and yet finds himself caught up in a multiplicity of claims. He will learn that while a conspicuous case such as that of Adams and Goldfine can make sensational headlines, the day-to-day lobbying that means large rewards for the lobbyist and the interests he represents goes on almost unnoticed. For that familiar stereotype, John Q. Citizen, the book should be a highly instructive lesson in the rudiments of how, the civics textbooks to one side, the country is actually governed.

MARQUIS CHILDS

PREFACE

The lives and well-being of individual citizens are affected by the activities of Washington lobbyists to a far greater extent than most Americans realize. As this book goes to press, lobbyists for special interest groups continue their unceasing battle against new proposals to advance the general welfare, to restore the nation's cities as decent places to live, to expand educational and economic opportunities for the underprivileged and to allocate America's material bounty more equitably. Lobbyists are working hard to prevent regulation of the interstate traffic in firearms and to block legislation protecting the consumer from hidden credit charges and misleading packaging. Lobbyists were also instrumental in delaying legislation to protect the public from dangerous drugs and to help the elderly meet the soaring cost of hospital and medical care.

The majority of Americans pay more taxes than they should because of special privileges arranged by lobbyists for wealthy individuals and powerful corporations. Congress feels the heat from automobile lobbyists when it has the temerity to question the slaughter on the highways, from tobacco lobbyists when it proposes to warn of the dangers of cigarette smoking, and from the aircraft industry when the Secretary of Defense tries to save billions of dollars by phasing out the manned bomber. A multi-million-dollar lobbying campaign seeks to deprive city and suburban dwellers of a full voice in the democratic process by reversing the Supreme Court's one-man-one-vote decision. Another grassroots pressure campaign defeats the interest and dividend withholding proposal intended to close a major tax loophole. Still another seeks to prevent federal regulation of natural gas prices. In these and many other ways, lobbying has a profound impact on your life and mine.

This book presents two major conclusions: First, that lobbying is an integral and often constructive part of the legislative process, both as a source of information that Congress must have in the enactment of sound laws and as an outlet for the aims and desires of special interest groups. If these important segments of the national life — businessmen, workers, farmers, doctors, veterans and the rest — were denied access to government or consistently frustrated in their legislative goals, there would be a strong tendency for them to form political parties or groupings of their own, and the consequence would be political fragmentation of the kind that has beset some European nations.

The second major conclusion is that lobbying's contribution to good government is flawed by many shortcomings. All too often the operations of large pressure groups prevent rather than encourage the balanced compromises that are the goal of the democratic system. All too frequently the legislative contests are uneven, and in too many instances the lobbyists serve to retard rather than advance the general welfare. There are other problems as well. The lobbying law is a shadow statute usually honored in the breach and lacking enforcement. Of the vast sums of money spent each year in the United States to influence legislation, only a pittance is disclosed to the public and the Congress. Moreover, the relationships between some lobbyists and legislators continue to mock our pretensions to political morality.

Much of this book is devoted to the abuses associated with lobbying. The emphasis on lobbying's faults is not intended to obscure its virtues, nor to suggest that the practice of influencing government is evil. But lobbying is an institution, and institutions are subject to frailties. The author pleads innocent of antipathy toward lobbying as such, and guilty of the belief that critical examination is the beginning of improvement. Thomas Hardy wrote that "if the way to the better there be, it exacts a full look at the worst."

A reporter who comes to Washington soon learns that the activities of lobbyists underlie most if not all of the legislative issues about which he writes. In that sense, this book is a distillation of my 12 years as a Washington correspondent for the *St. Louis Post-Dispatch,* including many long but stimulating hours in the committee rooms and offices of Congress. The actual research and writing of the book occupied the last four years and included interviews with dozens of lobbyists, Washington lawyers, foreign agents, public relations men, members of Congress and their aides, staff members of Congressional committees, academicians and newspapermen, as well as analyses of several recent lobbying campaigns.

To acknowledge the invaluable assistance and co-operation that I received in preparing this study of "the fourth branch of government" would require many pages. Most of the lobbyists, however, and many of the other sources, requested anonymity in return for candor. I do wish to express deep and continuing appreciation to Raymond P. Brandt of the *St. Louis Post-Dispatch* for his wise counsel and unfailing support; to M. B. Schnapper, editor of Public Affairs Press, for his help and confidence; to Spencer Rich of *Congressional Quarterly,* who offered many constructive suggestions and much valuable assistance; and, finally, to my wife, whose role in the research and writing of this book make it as much hers as mine, and for whose contribution no words of gratitude would ever suffice.

JAMES DEAKIN

CONTENTS

"There's getting to be a lot of dangerous talk about the
public interest"—a Herblock cartoon in the
Washington Post of April 10, 1966.

BILLIONS

"Congress shall make no law . . . abridging . . . the right of the people peaceably to assemble, and to petition the government for a redress of grievances."   — *First Amendment to the Constitution.*

"The business of influencing legislation is a billion-dollar business."
— *Representative Frank Buchanan, Chairman of a House investigation of lobbying.*

Politicians come and politicians go, as the public chooses. But the lobbyist — the hardy, resourceful agent of the non-public interest — goes on forever.

Lobbyists have been called a secret, invisible arm of government. Washington's lobbying corps has been nicknamed "the third house of Congress" and "the fourth branch of government." Both labels attest to the intimate relationship between lobbying and government. Often the nicknames have been less complimentary: "influence peddlers," "fixers," "five percenters" and, in an earlier day, "boodlers."

To apply these epithets indiscriminately to all lobbyists today is both inaccurate and unfair. The modern lobbyist is more likely to be a technician, competent and well informed in his field. He performs a vital function in furnishing Congress with facts and information. But he is more than a technician of facts. He is a technician of pressure. He exerts pressure on those who make the laws.

Washington swarms with lobbyists. It always has and probably always will. More than 1,100 individuals and organizations are currently registered as lobbyists, which means that, on the face of things, they outnumber the 535 members of Congress by two to one. But the real ratio is much higher than that. Because the law regulating lobbying is virtually a dead letter, a horde of company representatives, public relations men, lawyers and organizations engaged in influencing government in one way or another do not register as lobbyists. There are at least 8 to 10 lobbyists for every member of Congress.

No group in Washington is more controversial than these gentlemen. Their operations are scrutinized occasionally — and usually unfavorably — by Congress, the President and the press. But remarkably little is known about the lobbyists themselves and what they do.

They are an immensely diverse crew.

A lady named Margo Cairns has been gently pressuring Congress for years to adopt the corn tassel as the national floral emblem. She is a lobbyist.

Attorney Charles Patrick Clark represents Franco Spain and various well-heeled clients to the tune of $200,000 a year, about twice the salary of the President of the United States. He is a lobbyist.

A group of Washington teen-agers organized a campaign to persuade Congress to vote more money for the capital's dilapidated schools. Several of the students registered under the lobbying law. They were lobbyists.

Frank Ikard, a former Texas Congressman, registered as a lobbyist shortly after he became executive vice president of the American Petroleum Institute at a salary of $50,000 a year. While in Congress, Ikard was a member of the House Ways and Means Committee, which has jurisdiction over such matters as oil depletion allowances. At the present time he is president of the institute.

A "retired" couple, Harry and Ruth Kingman, pound the marble corridors of Congress in unceasing, selfless pursuit of votes for public interest legislation, including civil rights and federal aid to education. Kingman, a former Y.M.C.A. executive in his seventies, and his wife, in her sixties, are the entire staff of the Citizens' Lobby for Freedom and Fair Play. Their organization has an annual budget of just over $8,000, most of which comes from Kingman's pension. They are lobbyists.

Stephen G. Slipher, an assistant vice president of the powerful United States Savings and Loan League, is in the $40,000 to $50,000-a-year bracket. His assistant, Glenwood S. Troop, makes more than $25,000 a year. So does Sidney Zagri, legislative counsel for the International Brotherhood of Teamsters. Former Congressman Andrew Biemiller, head of the AFL-CIO's legislative department, draws about $20,000 a year. All these men are lobbyists.

Some very prominent citizens have registered as lobbyists in past years. Among them:

George Romney, "the Rambler Man," now governor of Michigan, who once represented the Automobile Manufacturers Association; Under Secretary of State George W. Ball, number two man in the State Department; United Nations Ambassador Arthur J. Goldberg, who registered for a minimum wage committee; Fowler Hamilton, former head of the foreign aid program; Wilson W. Wyatt, former mayor of Louisville, Kentucky, and campaign manager for Adlai Stevenson in 1952; and Esther Peterson, Assistant Secretary of Labor, who worked for the Amalgamated Clothing Workers. Other former lobbyists include J. Lee Rankin, Solicitor General in the Eisenhower administration; Joseph A. Beirne, president of the Communications Workers of America; Judges James Skelly Wright and John Minor Wisdom of the United States Court of Appeals; and Charles S. Rhyne, a past president of the American Bar Association.

The list of lobbying registrations in recent years includes Oscar Chapman, Secretary of the Interior in the Truman administration; former Senate Democratic Leader Scott W. Lucas; Thurman Arnold, an Assistant Attorney General in the New Deal; Abe Fortas, now a Supreme Court Justice; Paul A. Porter, former chairman of the Federal Communications Commission; Gerald D. Morgan, former deputy assistant to President Eisenhower, and Bryce N. Harlow and David W. Kendall, White House staff members in the Eisenhower administration.

Others recently registered as lobbyists, either personally or through their law firms, include:

Donald S. Dawson, a former administrative assistant to President Truman; Robert L. Farrington, chief counsel of the Agriculture Department in the Eisenhower administration; James H. Rowe Jr., an aide to President Franklin D. Roosevelt and later an Assistant Attorney General; Charles P. Taft, ex-mayor of Cincinnati and brother of the late Senator Robert A. Taft; James G. Patton, president of the National Farmers Union; Bernard L. Boutin, former head of the General Services Administration; Myer Feldman, a special assistant to President Kennedy; J. Edward Day, ex-Postmaster General; Frederick W. Ford, a former member of the Federal Communications Commission; and Richard M. Nixon. (Day's law firm has represented Inland Steel; Nixon's firm has been retained by Talisman Sugar).

Twenty ex-Senators and more than 70 former members of the House of Representatives have registered as lobbyists since 1946, when the law regulating lobbying was enacted. The former Senators, in addition to Scott Lucas, are:

Joseph H. Ball of Minnesota.
Prentiss M. Brown of Michigan.
Edward R. Burke of Nebraska.
Earle C. Clements of Kentucky.
John A. Danaher of Connecticut.
Sheridan Downey of California.
Felix Hebert of Rhode Island.
J. J. Hickey of Wyoming.
Edwin C. Johnson of Colorado.
Kenneth B. Keating of New York.

James P. Kem of Missouri.
Ernest W. McFarland of Arizona.
Francis J. Myers of Pennsylvania.
Herbert R. O'Conor of Maryland.
Joseph C. O'Mahoney of Wyoming.
Charles E. Potter of Michigan.
Kingsley A. Taft of Ohio.
Edward J. Thye of Minnesota.
Burton K. Wheeler of Montana.

Clements, one of the best known of legislators-turned-lobbyists, is a long-time friend of President Johnson. His daughter, Mrs. Bess Abell, is the White House social secretary, and his son-in-law is an Assistant Postmaster General.

Two Senators now serving, Sam J. Ervin Jr. and John Sherman Cooper, were once lobbyists for brief periods. Ervin, a North Carolina Democrat, was registered for the Southern Railway Company in 1947, before entering the Senate. He has said that he received no compensation for his lobbying and appeared in Washington on behalf of the railroad for only one day. "For my 24 hours of lobbying," he told Congressional Quarterly, "it took me five years to convince the Justice Department that I was not doing it permanently for a living." Cooper, a Kentucky Republican, was registered as a lobbyist for the Oceanic Steamship Company in 1950, while in private law practice in Washington. The case involved a claim against the government for the use of two ships during World War II. Cooper was not in the Senate at the time; he had been defeated in 1948 and was elected again in 1952.

Under another law, the Foreign Agents Registration Act, more than 400 individuals, law firms and public relations outfits are

registered with the Justice Department as agents of foreign
governments, companies or other interests abroad. Many of
these men do legal work, advertising, public relations or tourist
promotion for their foreign clients; others are lobbyists. Some
mix law and lobbying or public relations and lobbying.

The registered foreign agents have included former Secretary
of State Dean Acheson, who represented the government of
Venezuela; former Governor Thomas E. Dewey of New York,
the Republican presidential candidate in 1944 and 1948, who was
registered from 1955 to 1960 on behalf of the Republic of Turkey;
Rocco C. Siciliano, an Assistant Secretary of Labor in the Eisenhower administration; Charles F. Willis Jr., an aide to President
Eisenhower; and ex-heavyweight champion Joe Louis, whose
New York public relations firm, Louis-Rowe Enterprises, represented the National Tourist Commission of Cuba in 1960.
Another former foreign agent is Franklin D. Roosevelt Jr., now
head of the federal commission on equal opportunity in the
Johnson administration. Roosevelt registered for the Dominican
Republic in 1956 and 1957. He and Charles Patrick Clark re-
ceived a $60,000 fee for their work for the late Dominican dic-
tator, Rafael Trujillo. Roosevelt's brother, John, registered for
Haiti in 1958; his public relations firm was paid $150,000.

One incumbent Senator, Thomas J. Dodd, a Connecticut
Democrat, was a registered agent for the government of Guatemala in 1957 and 1958, before his election to the Senate. His
contract specified that he was to do no lobbying.

Between 1946 and 1965 a total of 7,591 individuals and organizations registered under the lobbying law. Congressional Quarterly, an authoritative reference service, eliminated the duplicate
registrations (individuals and law firms who registered for several clients) and counted a total of 4,962. Not all of these are
still active, but this is offset by the large number who do not
register.

All of these men and women were exercising their Constitutional right to petition the government. The fact that they were
doing it on behalf of others makes no difference.

Any discussion of lobbying begins with this point: it is entirely
legal. The right to petition government, guaranteed in the First
Amendment, is a broad right. It includes the right to seek to
influence legislation. Moreover, lobbying is an integral part

of modern government. If there were no lobbyists, as Voltaire said of God, we would have to invent some. In effect the founding fathers authorized lobbying. As a result of some frustrating experiences with George the Third, they decided the American people must have a guaranteed right of access to their new government. Lobbying followed, inevitably.

Today lobbying is so inextricably bound up with the governmental process that it is often hard to tell where the legislator leaves off and the lobbyist begins.

Lobbyists draft much of the legislation introduced in Congress. Some lobbyists estimate that fully half of the bills dropped in the hopper are written in whole or part by pressure groups. Lobbyists write and present much of the testimony heard by Congressional committees. Lobbyists and special interest spokesmen ghostwrite many of the speeches given in Congress.

The public relations firm of Selvage and Lee, Inc., representing the Overseas Companies of Portugal, admitted writing speeches on Portuguese policy in Angola for 14 legislators. One of them was Representative Joseph W. Martin Jr., Massachusetts Republican and former Speaker. Selvage and Lee boasted that Martin "used [our] stuff without change, apart from abbreviation."

Lobbyists have been known to use Congressmen's offices as their own, sometimes with long-distance telephone calls and stenographic help thrown in, all at the taxpayers' expense.

Lobbyists take an intimate part in the continual wheeling and dealing, the conferring, negotiating and compromising that go on in the formation of laws.

Not surprisingly, there are some distasteful connotations to the word lobbyist. In the minds of a good many Americans it conjures up disreputable images. It suggests a sinister character slinking through the halls of Congress, trailing behind the faint aroma of thousand-dollar bills. To the cringing Congressman, desperately in need of ready cash to meet his alimony, the overhead on his yacht and the demands of his Lolita, this crafty traducer dispenses the long green from a handy little black bag. In return for which the fawning legislator cheerfully sells the Republic down the river. After the vote, of course, there is the nightly orgy at the palatial manse of the beautiful Washington hostess who is having an illicit affair with this or that prominent Senator, and all clink glasses in a toast to another good day's work.

Bribes, blondes and booze — these are the durable ingredients in the popular image of lobbying and an everlasting boon to writers for slick magazines and Sunday supplements. The changing nature of American politics, however, has reduced the importance of all three as elements in pressure and power.

There are no reliable statistics on cash bribery and outright corruption, since the participants seldom advertise and cannot be depended upon to answer questionnaires truthfully. But students of government agree that the direct bribe — once a standard lobbying technique — is not a major factor today. The campaign contribution, perfectly legal and absolutely vital to most members of Congress, is another matter. The campaign donation, not the out-and-out bribe, is an important weapon in modern lobbying. But even it is far from being the only way in which money is used to influence the course of government.

Some authorities caution that the campaign contribution can be overrated as a means of gaining influence and exerting pressure. Professor Alexander Heard, who made a thorough study of money in American politics, concluded that "he who pays the piper does not always call the tune, at least not in politics. Politicians prize votes more than dollars." [1]

Nevertheless, many Washington lobbyists, as will be seen in a later chapter, are heavy contributors to the national party committees and to individual Congressmen. Furthermore, their contributions frequently go to members of Congressional committees which handle legislation directly affecting the interests of their clients. To interpret all campaign gifts by lobbyists as altruistic donations, as contributions given purely out of desire for good government, would be risky. But to view them only as bribes is to ignore the realities of government. They fall somewhere in between.

Sex is, if anything, a more dubious factor in lobbying today than the bribe. Sex is nice, but it doesn't necessarily swing votes.

There are several reasons for this. Extramarital dalliance is politically dangerous for the married Congressman. And if he is a chaser despite his vows, he does not have to depend on the lobbyist as a source of supply. Washington is freshly furnished

each year with a new stock of callipygian young things eager
to work on Capitol Hill. The amateurs always outnumber
the pros.

This is not to say that Washington is sexless. The amatory
proclivities of some lawmakers are an endless source of gossip
at the equally endless cocktail parties. But the lobbyist who
uses girls in his work is more likely to find himself obtaining them
for his out-of-town clients and employers on their trips to Washington than for Congressmen. There are exceptions, but generally
speaking, bedroom gymnastics have little real impact on the
business of making laws. For one thing, the older legislators
who dominate Congress, and who are the objects of the lobbyist's tenderest concern, are not easily swayed by women. They
have other vices, other rheums. Their main and enduring vice
is power.

There are differences of opinion about the third item in the
popular lobbying trilogy — entertainment (including, of course,
liquor). When political scientist Lester W. Milbrath interviewed
100 Washington lobbyists, he found that they gave entertaining
a very low rating. On an effectiveness scale of 0 to 10, entertainment scored a median of 1.17.[2] The lobbyists explained that
members of Congress and other top officials are deluged with
invitations, that some of these are "required" social events which
they feel they must attend, and that they are under such pressure to go to parties that an evening spent at home with the
family "seems like a gift."

Nevertheless the lobbyists do a lot of entertaining. It has
been estimated that 1,500 large cocktail parties complete with
receiving line and music — "alcoholic mass meetings," one reporter has called them — take place in Washington each year.
Besides these are numberless at-home dinners and parties, large
and small. Not all of these affairs are given by lobbyists. The
diplomatic corps, the military and the Mmes. Mesta and Cafritz
are unflagging. But lobbyists are among the most indefatigable
party-givers.

A veteran staff member of a Senate subcommittee subject to
intense lobbying pressures advised:

"Don't leave out the parties. They're damned important,
especially with the new Congressmen. The new man arrives
in town with his wife. They're both a little awed. And what

happens? All of a sudden, they are invited to a little dinner party given by the Washington vice president for a billion-dollar corporation. They're impressed, but there's more to it than that.

"Let's say the Congressman is a liberal. He's suspicious of big business. What does he find? The big shot is a darned nice guy. He doesn't have horns and a tail. He charms the wife and he's deferential to the Congressman. They go away feeling a little differently. Maybe it doesn't affect the way he votes, at least not right away. But it's a softening-up process."

Texas lobbyist Dale Miller and his wife "Scooter" are among Washington's best-known party givers. Each January for 18 years they threw a big birthday shindig for the late Speaker Sam Rayburn, at which the guest list was in the hundreds. Miller, of whom more will be said later, represents the Texas Gulf Sulphur Company, the Dallas Chamber of Commerce and the Intracoastal Canal Association of Louisiana and Texas, of which he is executive vice president.

Some lobbying entertaining is big and public. The Association of American Railroads, the American Trucking Associations and the National Association of Home Builders give large parties each year. The National Association of Manufacturers holds an annual reception for members of Congress (250 Congressmen attended a recent N.A.M. party). The United States Chamber of Commerce wines and dines the legislators about three times a year. Senator Stephen M. Young, Ohio Democrat, estimates that about 260 large national associations with Washington offices give at least one big dinner a year for members of Congress.

Often the partying is confidential. The very private Carlton Club in Suite 348 at the Sheraton-Carlton Hotel is a favorite gathering place for top lobbyists, especially oil lobbyists and their Congressional friends. Comfortable lounge furniture, paintings of Indian scenes, a well-stocked bar and tables for bridge and gin rummy make the Carlton Club a convivial and inconspicuous haven.

Hardly a day goes by without a batch of parties to which thirsty Congressmen can repair after a hot debate. Many of these small get-togethers are held in the Washington hotel suites maintained by large corporations. United States Steel, for instance, has a four-room refuge on the eighth floor of the Sheraton-Carlton, and Bethlehem Steel has a suite in the same hotel.

Or the legislator, if he has seniority, can relax with bourbon and branch water in the expensive surroundings of his Capitol hide-away, and invite his lobbyist friends in. There are 30 of these cozy retreats, assigned to senior members of Congress, in the new east front of the Capitol. The furnishings in some of them cost the taxpayer $15,000 and up; the drapes alone reportedly cost $700 a pair. Railroad lobbyists in particular find the little Capitol dens handy for a bit of quiet talk.

Consider the equally intimate Quorum Club, whose existence came to public attention when the case of Robert G. (Bobby) Baker first hit the headlines in 1963. Baker fell from power, grace and his position as secretary to the Democratic majority in the Senate when the Senate establishment found itself no longer able to ignore an embarrassing question: How had one of its employees, on a salary of $19,600 a year, accumulated assets of $2,166,886 in less than nine years?

Not lobbying so much as the ethical disrepair of Congress itself was the central issue in the Bobby Baker scandal; the country slicker from Pickens, South Carolina, was a product of the legislative branch and its mores. But the roster of the Quorum Club, together with data about some of Baker's business dealings, provide insight into the close social and working relationship between professional lobbyists and key staff personnel of Congress, the anonymous implementers of power.

For years one of the most influential staff aides on Capitol Hill, Baker was a charter member and leading light in the Quorum Club. Except for a sprinkling of Senators, Representatives, Generals and Admirals, most of the club's 200 members were lobbyists, "Washington representatives" and businessmen. Its members included Stephen Slipher and Glen Troop, lobbyists for the United States Savings and Loan League; Wayne L. Bromley, a lobbyist for the National Coal Policy Conference; Fred B. Black Jr., a consultant and government contact man for the North American Aviation Company; Thomas D. Webb Jr., Washington representative for Texas millionaire Clint Murchison Jr. and lobbyist for the Capital's mass transit system; Bedford S. Wynne of Dallas, one of Murchison's associates; Robert L. Humphrey, a lobbyist for the National Association

of Manufacturers; Lyle O. Snader, a lobbyist for the Association
of American Railroads; William Thompson, president of the
Florida-East Coast Railroad, and Scott I. Peek, former administrative assistant to Senator George A. Smathers of Florida.

Congressional members were Senators Daniel Brewster of
Maryland, Frank Church of Idaho, J. Howard Edmondson of
Oklahoma and Harrison A. Williams Jr. of New Jersey, all Demo-
crats, and Representatives William H. Ayres of Ohio and James
F. Battin of Montana, Republicans.

The Quorum Club, founded for "literary purposes, mutual improvement and the promotion of social intercourse," pursued
these laudable goals in unusual surroundings. Paintings of bare-
bosomed West Indian women adorned the walls of the club's
headquarters on the second floor of the Carroll Arms Hotel, just
across the street from the new Senate Office Building. There
was a small but elegant bar with three telephones on it and
plenty of masculine atmosphere.

The list of ways in which the lobbyist seeks to assure the
good life for the lawmaker and his staff is almost endless. Outdoor sports are not neglected.

One lobbyist for large textile interests maintains a large
county estate and fishing lodge with a 20-room house and its
own landing strip 200 miles west of Washington and flies his
guests to and fro in his private plane. Some years ago another
lobbyist, representing a shipbuilding firm, provided a sumptuous
fishing spot much favored by some Congressional leaders.

Entertainment plays a definite role in lobbying, but its pre-
sumed advantage to the lobbyist can be overrated. One evidence
of this is that entertainment often serves just as practical a purpose for the Congressman.

Everything in Washington is a two-way street. The legislators
use the lobbyists as much as the lobbyists use them. A cocktail
party — like an office conversation — may give the Congressman information that he needs. Or it may give him something
he needs even more: cash.

The Washington party has become an increasingly utilitarian
institution. Invited to a reception, the lobbyist may find that
he is giving more than he gets. The pressure boy is pressured.
As he leaves, pleasantly oiled, his attention is directed to a hat

in which he is expected to drop $50 or $100 for the Congressman's campaign.

Fund-raising parties have been held in recent years for Senators Thomas J. Dodd of Connecticut, Frank E. Moss of Utah, John O. Pastore of Rhode Island, William Proxmire of Wisconsin, Mike Monroney of Oklahoma, Gale W. McGee of Wyoming, Wayne Morse of Oregon, Alan Bible of Nevada, Warren G. Magnuson of Washington, George Smathers of Florida, Democrats, and Senators Everett M. Dirksen of Illinois, Thomas H. Kuchel of California and former Senator Homer E. Capehart of Indiana, Republicans, among others.

Washington is a very practical town, and money and votes mean more than liquor. In the final analysis, this is why bribes, blondes and booze don't rank as high as they once did in the lobbyist's scheme of things. They just aren't as important to the Congressman (to his political survival, which is his first law) as votes, and the money with which to get votes. The legislator may accept the lobbyist's entertainment, and gladly, but he is far more likely to do what the lobbyist wants if votes are involved.

Entertainment remains an important lobbying technique, but its principal function is to create and maintain good will. It is not usually a major determining factor in the legislative process. Some lobbyists explain that they wine and dine the lawmakers primarily because their clients expect them to, not because they believe it will have a direct impact on legislation. Many businessmen, they say, assume that what works corporately will work governmentally. The experienced lobbyist may consider this naive, but to tell the client would be to jeopardize the expense account, so the partying goes on.

There are always, of course, the sleazy, fly-by-night operators, holding forth over drinks in the crowded hotel bars on Capitol Hill, talking big, and willing, for a price, to try to "reach" a Congressman with a thinly-veiled campaign contribution, a drinking bout or a party girl. These are the shady, not-so-clever gentry who end up in the headlines. It makes spicy reading, but the point to remember is that this kind of thing seldom affects the course of government in any significant degree.

After an extensive investigation of lobbying, a House committee headed by the late Representative Frank Buchanan of

Pennsylvania discussed the changed character of lobbying. "In the 1870's and 1880's, 'lobbying' meant direct, individual solicitation of legislators, with a strong presumption of corruption attached," the committee said.³ But in the middle of the twentieth century, the Buchanan report went on, it means something quite different.

"Modern pressure on legislative bodies is rarely corrupt . . . it is increasingly indirect, and [it is] largely the product of group rather than individual effort," said the committee. The key words are "indirect" and "group."

Indirect pressure consists of campaigns to whip up public opinion for or against a piece of legislation. These campaigns almost always are organized and directed by lobbyists or lobbying groups. Indirect pressure, also known as grassroots lobbying, is one of the prime techniques of modern lobbying. In terms of the money spent and the impact on the public interest, it is the most important technique. It has the greatest effect on the legislator simply because it involves a large number of actual or potential votes.

Group pressure, as the Buchanan committee pointed out, means that large organizations, possessing the financial resources required to organize grassroots pressure, and commanding substantial blocs of votes, are the most significant factor in lobbying today. The massive, heavily-financed grassroots campaign is the trademark of modern lobbying, not the cash-under-the-table, babes-in-the-bedroom approach of the nineteenth century entrepreneur.

The individual lobbyist is, of course, still with us and always will be. He is as important as ever, but these days he usually operates with a big corporation, a trade association or a labor union behind him. He regularly combines direct lobbying and persuasion of Congressmen with organized indirect pressure from the legislators' constituents back home.

Although many Americans continue to think of lobbying almost exclusively in terms of the three B's, the gaudy corruption of another era, present-day definitions of lobbying are both inaccurate and unrealistic in the judgment of the Buchanan committee.

The conventional image of lobbying unfortunately misses both the good and the bad sides of the subject. Conceiving of the lobbyist only as tempter and corrupter, it ignores his very real contribution to the process of making laws. The Congressman, confronted with an annual mountain of complicated legislation and distracted by the problems of his constituents, must rely on the lobbyist for facts, statistics and information. This is the informational side of lobbying, and it is essential.

The immense complexities of the American economy make it impossible for Congress to legislate without informed, expert assistance. It must know, as accurately as possible, how a law will affect the diverse elements of the economy. One means of transmitting this information is the lobbyist.

In the case of federal highway legislation, for example, the late Senator Richard L. Neuberger of Oregon commented that three substantial segments of the economy felt that their interests were directly at stake: the truck lines, the railroads because the truck lines are their principal competitors for freight, and the American Automobile Association because the motorist pays most of the cost of building the highways.

"Lobbyists for these groups paraded to my office constantly," Neuberger reported. "They presented vast quantities of facts and figures — some of which I challenged, but a lot of which were accurate and impressive. No improper inducement ever was ventured. Without the data made available by railroads and truckers and the A.A.A., I doubt if I would have felt fully qualified to reach a decision on the kind of highway bill which was best for the nation." [4]

From the founding days of the Republic it has been recognized that special interest groups must be represented in some way in the councils of government.

In "The Federalist," James Madison spoke of "factions," describing them as groups which are "united and actuated by some common impulse of passion, or of interest." Madison believed that these interests would be "adverse . . . to the permanent and aggregate interests of the community" and must be counterbalanced by a strong federal government.

Nevertheless, Professor Heard has observed that "no popular government in history has yet survived that did not in some way permit such interests to exercise effective means of petition."

The interplay of special interests in the formation of laws is considered one of the strengths of democracy. It is vital to the

survival of the democratic system that groups with well-defined
interests — business and industry, labor, farmers, veterans,
teachers, professional men, women's groups and so on — have
a way of communicating with the legislature. Many devices are
used to make this communication possible. The lobbyist is one
of them. He is an agent of the special interest group, the non-
public interest.

When the popular image of the lobbyist casts him as a depraver
and procurer, it just as surely misses the bad as the good. There
are worse things than bribing a Congressman.

For one, the operations of lobbyists do not always serve a true
and fair interplay of interests. Equitable compromise as a goal of
the legislative process all too frequently is honored in the breach.
A good many lobbyists are rewarded not so much for their skill
in representing their clients' legitimate interests as for their talent
and experience in perverting compromise to grab.

For another, the conventional definition of lobbying ignores
the fact that the big grassroots pressure campaign can subvert
democracy as no nineteenth century boodler, in his wildest mo-
ments, ever dreamed of doing. From his bag of tricks, the
modern lobbyist pulls mass media to reach the people faster,
more often and in greater numbers than ever before, motivational
researchers to analyze their psyches and determine what will
excite them, and public relations experts to get them excited.
All the printed, broadcast, filmed and televised wonders of the
age are at his disposal. When the special pleaders want to mislead the people today, they can do so on a grand scale.

An example was the savings and loan industry's successful
grassroots lobbying campaign against the New Frontier proposal
to withhold federal income taxes on interest and dividends.
Millions of small depositors were artfully deluded into believing
that a new tax was to be levied on their savings. Actually, the
plan would only have added the withholding feature to collect
taxes already due on the interest. Another recent instance was
the American Medical Association's attack on the fiscal soundness of the social security system. In its efforts to block the
projected program of health care for the elderly, the A.M.A.
spread doubts about the stability of the social security fund,

on which millions of oldsters depend. The soundness of the fund has been attested to repeatedly by experts.

But despite lobbying's vastly expanded range, relatively few people are acquainted with its nature and scope. A Gallup poll has shown that 45 percent of the American people have no idea what the word lobbyist means.

"Whenever I tell people I am a lobbyist, there is an embarrassed pause," said Arnold Mayer, a labor lobbyist. "Then a barrage of questions. Some people think lobbying is one of the romantic careers of the twentieth century: 'Do you meet all the important people?' Some indicate that they consider lobbying only a little short of the devil's work: 'Do you bribe Congressmen?' Lobbying is something very mysterious, very suspicious and very unknown to the average American — even to those who follow current events."

Partly because of the opprobrium attached to the word, today's lobbyists generally call themselves by a set of more respectable-sounding names: legislative representative or legislative consultant, governmental relations consultant, legislative counsel, legislative liaison man, Washington counsel or Washington representative.

Reluctance to use the word "lobbyist" is pointed up in a study by the Brookings Institution. Nineteen Washington representatives employed by large corporations were interviewed. Their identities were kept secret to encourage frankness.

At first, most of them made "a general disclaimer that they ever engage in lobbying," the Brooking researchers reported. Only two of the 19 were registered as lobbyists and accepted the designation. But as the interviews progressed and the "company reps" lost their uneasiness, it became evident that "virtually all of them deal in some degree with legislative matters, although some of them do so indirectly through trade associations or through company personnel back home. It developed that the disclaimer with respect to 'lobbying' went to the point that only a small minority attempt as a regular part of their duties to influence *directly* the passage of specific legislation."[5]

The Washington representatives, it turned out, had a role in indirect, grassroots lobbying. Almost all of them said they kept an eye on legislative matters that might interest their companies and reported them to the home office, so that the company could take any action it deemed necessary. One company rep described his listening and reporting function: "We send in a weekly report on bills that we are following; of the 10,000 public bills that were introduced in the first session of the Eighty-fifth Congress, we were actually following about 1,500."

This deserves special note. Again and again, Washington representatives of large corporations, public relations men and some trade association officials assert that their legislative function is confined to reporting to their employers, clients or members on the status and prospects of pending legislation. They say they do not attempt to influence the passage or defeat of specific bills, so they do not register under the Lobbying Act.

"It also appeared," the Brookings study said, "that, in common with the popular view, or perhaps because of it, the (company) representatives regard 'lobbying' as that segment or type of legislative activity that is not quite 'nice.' It is not surprising, therefore, that most representatives do not wish to be classified as lobbyists."

What accounts for the out-of-date view of lobbying? There are many possible explanations.

The ignorance of the American people about their government certainly is a factor. Ignorance contributes to misconceptions about lobbying, just as it contributes to misconceptions about politics in general. From time to time, we are told that Americans are growing more knowledgeable about their government, and hopefully this is so. But a poll by Elmo Roper and Associates found that only 33 percent of the adult population knew the length of term of a United States Senator. Forty-seven percent gave incorrect answers and 20 percent had no idea at all. A poll by Dr. George Gallup's American Institute of Public Opinion disclosed that 54 percent of adult Americans could not name even one branch of the federal government. Twenty-seven percent could identify one or two. Only 19 percent correctly identified all three branches. Gallup found that 31 percent of the adults did not know who was vice president of the United States.

Cynicism about government also contributes to misunderstandings about lobbying. Professor James MacGregor Burns has referred to this as political alienation — "the feeling that politics is a racket for a few insiders and is meaningless to the rest of the people."⁶

The past excesses of lobbyists and the special interest groups that they represented are another cause of current distrust. Politics, law-making and lobbying in nineteenth century America were raw and rough. It was, as Heard has said, the period of our late youth — a brawling youth. But new excesses replace the old, and new attitudes are slow to catch up.

A deeper and more complex cause of misconceptions about lobbying is the fact that the role of organized special interest groups in American government has never been adequately defined. There is no question that they have a role and an important one, but the rules of the game have never really been drawn up. "The American government does not accord formal recognition in its legislatures to the 'instruments of power' that undergird the nation's social, economic and political life," Professor Heard points out. "The question," he adds, "is . . . not whether special interests shall be represented in a democratic government, but how."

Those who believe that lobbying is bad *per se* — Justice Hugo L. Black of the Supreme Court, as a Senator, once suggested that lobbying be outlawed — would not subscribe to the logical conclusion, repeal of the First Amendment.

But there remains a fundamental problem: to what extent should private interests composed of the few be permitted to influence the course of government? Perhaps the problem defies a complete solution, but so far as Congress is concerned, there has been a remarkable paucity of effort. The lobbyist, as the agent of the private interest, operates without any effective rules or limitations. There is a lobbying law, but it is a mockery.

All these things contribute to the citizen's attitude toward lobbying and lobbyists. But even this incomplete list indicates that the public and the Congress share a good part of the responsibility for whatever disrepute attaches to the business of influencing government.

There is another side to the coin, however. On the few occasions when Congress has tried to come to grips with the problem of pressure on government, it has encountered a jungle of difficulties and a morass of contradictions.

Webster's New International Dictionary defines lobbying in

these words: "To address or solicit members of a legislative body in the lobby or elsewhere, as before a committee, with intent to influence legislation" and "to urge or procure the passage of [a bill, measure, etc.] by lobbying; also to influence or persuade [a legislator] by lobbying."

This, it should be noted, is what any citizen does when he journeys to Washington and talks to a member of Congress about a bill. According to Webster, this is lobbying activity, but the voter does not think of himself as a lobbyist. He is exercising his constitutional right of petition. In addition, many persons, either because of their interest in a particular piece of legislation or because they are authorities on some subject, testify each year before committees of Congress. Most of them do not consider themselves lobbyists.

Moreover, the dictionary definition says nothing about indirect, grassroots lobbying, by mail, phone call, telegram or petition.

In 1946, after several false starts, Congress defined lobbying. In an attempt to distinguish between the professional lobbyist and the ordinary citizen petitioning his government, Congress added two factors. It defined a lobbyist as a person or organization whose principal purpose is to influence the passage or defeat of legislation and who receives money for that purpose. As enacted, the lobbying law covered indirect, grassroots pressure campaigns as well as the traditional direct contact with members of Congress.

Under the law, lobbyists were required to register with the Clerk of the House and the Secretary of the Senate and to report the amount and sources of their income, as well as the amounts they spent on lobbying. Congress made no effort to limit lobbying or to place any restrictions on the practice, since it is an exercise of the First Amendment's right of petition. The only requirement was disclosure, so that the legislators and the public would know the identity of the pressure boys and their employers, and where the money went.

But like all laws, the Lobbying Act wasn't perfect. It was even less perfect than most. Many veteran lobbyists say they are still not sure what it means, and virtually every Congressman, lobbyist and government official to whom this writer talked described it as a vague and badly-worded statute.

The prime cause of confusion over the years has been the "principal purpose" clause. In a great many instances, it is next to impossible to demonstrate that the principal purpose of an individual or organization is lobbying. One of the principal purposes, perhaps, or a substantial purpose, but the Lobbying Act hung itself up on the words, "*the principal* purpose."

Every trade association and business organization provides important services for its members that have little or no bearing on legislation. Most if not all Washington lawyers engaged in lobbying for some clients have other clients for whom they do no legislative work. The Washington representative of a large corporation may spend more time at the Pentagon, where the lobbying law does not apply, than on Capitol Hill. Yet many of these individuals and organizations would be out of business or would close their Washington offices and go home if Congress outlawed lobbying.

Nor does the confusion end with the uncertain wording of the lobbying law.

In 1954, the Supreme Court held that the Lobbying Act applies only to direct communication with members of Congress to influence legislation. The court, in the case of U.S. v. Harriss, threw out that part of the act which required registration and spending reports by those who seek to influence Congress by indirect means. The lobbying technique involving the largest amounts of money — indirect, grassroots pressure — was removed at one stroke from public scrutiny.

What was left was a shadow law with a limited and highly unrealistic definition of lobbying. Dean Robert F. Drinan of the Boston College Law School has described the Lobbying Act as a "judicial shambles."[7]

Together, the principal purpose clause and the Supreme Court decision have created situations such as these:

For three months, Crawford H. Greenewalt, president of the mammoth E. I. du Pont de Nemours, lobbied intensively up and down the halls of Congress to put through the du Pont stockholders tax relief bill. The bill, which was passed and signed by President Kennedy, permitted du Pont stockholders to pay a lower capital gains tax rather than straight income tax on

General Motors stock they received under a court divestiture order.

Greenewalt visited more than 50 Congressmen and top government officials to plug for the bill. He talked with the late Speaker Sam Rayburn, Senate Majority Leader Mike Mansfield and most of the other Democratic and Republican leaders of the House and Senate. He conferred several times with Chairman Wilbur D. Mills of the tax-writing House Ways and Means Committee, and he saw almost all of the 15 Democratic members of Ways and Means.

Several of these Democrats said later that Greenewalt's persuasiveness was the main reason they voted for the bill. There was one dissenter — a Midwestern liberal who reported that he was "properly impressed" when the du Pont chieftain dropped in, "but it didn't change my vote."

Greenewalt did not neglect the executive branch. He visited then-Secretary of the Treasury Douglas Dillon; former Attorney General Robert F. Kennedy; Byron R. (Whizzer) White, then deputy attorney general and now a Supreme Court justice; Lee Loevinger, then assistant attorney general in charge of the antitrust division, and Robert H. Knight, general counsel of the Treasury Department.

This was lobbying activity of a sustained sort but Greenewalt did not register under the Lobbying Act. One of his associates explained that the du Pont president is not paid his salary for the principal purpose of lobbying. That is obviously true, so, in the Alice-in-Wonderland world of lobbying, he was lobbying but was not a lobbyist.

Or take the case of Hill and Knowlton, Inc. This big public relations firm masterminded the drug industry's grassroots lobbying campaign against the drug regulation bill sponsored by the late Senator Estes Kefauver of Tennessee. Bert C. Goss, president of Hill and Knowlton, directed the campaign, and the fee was $5,000 a month. But Hill and Knowlton did not register under the lobbying law on behalf of the Pharmaceutical Manufacturers Association, its client. The Supreme Court decision removing indirect pressure from the purview of the Lobbying Act meant that it did not have to do so.

Earlier, Hill and Knowlton had mapped the oil industry's grassroots lobbying campaign to put through the Harris-

Fulbright bill exempting natural gas producers from federal
regulation. The fee was $85,000. Again, Hill and Knowlton did
not register under the lobbying law. As a matter of fact, H. and
K. has not registered as a lobbying organization for any of its
clients since 1950, when it filed a lobbying report on behalf of
the American Butter Institute.

In 1963, the Selvage and Lee public relations firm sent every
member of Congress a large amount of material on the Angola
situation, including reprints of a column by Robert Ruark,
copies of a resolution passed by Portuguese-American groups and
editorials from American newspapers supporting the Portuguese
position on Angola. The material was mailed out on behalf of
Selvage and Lee's client, the Overseas Companies of Portugal.

Selvage and Lee distributed 40,000 copies of a necrotic pamph-
let, "On the Morning of March 15," dealing with atrocities in
Angola; 10,000 copies of another booklet, "The Communists and
Angola"; 5,000 copies of a speech, "Portugal and Her Overseas
Provinces"; 15,000 reprints of articles on Angola from Catholic
newspapers; 10,000 copies of a booklet, "Angola: A Challenge
and Opportunity"; 15,000 reprints of a Reader's Digest article,
"'Behind the Terror in African Angola," by Brig. Gen. Frank L.
Howley; 5,000 reprints of speeches in the Congressional Record
by Representative Hastings Keith, Massachusetts Republican,
and 52,500 copies of various other press releases, pamphlets,
letters, speeches and reprints of newspaper and magazine articles
on Angola. Selvage and Lee registered under the Foreign Agents
Act and reported the distribution of this material. But it did not
register or report under the Lobbying Act on behalf of the Portuguese companies, although members of Congress received
many of these pamphlets and reprints.

The National Association of Manufacturers, about three-fifths
of whose annual budget goes for grassroots lobbying or public
opinion formation, has not registered or reported any spending
under the lobbying law since 1950. Several other large organizations have followed the N.A.M.'s lead and do not file lobbying
reports. However, some individual employees of the N.A.M.
and the other non-reporting groups are registered and report
portions of their salaries.

The legal uncertainty over what constitutes lobbying means

that it is impossible to determine the number of pressure boys who are operating.

From the standpoint of the public interest, there is an even more significant consequence. It means that there is no way to tell how much money is being spent to influence government in the United States. All that can be said with certainty is that the amount reported to Congress and the public is a very, very small fraction of the total.

The American Medical Association is estimated to have spent between $7,000,000 and $12,000,000 in 1962 to lobby against the health care plan. By its own admission, the big medical group coughed up $1,300,000 in that year for just one item — public relations — in its grassroots campaign against Medicare. The A.M.A. reported total 1962 lobbying expenditures of $83,076. Similarly, the oil industry spent at least $20,000,000 and probably $25,000,000 or more to lobby for the Harris-Fulbright bill. The total amount reported under the lobbying law was $118,625.

The Washington office of the United States Chamber of Commerce estimates that about 75 percent of its time (and money) is spent on research on governmental matters, including legislation. Said Theron J. Rice, former chief lobbyist for the Chamber: "We did not consider that lobbying, and we did not report the money we spent on it." But Rice acknowledged that the research "went into all the material that we sent out to members to keep them informed about legislation, to keep them interested, aware and active. This was in the hope that they would exert their influence on legislation."

When the Chamber learned that a Senate-House conference committee had deleted an amendment it favored from a federal welfare and pension act, it sent telegrams to local chambers in 30 or 35 key Congressional districts, "suggesting," in Rice's words, "that they do whatever they could to try to get the conference report rejected."

The Washington office had no way of knowing whether the local units followed up the suggestion, Rice said. For this reason the Chamber did not interpret the telegrams as lobbying and did not report the cost of sending the wires. The Chamber's Washington office had not been in direct contact with Congress, and direct contact is all that's left of the lobbying law.

In any session of Congress there are hundreds or thousands

of instances of this kind of grassroots pressure, suggested or organized by Washington lobbyists. But the money spent on this kind of lobbying does not have to be reported to Congress or the public.

After the Lobbying Act had been on the books for three and a half years, the Buchanan committee sent questionnaires to 173 large corporations, dealing with their expenditures to influence legislation, directly or indirectly. Only 37 of these companies had filed lobbying reports in the period from January 1947 through May 1950, and the total amount of spending listed in these reports was $776,466. Replies to the committee's questionnaire were received from 151 of the corporations. They showed actual lobbying outlays of $32,124,835 in the same period.

The amounts spent by corporations and labor unions on programs and activities with such high-sounding names as "public information," "political education," "employee information" or "employee education" continue to be a huge but inaccessible element in the grassroots lobbying picture.

It was estimated in one year for instance, that 10,000 corporation executives and lesser fry were receiving instructions in government and politics, using material supplied by the Chamber of Commerce and the N.A.M.

In that same year, political activity programs were operating at the Ford Motor Company, General Motors, Chrysler, Gulf Oil, General Electric, Johnson and Johnson, Bristol-Myers, Allied Chemical, Allied Paper, Kaiser Industries, American Can and National Steel, to name only a few.

Gulf Oil distributed to its employees, stockholders and dealers a pamphlet entitled "A Political Program for Gulf Oil Corp." It outlined a broad program under which the oil company would assign its executives on a regional basis to stimulate political action by Gulf employees. The company also said it would station a registered lobbyist and a public relations man in Washington and would supply "Gulf's people" with the voting records of members of Congress (a lobbying tactic, by the way, which the lobbyists themselves do not find very effective).

In the same year General Electric distributed an eight-page booklet to its "people," urging them to complain to their Senators and Representatives about "high federal spending."

The Buchanan committee, in masterfully restrained language,

concluded that the amount of money publicly reported as having been spent to influence government provides "a very incomplete picture of the realities of lobbying."

"If the full truth were ever known," its report said, "this committee has little doubt that lobbying, in all its ramifications, would prove to be a billion-dollar industry. This figure is not offered in an effort to shock the complacent, but as a sober estimate."

Using the committee's estimate the pressure boys spent some 18 billion dollars between 1947 and 1964. The amount disclosed to Congress and the public in this same period was approximately 93 million dollars.

It should be noted that this refers only to the money spent to lobby Congress. This is another big loophole in the lobbying law: it applies only to those who seek to influence legislation.

Considering the tremendous pressures on the executive branch — especially the Defense Department — and the federal regulatory agencies, this is a staggering defect.

Lobbying in the Pentagon and elsewhere in the executive arm of government is, of course, beyond the scope of the present study. This book deals primarily with the professional lobbyist practicing his arts on the Congress of the United States, where the money, and therefore the pressure, originates.

2

PRESSURES

"The Presidency is . . . pre-eminently a place of moral leadership."
— *Franklin D. Roosevelt in 1932.*

"Between the idea and the reality . . . falls the shadow."
— *T. S. Eliot, "The Hollow Men."*

Stately, plump Alexander Wiley seemed pleased with himself as he came out of the committee room.

Although his Wisconsin constituents were soon to replace him, Wiley at this time was the senior Republican member of the United States Senate, with almost 24 years tenure. He was the ranking G.O.P. member of three important committees — Foreign Relations, Judiciary, and Space Sciences. The last-named committee was considering a bill to put the communications satellite (Telstar) program in the hands of a private corporation dominated by the American Telephone and Telegraph Company.

Waiting for the Senator as he emerged from the space committee meeting was a younger man, well-dressed and extremely personable. He was a lobbyist for A.T. and T. The two men walked down the hall to Wiley's office, chatting amiably.

Months before the Telstar bill came to a vote, the lobbyist became a regular visitor to Wiley's office. He dropped in at least once a day, and sometimes twice, for a period of several months. "He called on Wiley constantly," said a former member of the Senator's staff. "He was a very pleasant person, very sophisticated. He made himself useful to Wiley in a multitude of ways."

The lobbyist assigned to Wiley was one of a team of A.T. and T. men who fanned out quietly and efficiently through the halls of Congress to help smooth the passage of the Telstar measure through an already-complaisant legislature.

From the home states and districts of members of Congress came vice presidents and managers of local telephone companies,

26

solid men of good standing in the community, often long-time friends or acquaintances of the Senators and Representatives. Virtually every member was visited at least once.

Within a week after the Telstar bill was introduced in the House, a Texas Congressman was contacted by every important businessman in his district, with only three exceptions. Curious about the three, he checked and found they were on a fishing trip. The calls and letters from the businessmen, urging him to support the Telstar measure, were prompted by a telephone company executive in his district.

Much of the lobbying in this connection was on a geographic basis. Southern Senators, for instance, were visited by an executive of the Southern Bell Telephone Company. Often he brought along a vice president of the Bell System located in the Senator's area. The conversations were invariably cordial. Most of the time, said a participant in several such conferences, the telephone officials simply probed, pleasantly but persistently, into the Congressman's stand on the Telstar measure. Their visits served, of course, to remind the legislator of the political and economic importance and pervasive influence of a corporation whose operations extend into almost every hamlet in the land and whose assets total some 26 billion dollars.

In arguing for private ownership of the burgeoning space communications industry, the A.T. and T. men emphasized that their corporation had spent $50,000,000 on space communications research between 1957 and 1962. Rarely did they mention the amount contributed in the same period by the American taxpayer — $175,000,000 on space communications technology specifically and a staggering 25 billion dollars on the general space program, many aspects of which were closely related to communications.

The A.T. and T. lobbyists were discreet, unobtrusive — "They always used a soft sell approach," a committee staff aide commented — and unfailingly helpful. They were particularly attentive to Senators who appeared to be wavering on the Telstar bill.

Did the Senator want information about Telstar? The lobbyists supplied it promptly, sometimes instantly, and then followed up with telephone calls several days later to see if any more statistics were desired. "The most striking thing about the A.T. and T. material," said one Senator, "was that it almost completely ignored everybody else who had contributed to the space communications program."

A.T. and T.'s blanket lobbying for the Telstar bill paid off handsomely. The space committee reported out the measure unanimously, and later the Senate approved it by a vote of 66 to 11. Amendments offered by a small band of liberals to protect the public interest were defeated by similarly lopsided margins. A filibuster effort by the liberals was brushed aside contemptuously. For the first time since 1927 cloture was voted to cut off debate.

One of the questions most frequently asked about lobbying is simply: what does a lobbyist do? The A.T. and T. lobbying provides several answers. To begin with, the lobbyists supply Congressmen with a great deal of information about complex subjects. It is usually self-serving information, and the legislators know that, but it is data they need and they could not possibly put together comparable facts and figures by themselves. Another cardinal function of the lobbyist is to create and maintain cordial relations with members of Congress, their staffs and the staffs of committees. Good will is one of his chief stocks in trade.

The lobbyists are out to make life easier for the Congressman and his assistants, in large things and small. The telephone company lobbyist sets up conference calls so that the legislator can address meetings in his home state; the airline and railroad lobbyists arrange plane and train tickets; the trade association lobbyist sees to it that the key Senator or Representative is invited to address his organization's annual convention for a substantial fee; the "company rep" may be instrumental in throwing some business to the Congressman's law firm. And almost all lobbyists are keenly concerned about the political future of legislators friendly to their clients; campaign contributions reflect such concern.

A new member of Congress soon finds that, if he chooses to have it so, a good many of the little niceties of life will be provided for him by the agreeable gentlemen waiting for him in the outer office. His staff, if he permits, is remembered at Christmas and other times throughout the year. A few members, notably Senator Paul H. Douglas of Illinois, put a limit on the cost of gifts; most don't.

Sometimes lobbying largess is harmless. A representative of

a food manufacturing company regularly breezes into Congressional offices with a pocketful of prepared soup mix samples which he distributes to the secretaries. One day a young Senatorial aide inquired whether he was trying to buy votes this way. "Son," replied the lobbyist in booming southern accents, "if ah can buy your vote for 80 cents worth of soup, it's not worth buyin'."

What does a lobbyist do? There are still more answers.

"A good part of my work," said a lobbyist for one of the nation's largest corporations, "consists of constantly broadening my contacts — getting to know more people and establishing friendly relations with them. It's like throwing a stone into a pond. One contact leads to another. Suppose I need some information about a particular matter. I think of a guy I know on the Hill who may have it, so I call him. He doesn't have it, but he refers me to another man, whom I don't know. I call the second fellow, introduce myself and ask him the question. But I don't drop it there. I invite him to lunch and get to know him. Making new contacts is an endless process."

This lobbyist specializes in three governmental areas for his corporation. He estimates that he spends 60 to 75 percent of his time dealing with the members and staffs of the Congressional committees that handle legislation in these three fields. When other chores come along, he is adaptable.

"I catch whatever comes along" he said. "There's a good deal of variety. The other day, for instance, my boss called from New York and said he was sending two men down to Washington to look into the automatic vending machine business. The company was thinking of going into automatic vending machines.

"So I spent a day at the Commerce Department, putting together information on automatic vending machines, and over at the Agriculture Department getting a lot of stuff on institutional feeding. You know — feeding large numbers of people with a batch of these machines, some for sandwiches, some for coffee, and so on.

"Another part of my job is to iron out disputes between company plant managers who come to Washington with Congressional problems. Two of them will come in. They're both pushing a particular section of a bill, but they have different ideas of how to go about it, what approach to take. I sit down with them and try to persuade them to agree on one tack. I tell them I don't care what they decide, as long as they go up there with one approach. I don't want it to appear that the company can't make up its mind.

"Then you have this kind of thing. An assistant to a Congressman called me the other day and said the Congressman wanted to poll his constituents on how they felt about various issues. He said they were short of money for the poll and needed another $250. My firm has plants or facilities in more than 100 communities, and one of them is in this Congressman's district. I called the manager of that plant and told him about it. About a week later, I ran into the assistant, and he said: 'I don't know who you called, but it certainly did the trick. We got the $250 in a few days.' "

Most examples of this type involve direct contact lobbying — personal contact between the lobbyist and the legislator or his aides. This is the lobbyist as persuader more than technician of pressure.

In almost all struggles over important legislation the lobbyist regularly mixes the direct contact technique with another important method — the indirect contact or grassroots lobbying. This is another answer to the question, what does a lobbyist do? He organizes grassroots pressure on Congress.

The United States Chamber of Commerce is masterful at the grassroots technique. In the expert hands of its lobbyists, indirect lobbying is a highly specialized, intricate affair.

In June 1963, the House of Representatives handed President Kennedy a major defeat by turning down his request for an additional $450 million to aid economically depressed areas. Grassroots lobbying by the Chamber of Commerce, including pinpointed pressure on key Congressmen, played an important, behind-the-scenes role in turning a close vote against the President. The strategy was mapped out in a meeting between "Judge" Howard Smith, the conservative chairman of the House Rules Committee, and Theron J. Rice, then chief lobbyist for the Chamber.

As part of the campaign, the Chamber sent a three-page letter signed by its president, Edwin P. Neilan, to all 435 members of the House, urging them to vote against the depressed areas bill. Another letter went to about 800 chairmen of Congressional Action Committees of local chambers of commerce. These chairmen were urged to whip up grassroots pressure on the House. "A substantial volume of letters, wires and phone calls to your Congressman will be a key factor in the outcome," said the letter.

All this was standard grassroots lobbying procedure. But the Chamber does more than issue general appeals. It breaks things down into little pieces for greater effect. The important point about the second letter was not who received it, but who didn't. It went to local committes in 39 states; it did not go to any in the 11 southern states.

A third letter was sent to about 200 Congressional Action chairmen in the south. The appeal in this letter was more specialized. It emphasized the "big federal spending" argument so persuasive to southern conservatives — and then it got down to cases. In one sentence, it flicked Dixie nerve endings where they were sure to hurt most: "The outcome of the vote depends in large measure upon how many southern conservatives vote their convictions and how many knuckle under to administration pressure . . ."

The Chamber's next letter zeroed in even more closely. In 1961, 43 Republican members of the House had voted for the original depressed areas bill. Thirty-six of them were still in the House. So a fourth letter went to the chairmen and all members of Congressional Action Committees in the districts of these 36 Republicans. It suggested that the local businessmen point out to these Congressmen that they had voted for a four-year "experimental" program and that they should see how it worked before approving more money for it.

Finally, a fifth letter went to chairmen and members of Congressional Action Committees in the districts of four House Republicans who had voted more recently for a stepped-up program of public works and presumably were flirting with dangerous thoughts. The Chamber was taking no chances.

The wording of each of the five letters was different. Each was tailored to a specific situation; each took into account a different set of factors.

This was lobbying.

And it paid off. The bill was defeated on a close vote, 209 to 204. For the first time in the Eighty-Eighth session of Congress, Republicans and southern Democrats resurrected their old coalition — which was what Judge Smith and Terry Rice had in mind — to defeat a New Frontier bill. Of the 57 Democrats who voted against the measure, all but three were from the south. Equally important, of the 36 Republicans singled out in the fourth letter, 19 switched and voted against the additional money for depressed areas. If only three more of the 36 had stuck by their 1961 vote, the bill would have passed. Administration leaders in the House had counted on about 20 Republican votes and a close win — which gives a good idea of the importance of well-organized grassroots lobbying.

If these have been examples of what lobbyists do, what do non-lobbyists do? It's an important question; Washington abounds with non-lobbyists, too. That is, there are a great many men and organizations whose work brings them into the legis-lative arena in one way or another, often intimately, and yet they do not register under the Lobbying Act.

It was noted in the first chapter that although the public rela-tions firm of Hill and Knowlton conducts large grassroots lobby-ing campaigns it has not registered as a lobbying organization. What do the Washington representatives of this firm do?

"The reporting function is 99 percent of our work," said Robert K. Gray, vice president in charge of the Washington office. "One man in the office goes through the Congressional Record every day looking for anything that might affect Hill and Knowlton's clients. We look over all government press releases. We report to our clients on upcoming appointments to federal posts that might be of interest to them and on actions by federal regula-tory agencies that might affect them. On legislation, we may check with the sponsor of a bill to see whether he intends to push it, but we make no attempt to influence legislation."

There is a fine line here. When Hill and Knowlton expresses interest in a bill by checking with its sponsor, is that pressure of a sort? Many Congressmen are fully aware that H. and K. represents some of the largest and most powerful corporations in the country. It is hardly a secret that Hill and Knowlton's clients account for more than 10 percent of the gross national product of the United States, that it represents seven large oil companies and that among its trade association clients are the American Petroleum Institute, the American Iron and Steel Institute, the Tobacco Institute, the Aerospace Industries Association and, until recently, the Pharmaceutical Manufacturers Association.

Gray, a compact, wiry man with a pleasant but rather cautious manner, was secretary to the Cabinet in the latter years of the Eisenhower administration and has extensive contacts in Republican circles. To illustrate his point about the reporting function, he described his activities on a fairly typical morning:

"To start with, I spent a half hour at the Interstate Commerce Commission trying to determine the schedule of hearings on a parcel post increase — whether they had a list of witnesses, and so on. Then I went to the Hill and talked to two Congressmen about a related parcel post matter. After that I talked to a Senator on a purely political matter.

"But I didn't give the ICC or the Congressmen any arguments against the parcel post increase. We never give arguments for or against legislation. That's up to our clients. We advise them. I don't consider myself a lobbyist as defined by the Lobbying Act or the Supreme Court. We don't testify before Congressional committees. We do have contacts with members of Congress, but this is for the purpose of obtaining information on legislation."

A booklet put out by Hill and Knowlton describes the services of its non-lobbying Washington office as follows: "Counsel on Congressional hearings, legislation and developments; intelligence concerning government activities, policies and decisions, and representation of clients in these areas; Washington press relations — counsel and operations."

One of Gray's associates explained that the Washington office advises Hill and Knowlton clients on how to make their testimony before Congressional committees more effective. "We don't usually write the testimony," he said, "but we go over it and liven it up if necessary, to make it more presentable. Then we get it out to Washington newspapermen in the form of press releases. We have lists of reporters and writers who will be interested in specific topics — steel, tobacco, etc.

"A more important part of our job is reporting to clients on governmental developments. Among other things, this involves attending hearings, as well as careful, selective reading of newspapers. The Southern Railway, for instance, was very interested in the transportation bill. So one of our men attended the hearings on the bill, prepared thumbnail summaries of the hearings and reported on the progress of the bill. We're sort of resident representatives. We can't speak for the client, but we can certainly keep his interests in mind in everything we do. It's a matter of staying in touch with everything that's going on."

Nowadays practically everybody belongs to a pressure group. If you have reached the age of discretion and are gainfully employed, the odds are heavy that you are an active or passive member of a special interest group that attempts to impose its will on government.

There is an association, union, society, league, conference, institute, organization, federation, chamber, foundation, congress, order, brotherhood, company, corporation, bureau, mutual, cooperative, committee, council, plan, trusteeship, movement, district, assembly, club, board, service or tribe for every human need, desire, motive, ambition, goal, aim, drive, affiliation, occupation, industry, interest, incentive, fear, anxiety, greed, compulsion, frustration, hate, spirit, reform and cussedness in the United States. Most of these groups sooner or later decide that they need someone in Washington to look after their special interests.

The Washington telephone directory lists some 1,200 trade, business and professional associations and more than 100 national labor organizations with offices in the nation's capital. The list takes up five pages. Only 304 of these organizations filed lobbying reports in a recent year. The list of associations does not include individual corporations maintaining Washington offices.

The best known pressure groups are such titans as the United States Chamber of Commerce, the National Association of Manufacturers, the American Federation of Labor-Congress of Industrial Organizations, International Brotherhood of Teamsters, American Medical Association, United States Savings and Loan League, National Association of Home Builders, National Association of Real Eestate Boards, American Trucking Associations, American Petroleum Institute, American Farm Bureau Federation, National Farmers Union, American Legion and National Education Association — the big-membership, big-league lobbying groups.

But the list just begins with these well-known names. The procession of special interest groups is almost endless. There are associations and organizations representing the electrical industry, the railroad industry, the airline industry, the drug industry, the insurance industry, the shipping industry, the trucking industry, the food industry, the automobile industry, the hotel industry, the cotton industry, the paper and pulp industry, the sugar beet industry, the publishing industry and the shoe industry, to mention only a few.

Further on, the list gets quite specialized: The American Carpet Association, the Wherry Housing Association, American Tramp Shipowners Association, Clay Pipe Industry Depletion Committee, Society for Animal Protective Legislation, Cross Florida Canal Navigation District, the Apache Tribe of the Mescalero Reservation, Bulgarian Claims Committee, Arthritis and Rheumatism Foundation, Liberty Lobby, Southwest Peanut Shellers Association, Committee to Support U.S. Congress Bill Creating a Commission on Obscene Matters and Materials, the Canal Zone Central Labor Union and Metal Trades Council, National Turkey Federation, Burley and Dark Leaf Tobacco Export Association, Council of Mechanical Specialty Contracting Industries, Inc., Junior Order of United American Mechanics, Armored Carrier Corporation (which, presumably being protected against life's vicissitudes by more effective means, reported spending only $17 for lobbying in 1961), Corn Starch Industry Committee, American Justice Association, American Thrift Assembly, New York and New Jersey Dry Dock Association, Home Town Free Television Association, and the Pitkin County Water Protective Association.

There are lobbies for children and old folks, for the unemployed and the affluent, for families and religious groups, for owners of confiscated German and Japanese property, for Negroes, Indian tribes, reserve officers, social workers and veterinarians. There are lobbies for foreign aid, for the World Court, and for home rule for the District of Columbia. There are lobbies for lighthouse employees, musicians, county supervisors, real estate dealers, osteopaths, sailors, government employees, bankers, bus drivers and librarians. And there are lobbies against all sorts of things — high tariffs and low tariffs, alcoholic drinks, air pollution, etc., etc.

In all probability more Americans pay dues and fealty to private interest pressure groups than go to the polls to vote for President of the United States and for their representatives in Congress.

The question is not whether these organized Americans *think* of themselves as Americans first and members of special interest groups second. Undoubtedly they consider themselves Americans first. The question is how they *act* — or if you will, how their special interest groups act.

The appeals and exhortations that go out constantly from lobbying organizations to their members place primary emphasis on the specific interests of the group, not the whole. Lip service is paid to the national welfare, but the fundamental appeal is to the economic or social well-being of a faction.

Pressure groups, Professor V. O. Key Jr. has written, have become the "true demagogues in our politics, in the sense that they appeal to the immediate selfish interests of their constituents to a far greater degree than do ordinary politicians."[1]

Some political scientists have concluded that the pressure group at work is the most realistic picture of government in the United States. They argue that no governmental decision (with the possible exception of a few of our wars and in spite of Lyndon Johnson's "consensus") ever results from a broad, generally-held belief that it is in the national interest. The actions of government, they contend, are produced solely by the mechanistic interaction of competing pressure groups. In the final analysis, some political scientists say, "the public interest" and "the national welfare" are euphemistic flag waving terms.

An interpretation of American government as merely the interplay of group pressures, nothing more, was propounded as early as 1908 by A. F. Bentley. His book, "The Process of Government," has had a substantial influence on political thought in the United States. To him there was no such thing as "government by the people." This, he believed, was nothing more than "a slogan and a rallying cry for some particular groups at special stages of their activity."[2]

The entire governmental process, Bentley argued, could be explained in terms of the action and reaction of interest groups. All legislative decisions could be traced to the influence of pressure groups at work — jockeying for advantage, trading and compromising, with one group gaining temporary dominance, then losing it to another in an endless struggle.

Discussing log rolling, or legislative trading, Bentley asserted: "When one condemns it 'in principle,' it is only by contrasting it with some assumed pure public spirit which is supposed to guide legislators, or which ought to guide them, and which enables them to pass judgment in Jovian calm on that which is best for 'the whole people.'" But, said Bentley, there is nothing that can be demonstrated to be best for "the whole people." Government, he concluded, "is trading. It is the adjustment of interests."

This thesis left little room for a broad concept of the national welfare as a backdrop against which disagreements over transitory, specific issues are fought out, and it gave precious little encouragement to the idea that there is such a thing as an overall public interest.

Bentley's view has not, of course, been accepted unanimously.

"The whole logic of democracy," Professor R. M. MacIver has commented, "is based on the conception that there is still a national unity and a common welfare . . .

"The fact that the interest in the common welfare cannot be organized after the fashion of specific interests should not conceal from us either its existence or the need to sustain it. Democracy itself is the final organization of the common interest. In a democracy, every specific interest, being a minority interest, must appeal to the whole (to get what it wants). In a democracy, certain values are accepted as being superior to minority interests."[3]

Among the superior values cited by MacIver are the right of every man to his own opinion and the right of free relationships. In other words, the very existence of a multitude of special interest groupings (free relationships) affirms the existence of democracy and, therefore, the existence of the public interest.

Professor Key weaves the two concepts together and arrives at what is probably the most widely accepted definition of the relationship between the general public welfare and the special interest.

"The promotion of the public good cannot be accomplished apart from class or special interest," Key says. "The public good is, after all, a relative matter. It rarely consists in yielding completely to the demands of one class or group in society. It more often consists . . . of compromise between conflicting groups.

"The principal driving forces in politics are class interests and group interests . . . It is a function of government to attempt to reconcile the interests of these groups, to devise policies that provide an accommodation among conflicting drives, to maintain social unity despite the inevitable diversity of interest . . ."

E. H. Carr makes the same point in this way: "If we wish to get a correct picture of the structure of the modern world, we must think not of a number of individuals . . . but of a number of large and powerful groups, sometimes competing, sometimes cooperating, in the pursuit of their group interests, and of a state constantly impelled to increase the strength and scope of its authority in order to maintain the necessary minimum of cohesion in the social fabric."[4]

There is no doubt that pressure groups make it difficult to achieve broad national agreement on which governmental actions are best for "the whole people." They always have and they always will. But given the immensely diverse, pluralistic nature of modern society, it is a waste of time to talk about this in terms of flat moral judgments. Special interests, like their agents, the lobbyists, are neither good nor bad; they just *are*.

The more productive line of inquiry would seek to draw up legislative ground rules that would define a balanced working relationship between special interests and government, that would prevent pressure groups from unduly delaying or diluting vitally-needed legislation and that would give Congress a greater measure of independence from these groups. This admittedly large order Congress traditionally has been unwilling to undertake.

There are two basic definitions of the public interest. Explicitly or implicitly, every special interest group relies on one or the other to justify its attempts to influence government. One definition holds that the public welfare consists of the greatest good for the greatest number. The other states that the public interest is composed of the sum of all the private interests.

The latter definition apparently originated with the British utilitarian philosopher, Jeremy Bentham, who wrote that "the interest of the community [is] the sum of the interests of the several members who compose it." Ironically, Bentham also propounded the doctrine of "the greatest happiness [good] of the greatest number." As a matter of fact, he spent a good deal of time trying to reconcile the two. The predictable result was that he incurred the hostility of both sides.

In lobbying parlance, those who rely essentially on the "sum of the private interests" definition are commonly referred to as profit or status quo lobbyists. The shoe usually fits, since their legislative interests, when the verbiage is stripped away, usually come down to the protection of profits or private property.

Those who invoke the rallying cry of the greatest good for the greatest number generally are referred to as non-profit lobbyists, or sometimes *pro bono publico* lobbyists. They are fewer in number, and their right to the title of *pro bono publico* depends on your political and economic views. The fight over the Telstar bill was a classic illustration of a clash between private and public interests.

The private interest, or profit, definition leaves much to be desired. There are all sorts of conflicts of private interests — economic, regional, social. The truckers and the railroads are at each other's throat; the Chamber of Commerce supports one tax bill, the N.A.M. another; the butter men snipe at the oleomargarine men. Some manufacturers want high tariffs, others low tariffs; the N.A.M., for instance, took no position on President Kennedy's tariff program — the Trade Expansion Act — because it could not get the required two-thirds majority of its board of directors to come out for or against the measure. And so it goes. The sum of the private interests is the same confusion and disagreement as the parts.

Although Professor Key correctly points out that "no universally acceptable definition of the general welfare could be formulated," he adds that "the doctrines of American democracy give weight to the notion of the greatest good for the greatest number."

The greatest good for the greatest number remains the best definition of what constitutes the public interest. This definition keeps the emphasis where it should be — on the substance of the legislation, what it would do and for whom. If the greatest good principle is kept in mind, it is easier to spot the camouflaged appeals of privilege. Moreover, the greatest good doctrine is a safeguard against the transaction of public business in private. Special interest legislation has a way of originating under conditions that are, in Daniel Webster's words, "as private as murder."

Finally, the greatest good definition helps protect the many from the few. Governmental action benefiting the few must be considered in the light of what it adds to what they already have.

Conventional beliefs don't jibe with the greatest good definition. A current American mystique is that ours is a happily affluent society in which the nation's wealth is constantly being distributed more equally. Those who believe this cherished myth of the middle class cite the 70,000,000 personal bank accounts in the United States, the 115,000,000 life insurance policies, the 3,500,000 unincorporated businesses and the fact that about 17,000,000 Americans, one out of every six adults, now own corporate stocks.

But John G. Fuller has pointed to a lesser-known statistic: about 1½ percent of the adult population of the United States owns approximately 80 percent of the corporate stock.[5] In 1922, economist Robert J. Lampman found, 1 percent of the adult population owned 60 percent of the stock in corporations; by 1929, just before the bust, this same 1 percent held 66 percent of the stock; by 1953, its share had risen to 76 percent.[6]

Those who hold fast to the conventional outlook like to point out that the wealthiest 10 percent of the nation's population received only 29 percent of the national income in 1959, compared with 39 percent in 1929. But historian Gabriel Kolko has noted that the big gainers at the expense of the wealthy have not been the poor. The second and third tenths of the population — the middle class — increased their share from 22 percent in 1929 to almost 28 percent in 1959. The poorest three-tenths saw its share of the national income actually drop — from 14 percent in 1910 to 10 percent in 1929 to 9 percent in 1959.[7] The income of the non-affluent has risen, to be sure, but at a much slower rate than that of the affluent.

The Department of Commerce's annual survey of the distribution of income in the United States reveals that the wealthiest 5 percent of American families receives about 20 percent of the national income and the poorest 20 percent of the families get about 5 percent of the total income. In 1953, Kolko has pointed out, 9 percent of the people owned 46 percent of the nation's net

private assets. Since World War II one-tenth of the population
has owned, on the average, two-thirds of all liquid assets. Lampman found essentially the same thing: one-tenth of the population owns fully half of all the wealth in the United States,
including 80 percent of business and investment assets.

The many still need protection from the few. How are they
to get it?

The civil rights revolution has demonstrated that one way for
the disadvantaged to protect themselves is through direct action
outside the regular political channels. As a Negro lobbyist put
it in a conversation with this writer: "Most colored people regard
both political parties as fakers on the issue of civil rights." The
Negroes, who comprise a substantial part of the unprotected
many, had until recently given up hope that the normal political
and legislative apparatus would help them. This was one of the
main reasons they took to the streets.

Within the regular framework the traditional answer to the
question, how can the many protect themselves, has been:
through the ballot. And since the President of the United States
is the office-holder elected by a national constituency, the Presidency increasingly has become the key to whether, in our time,
the traditional answer suffices.

Strong Presidents, aware of their national constituency, have
asserted a claim to representing the national interest. Franklin
Roosevelt's New Deal and Harry Truman's Fair Deal, as Karl
Schriftgiesser and others have pointed out, set forth broad concepts of the national welfare, at least by implication, and fought
it out with powerful opposing concepts.[8] Roosevelt's early "fire-
side chats" inveighed not against Congress but against narrow
economic interests which he said were trying to block programs
that would benefit the vast majority of Americans.

After Truman left the White House, he said he hoped to be
remembered as "the people's President," adding: "There are
a great many organizations with lots of money who maintain
lobbyists in Washington. I'd say 15,000,000 people in the United
States are represented by lobbyists. The other 150,000,000 have
only one man who is elected at large to represent them — that is,
the President of the United States." Truman's first figure was
too low, but his points were clear: the public interest consists

of the greatest good for the greatest number, and the President is, or should be, the lobbyist for the public interest.

During the 1960 Presidential campaign John F. Kennedy asserted the same claim. At Wittenberg College in Ohio, he declared that "the consumer is the only man in our economy without a high-powered lobbyist in Washington. I intend to be that lobbyist." Again in 1960 he told an audience at the National Press Club that the American people "demand a vigorous proponent of the national interest — not a passive broker for conflicting private interests."

While Kennedy embodied Franklin Roosevelt's definition of the President as moral leader, he was not equally impressive as a lobbyist for the people's interest. Some of his accomplishments were notable and imaginative — the nuclear test ban treaty, the trade bill, the Peace Corps — but most of the progressive domestic measures he proposed lacked vigorous support and were often blocked in Congress by recalcitrant old men.

Lyndon Johnson has yet to capture the heart and spirit of the American people as a moral leader, but his achievements as chief lobbyist for the national welfare far exceed Kennedy's. It is a striking contrast: Kennedy, the brilliant, charismatic young leader thwarted again and again in his efforts to translate his vision into law; and Johnson, the singularly unlovable, uncaptivating figure who nevertheless has put on the books a massive increment of long-overdue social legislation.

How has Johnson done it? The answer is as many-sided as the man himself.

In a very real sense much of the spadework that led to Johnson's legislative victories in 1964 and 1965 had been done in the Kennedy administration. It's true that Congress stalled or rejected Medicare, federal aid to education, civil rights legislation, tax reduction and other major New Frontier programs, but hearings had been held, labor and civic organizations aroused public concern, and the White House created lobbying groups with ongoing influence. Softening up of Congress and moulding of public opinion were set in motion. Moreover, the legislators, like the rest of the country, were shocked by Kennedy's assassination and ready to do for him in death what they had been reluctant to do in life — a situation on which Johnson capitalized shrewdly in the early months of his administration. Yet these

things do not fully account for Johnson's legislative triumphs.
Of primary importance are the qualities, skills and experience
that he brought to the Presidency.

Although Kennedy worked hard at the business of lobbying
Congress, he was not a Congressional insider during his years
in the legislature. Congress was not the final goal of his ambition — that was reserved for the Presidency — and his detached
and ironic nature, the cool inner reserve of the superior man,
did not accord well with an invincibly middle-class legislature.
Kennedy knew what had to be done — knew it as well, perhaps,
as any American of his generation, knew it far better than most
members of Congress — but between the thought and the action
was a large gap. When he called in one of Capitol Hill's rough-
hewn rural barons for a chat, he outlined his ideas in quietly
rational terms, presented his arguments dispassionately and
wound up with a calm, even a diffident, plea for support. He and
the committee chairmen just didn't talk the same language, and
there was no help for it. Kennedy's New England reserve or
personal dignity made it difficult for him to harangue, bluff,
bluster and plead. He had the self-consciousness of the intellectual who watches himself at arm's length and draws away from
political brawling.

No compunctions of self-consciousness, intellectual pride or
cultural restraint encumber Lyndon Johnson. He has made his
way — bulled his way — through 30 years of the roughest kind
of politics, starting in the bash and smash abattoir of Texas. He
once told a political associate who had played around with the
opposition, "I'm gonna give you a little two-minute lesson in
integrity. And then I'm gonna *ruin* you."

The lessons that Lyndon Johnson learned in his hard school
were these: First, define the differences between the parties in
a dispute. Then see what each side will give up and what it will
insist on. Then find the pressure points that will compel each
side to give up a little more. Know their weaknesses. Then work
out a compromise. Then press, press, press to get the compromise
accepted.

It is this unselfconscious willingness to press, press, press —
never mind dignity, never mind the niceties, there's a job to be
done — that is the essence of "the treatment," as Johnson's technique came to be called when he was Senate majority leader.

As President, he has seen no reason to abandon the treatment.

After a White House meeting with Congressional leaders in 1965, Johnson called in reporters and cameramen to hear the legislators comment on the pending Medicare bill. One of those present was Virginia's conservative Harry F. Byrd Sr., then chairman of the Senate Finance Committee, which would have first crack at the legislation after it passed the House. Byrd was opposed to the health care measure and could delay, although probably not defeat it.

Did Byrd have any "observation" to make about the bill, the President inquired.

"There is no observation I can make now, because the bill hasn't come before the Senate," Byrd replied.

"But you'll take an interest in this?" Johnson asked.

Byrd, beginning to turn red as the reporters leaned forward to hear the exchange, responded: "All I can say is that I will see that adequate and fair hearings are held."

"It's true, isn't it," Johnson pressed on, "that there's nothing ahead of this, and that in a reasonable time you will arrange prompt hearings? You have nothing that you know of that would prevent that coming about in reasonable time, not anything ahead of it in the committee?"

The Senator, publicly on the spot, gulped, nodded and said: "Nothing in the committee right now."

"So when the House acts on this and it is referred to the Senate Finance Committee, you will arrange for prompt hearings and thorough hearings?" Johnson continued urgently.

Reduced by now to flushed and dumbfounded silence, Byrd nodded.

"And those hearings will be held promptly?" the President insisted again.

Byrd said something inaudible and nodded again.

"Good," said Johnson. Then, having hammered the opposition into incoherence, he banged the table, addressed the cameras, and tossed out the carrot. "I believe these responsible men will be responsible in meeting the needs of the country," quoth the President.

This was "the treatment," one of the few times it has ever been seen publicly. It was hard, it was harsh, it was undignified. John Kennedy could never have done it. But it worked. Johnson

got what he wanted — a public promise from Byrd not to delay
hearings on the bill, and he knew that the Virginia gentleman
would honor the pledge, albeit under duress. "The treatment" —
insistent pressure for action — has probably accomplished more
for Johnson than outright armtwisting or threats.

To get his astonishing way in the Congressional sessions of
1964 and 1965, Johnson had many things going for him, not the
least a huge Democratic majority in the House that Kennedy
never enjoyed. But it was Johnson himself, pressing, cajoling,
wheedling and exhorting the legislators in innumerable telephone
calls and at White House parties and briefings, dancing with their
wives and flattering the ladies outrageously, skillfully marshaling
his knowledge of each man's political background (a Senator
once commented that Johnson, as majority leader, ran his own
F.B.I. on Capitol Hill) — it was Lyndon Johnson, "old Lyndon," the cynical, shrewd veteran of a thousand battles and a
thousand deals, who got the votes when they were needed most
and turned in the most impressive legislative record since Franklin D. Roosevelt's Hundred Days.

It is a tribute of some kind to Johnson's monumental self-
confidence that he denies all — or most — of this. He has told
reporters blandly that "I haven't insisted on a single bill. I don't
believe in must bills. I never wanted the President telling me
it had to be done. We take the position with these people [Con-
gress] that we propose and they dispose. It's a matter of principle with me." On one occasion, he told reporters that the
stories about his marathon telephone calls to Capitol Hill were
a fiction nurtured by Senate Republican Leader Everett M.
Dirksen. The President insisted that he had made only two
telephone calls to members of Congress in one entire session.
He did not ask the reporters whether they believed in Santa
Claus, too.

Under Kennedy, liaison with Congress — the White House's
euphemism for lobbying — was a well-organized effort by a five-
or six-man staff headed by Lawrence F. (Larry) O'Brien, veteran
political strategist and a charter member of the "Irish Mafia."
When Johnson became President, O'Brien stayed on at the White
House. Although the personable Irishman is now Postmaster

General, he continues to serve as the administration's chief lobbyist, after Johnson himself.

When an administration bill is introduced in Congress, the White House staff leaves the early stages largely to another group of lobbyists, the Congressional liaison officers for the Cabinet department or executive agency involved — State, Treasury, Agriculture, and the rest. These departmental lobbyists have primary responsibility for getting bills through the subcommittees and committees, although O'Brien and his men are ready to lend a hand where needed. When the bill nears the floor for a vote, the White House staff joins forces with the agency lobbyists. There are about 35 of these departmental liaison officers, not all of whom devote full time to legislation. Together with O'Brien's staff, they comprise the "vast horde" of administration lobbyists which on occasion brings cries of anguish and indignation from the pitifully outnumbered Republican members of Congress and the brave little band of business lobbyists.

One of the departmental liaison men is Kenneth M. Birkhead, a sure-footed operator in the labyrinthine world of farm legislation as chief lobbyist for Secretary of Agriculture Orville L. Freeman. Generally ranked among the ablest of the liaison officers, Birkhead is one of Washington's anonymous old pros, a skilled tactician who held the Democratic Senatorial Campaign Committee together in the lean Fifties. "He ran the only effective political operation the Democrats had while Ike was President," a White House staff member said admiringly.

Until recently the many-sided legislative interests of the Health, Education and Welfare Department were in the dainty hands of James Grant Bolling, a wealthy, cigar-smoking Texan. She didn't take offense at newspaper stories that described her pretty or petite; she just smiled and lit up another black stogie.

To the American Medical Association, which outrages easily, lobbyist Jim Bolling was insult added to injury added to indignity. Here was a government agency trying to foist health insurance on an unsuspecting public, the A.M.A. snorted. And they were using a woman to do it. Snort. And she smoked cigars. Snort. Judging from the A.M.A.'s huffy tone, the cigars bothered the doctors almost as much as the socialistic shame of it all.

Jim Bolling, a personable brunette in her mid-thirties, explains that she was an only child and was named for her "badly disappointed" father, James W. Grant, a Texas oil man. Mrs. Bolling, who "loves politics violently," entered the University of Chicago as a political science student at the age of 15. An all-American skeet shooter in 1952-54, she has served as Democratic finance chairman for Texas. She left the HEW when she married Representative Richard Bolling, a Missouri Democrat. She has two children by a previous marriage to William B. Akin, an independent oil operator.

The basic legislative pattern under Kennedy and now under Johnson is familiar and, in broad outline, not too different from that of President Eisenhower. A proposal is announced, usually in general terms in the President's State of the Union address and then in greater detail in a special message. An administration bill embodying the proposal is introduced in Congress and referred to the appropriate House and Senate committees. The secretary of the department involved, flanked by his assistants, testifies at great length before each committee, and later he may do some top-level lobbying himself.

If the recommendation is a major part of the President's legislative program, a departmental task force is usually set up to push it. An example was the adminstration team assembled by Under Secretary of Health, Education and Welfare Ivan A. Nestingen to beat the drums in Congress and at the grassroots level for the King-Anderson Medicare bill. Nestingen himself traveled widely in 1963, making speeches to whip up local support for the health care measure.

Another standard administration lobbying technique is the ad hoc citizens committee set up or encouraged by the White House to plug for a particular piece of legislation. To help Kennedy's beleaguered tax bill, for instance, a Business Committee for Tax Reduction was organized in the spring of 1963 under the impressive auspices of Henry Ford II, chairman of the Ford Motor Company, and Stuart T. Saunders, new head of the Pennsylvania Railroad, and with a membership list of some 2,400 businessmen. Discreetly in the background was the man who had first spread the word in the business community that such a committee was needed — Under Secretary of the Treasury Henry H. Fowler, who later became Treasury Secretary in the Johnson Cabinet. Johnson has made good use of this technique of ostensibly independent lobbying groups actually operating under White House auspices.

Probably the best organized White House lobbying operation in the Kennedy administration was the successful campaign to put through the Trade Expansion Act of 1962. The planning began in August 1961, more than a year before the tariff-cutting bill was passed, when Howard C. Petersen was appointed special assistant to the President for trade policy. Petersen, who is widely known in business and financial circles, took a leave from his job as president of the Fidelity-Philadelphia Trust Company. He rounded up a small staff of experts for a special task force on trade and enlisted an energetic "company rep," Carl Levin, as publicity director. Levin, Washington vice president of Schenley Distillers, Inc., persuaded public relations firms in New York, Chicago, Los Angeles and New Orleans to do volunteer grassroots work for the trade bill.

While Levin was mobilizing public opinion behind the trade program, Petersen's experts prepared statistical material for members of Congress, giving detailed breakdowns on how exports and imports affected their districts and states. In almost all cases the figures showed that expanded American trade abroad would benefit both management and labor at home. When the floor debates began the Senators and Representatives quoted these statistics to allay the fears of local industries and labor unions, pointing out that although a few might be hurt by lower tariffs, the over-all impact would be heavily on the beneficial side.

During the fall and winter of 1961-62, Petersen quietly lined up support for the bill in conversations with the heads of organizations whose backing would be vital. Former Secretary of State Christian A. Herter, a Republican, and former Under Secretary of State William L. Clayton, a Democrat, made speeches on behalf of the trade program and wrote a widely-distributed pamphlet calling for a "giant step" to form a trade partnership between the United States and Europe.

In this lobbying campaign, as in many others, the White House's task was to win the support of as many large special interest groups as possible. Alliances between the President and the big organizations are constantly shifting. When their interests coincide with his, or when they can be persuaded that this is the case, they are with him; if not, they fight the White House or remain neutral.

On the trade bill, administration forces did very well. The AFL-CIO and the U.S. Chamber of Commerce, institutionalized opponents on most issues, worked hard for the tariff measure. Equally important was support from two highly unlikely quarters — the American Cotton Manufacturers Institute, representing 80 percent of the nation's textile industry, and the American Petroleum Institute.

To win over the traditionally high-tariff textile men, the White House approved a series of executive actions to help the ailing textile industry. To woo the domestic oil industry, which wants tighter restrictions on oil imports, a study of existing curbs on oil imports was undertaken. All these actions were announced and publicized well before the trade bill came to a vote.

The basic aim of the Kennedy and Johnson administrations in their dealings with Congress has been to cooperate with the legislative branch, not challenge it. In the pursuit of this elusive goal, the determined motto of the White House lobbying staff is service — with a smile. As one Presidential aide put it: "We say to the Congressman, in effect, 'what can we do for you?'" There is, of course, plenty that the President of the United States can do for a member of Congress, and the White House staff is tirelessly alert to the possibilities, large and small. Does the Congressman have some important constituents in town? A call to the White House gets them on one of the private "V.I.P. tours" of the executive mansion, sparing them a long wait in the line for the public tour. If the constituent is really important, he may get a few minutes with the President himself, while the Congressman basks in the reflected glory.

A member who faces a tough fight for re-election may call on the White House for help. Perhaps he wants his picture taken with the chief executive, for use in hometown newspapers. Or the President's personal endorsement of his candidacy. Or a few well-known administration officials, who command headlines, to make speeches for him. Or a quiet word from the White House to the Democratic National Committee, to jar loose a little more campaign money. The White House lobbyists usually do not make the initial moves: "We simply put ourselves in a receptive posture if the Congressman wants to ask for something," one of them explained.

Predictably, the President's lobbyists contend that they do not expect White House favors to bring any direct or immediate advantage. They emphasize that a favor is seldom accompanied by a request for a *quid pro quo*. They insist all that is involved is building up good will and friendly relations, in the hope that the Congressman at some later date will vote with the administration on a tough bill.

"There are far fewer deals — for patronage, federal projects, that kind of thing — than you would think," said one Presidential legislative aide. "There are some — a few — but I rank deals at the bottom of the list in effectiveness." The most effective weapons in the White House arsenal, he continued, are, first, "the prestige of the national administration, with all its real but intangible power." Then, "We try to have a thorough knowledge of each member of Congress — his personality, his outlook, his background and his problems. Every Congressman has problems involving his area and his constituents. Maybe we can help him on some of them, others not. But at least we can understand him better if we know what his problems are." Next, "We want to have the same thorough knowledge of his district or state, especially its economics and politics." And finally, "We want a clear understanding of the two together — what is the Congressman's political situation at home? Does he have a hard fight coming up? What groups will be most important in determining whether or not he is re-elected?"

With the exception of the first item, all these are standard techniques for every experienced lobbyist. The business lobbyist and the labor lobbyist are just as intent on acquiring — and using — the same knowledge of Congressional attitudes and problems. For power and profit, Congress is one of the most assiduously cultivated institutions on earth.

As his own chief lobbyist, President Johnson cites the Great Society record with justifiable pride: of the 88 major legislative proposals backed by the White House in 1965, 84 were enacted. Among them were such landmark measures as the Medicare program, the most comprehensive voting rights bill in 90 years, the general school aid bill, new programs for higher education, a cabinet department of housing and urban development, regional medical centers, revision of the immigration system and many others. With good reason, the President called this session of Congress "the fabulous Eighty-ninth."

In the domestic arena, where he operates with such skill, Johnson has performed impressively. If his methods and manners offend some, only the unreconciled few can quibble with the results. The Texan with the bad grammar and worse pronunciation, the heavy hand, the low-brow tastes and the mock humility, has nevertheless labored mightily to improve the quality of life in the United States. If he cannot be loved, he can be admired.

But in the most important problem that has confronted his administration thus far, the sure hand of Lyndon the lobbyist has faltered. Despite the most strenuous efforts, he has not succeeded in persuading a number of leading members of Congress, and an important segment of the American people, that his Viet Nam policy is a wise and realistic one. Johnson and his national security advisers have briefed dissident Senators and Representatives an infinity of times, displayed a forest of charts, rattled off reams of intelligence reports, preached hundreds of sermons about dominoes and heathen Chinese, and offered dozens of rosy predictions, few of which have come true.

But the doubts remain. And unless they can be resolved, the catastrophe of Viet Nam could overshadow, in the final reckoning, all of Johnson's domestic achievements. It is not enough, in a pluralistic world, to assign all men and all nations to the pigeonholes of good and bad, friend and foe. It is not enough, in a revolutionary world, to respond to social upheaval with gunboats and Marines. It is not enough, in an age of nuclear overkill, to conduct holy wars against ideologies. The Saracens still held Jerusalem after all the shining knights had fallen. It is not enough, since man and his condition are volatile, to cling to old policies possessing only the dubious virtue of seniority. In these respects does moral leadership yet elude Lyndon Johnson.

HISTORY

"He who is disposed to ignore history must be prepared to repeat it."
— *George Santayana.*

"History is more or less bunk." — *Henry Ford in an inteview in 1916.*

Time has done wonders for Daniel Webster. Stephen Vincent Benet portrayed him as an incorruptible, granitic New England Puritan thundering the devil to a standoff, and it is this image that has persisted.

Historians have put Webster in a somewhat different light. The great orator was chronically short of cash and not a bit particular about how he got it. Webster's financial relations with the wily Nicholas Biddle, president of the second Bank of the United States, typify the great boodle and bribe era of American lobbying: the freewheeling nineteenth century.

At the beginning of his second term, President Andrew Jackson resolved to break the power of Biddle's bank and the "Nobility System" it represented. His first move was to withdraw the federal government's deposits from the bank. Biddle retaliated by using his institution's great power over state banks in an attempt to create a financial panic and coerce the government into renewing his charter. By the winter of 1833 the battle was raging in Congress.

On December 21, 1833, Webster, then a Senator from Massachusetts (he later was to serve twice as Secretary of State), wrote a confidential letter to Biddle. A model of brevity, it read in full: "Sir: Since I have arrived here, I have had an application to be concerned, professionally, against the Bank, which I have declined, of course, although I believe my retainer has not been renewed, or REFRESHED as usual. If it is wished that my relation to the Bank should be continued, it may be well to send me the usual retainers."

Webster got the money. The day after his greatest oratorical effort on behalf of the bank, Biddle handed him $10,000. Altogether he received $32,000 from the bank while it was under fire in the Senate. These were not loans; Webster never repaid anything. Arthur M. Schlesinger Jr., in "The Age of Jackson," has commented that Henry Clay fought for the bank "because it fitted in with his superb vision of America, but Webster fought for it in great part because it was a dependable source of private revenue." [1]

The great debater saw nothing wrong at all in what he did. Historian Gerald W. Johnson has observed: "The fact that he [Webster] had already sold his services to the people when he drew his salary as a United States Senator, and had, therefore, no right to resell them, affected him not at all . . . As for the people, he believed that in protecting the rich, he was protecting them . . ." [2] That was the feeling of other nineteenth century Congressmen who accepted "fees" and "retainers" and free stock from railroads, banks and other business interests while at the same time voting on legislation affecting these interests. They were men of their times, and the prevailing temper of the age did not find anything particularly unprincipled about this behavior.

The business of the United States in the nineteenth century, as a later President said of the twentieth century, was business. More accurately, the business of nineteenth century America was to grow, and the bankers, the industrialists, the railroad men, the factory owners, even the Wall Street speculators, were making America grow. The lobbyists swarmed over Capitol Hill putting this message across. Congress was a willing listener.

This was the "classic" era of lobbying in the United States. In these gaudy, corrupt years, government generally stood aside. The nation grew, and some men prospered. But in the process the public at large was victimized, and natural resources belonging to all were plundered by a few.

No one knows who the first lobbyist was, or the first pressure group. The only certainty is that both are virtually as old as government itself. The priestly Egyptian brotherhood conspiring against Akhenaton's monotheism was a pressure group. The courtiers seeking favors at Versailles were lobbyists of a sort.

Plato wrote that the real rulers of men usually are unseen and unknown, but "always they are there and always they are few."

The word "lobby" first appeared in the English language around the middle of the sixteenth century. It apparently was derived from the medieval Latin word "lobium," a covered walk or cloister in a monastery. With the development of the parliamentary system in Britain, the word came to refer to the halls and corridors in the House of Commons. In Britain, however, the word lobbyist means a newspaperman gathering information in the corridors of Commons. What we call a lobbyist the British call a lobby-agent.

According to the "Dictionary of American English," the first recorded use of lobby as a legislative word in the United States was in 1808, when it appeared in the annals of the Tenth Congress. By 1829 the word lobby-agent was in use at the New York state capitol in Albany, and was soon shortened to lobbyist. At other times in the nineteenth century lobbyists also were known as lobbyers, lobby members and "strikers."

Where the right to petition government is guaranteed, the right to engage in lobbying is similarly guaranteed. For the English-speaking democracies, the basic right of petition was set forth in Magna Carta, the Great Charter wrung by the British barons from blundering King John on the field of Runningmead (Runnymede), on June 15, 1215. After permitting the barons to set up a 25-member committee to "keep and cause to be observed, the peace and liberties which we have granted to them," John further granted them the right to petition him for redress of any violation of their rights. The charter, as W. S. McKechnie and others have pointed out, was not a broad affirmation of human liberties. It contained no reference to habeas corpus, jury trial in criminal cases or parliamentary control over taxation.

For two or three centuries after Runnymede, the charter was all but forgotten, blotted out by the Wars of the Roses and the strong arms of the Tudors. "It remained for the Puritans of the seventeenth century, in their contest with the Stuarts, to resurrect Magna Carta and interpret it as an impregnable bulwark of democracy," McKechnie has noted. "Many of these Puritans migrated to the New World and imbedded their ideas in American political philosophy. And when the United States came into being, Magna Carta was viewed as a priceless heritage, never to be lost sight of, and bravely to be defended." [a]

The right of petition was claimed and exercised in the British portion of the New World at least as early as 1619, when Virginia's first House of Burgesses took this as its prerogative. The colonial assemblies, particularly in Puritan-dominated New England, came to regard themselves as the custodians of popular rights under the colonial charters granted by the King of England. Thus, the Massachusetts general court was petitioned in 1646 by a Dr. Child, who hoped that in this way his plea might reach the British Parliament.

With this background, it was a matter of course for the right of petition to be affirmed in the colonial Declaration of Rights in 1765. It was mentioned in the Declaration of Independence and then secured formally in the First Amendment to the Constitution. The right of the American people to bring any and all matters to the attention of their government thus is among the oldest of our liberties. Equally hoary is the less worthy practice of seeking special or excessive privileges from government.

Hardly was the United States of America under way as a going concern when a monumental lobbying and bribery scandal rocked the new nation. President Washington was indignant, and the aroused citizens of Georgia finally tossed out a corrupt and faithless legislature whose members had been bought — lock, stock and vote — by land speculators.

Georgia had been having trouble with its vast western lands. After an unsuccessful effort to sell part of its western holdings to the federal government (Congress turned down the offer), the state finally decided, in 1789, to sell three huge tracts of land to three groups of speculators. The three groups came from three states, and since part of the land involved lay along the Yazoo river, each had the word Yazoo in its name — the South Carolina Yazoo Company, the Virginia Yazoo Company and the Tennessee Yazoo Company. The South Carolina group was led by Thomas Washington, alias Walsh, later hanged for counterfeiting. Patrick Henry was in the Virginia group. These three public-spirited companies proposed to buy some 20,000,000 acres of land for a total of $207,000, or about a penny an acre. They almost succeeded, but the deal fell through at the last minute.

A few years later, in 1795, the speculators were back, and heavy pressure began. Four companies were organized this time, to buy 35,000,000 to 50,000,000 acres for a non-inflationary total of $500,000. A bill was introduced in the Georgia legislature, authorizing sale of the land to the speculators, but its title did not mention the sale.

"Bribery and fraud appeared in the title of this act, in its body, and accompanied its passage," remarks E. Merton Coulter in his history of Georgia.[4] Reluctant members of the legislature were won over with bribes of land (75,000 acres to one legislator), slaves, barrels of rice, and, of course, money. David Loth reports that every member of the legislature but one was bribed.[5] A chief lobbyist for the speculators was James Gunn, a United States Senator from Georgia.

The bill passed and was signed by the governor, at which point the people of Georgia woke up. Grand juries acted against some of the legislators; one member was driven out of the state by his enraged constituents, and at the next election the entire legislature was heaved out. The people were quite upset. They burned the bill at a public ceremony, expunged all references to it from the state records and passed a law providing a $1,000 fine for any subsequent legislator who even mentioned it.

But lobbying persisted in Georgia, as elsewhere. By 1877 things had got so bad in the Peach State that the voters wrote an unprecedented clause into their constitution. "Lobbying is declared to be a crime," it said simply. When the state constitution was revised in 1945, however, this pithy little sentiment disappeared.

The lobbying activities of wealthy merchants during the First Continental Congress were not lost on the founding fathers when it came time to draft the Constitution and persuade the states to ratify it. James Madison, one of the chief architects of ratification as a co-author (with Alexander Hamilton and John Jay) of the Federalist papers, was clearly aware of the potentially divisive consequences if special interest groups were not restrained by some equal or superior governmental force. In the tenth of the Federalist essays he wrote:

"Among the numerous advantages promised by a well-constructed union, none deserves to be more accurately developed than its tendency to break and control the violence of faction . . . By a faction, I understand a number of citizens, whether amounting to a majority or minority of the whole, who are united and actuated by some common impulse of passion, or of interest, adverse to the rights of other citizens, or to the permanent and aggregate interests of the community."

What to do about factions? "There are," Madison said, "two methods of curing the mischiefs of faction: the one, by removing its causes; the other, by controlling its effects." To remove the causes, he wrote, it would be necessary either to destroy liberty or to see to it that every citizen had the same opinions, the same passions, and the same interests. Both of these cures Madison rejected as worse than the disease. "The inference to which we are brought," he concluded, "is that the causes of faction cannot be removed, and that relief is only to be sought in the means of controlling its effects." A strong union — a strong federal government — he saw as the only feasible counterbalance to powerful factions.

With the industrial revolution came big-time lobbying at the national level. The phenomenal growth of industry and commerce in the United States in the nineteenth century created so much money and put it in the hands of so few people that their need for protection immediately became apparent. The chief characteristics of lobbying throughout the century were the preservation and encouragement of private property.

As soon as there was property to protect — new property in the form of manufactured goods, industrial plants, mines, smelters, railroads, as opposed to land — there were organizations and lobbyists to see to it that the federal government protected it. Alexander Hamilton's Philadelphia Society for the Protection of National Industry was founded in the early 1800s, as was the Pennsylvania Society for the Encouragement of Manufactures and the Mechanic Arts, spiritual forbear of the National Association of Manufacturers.

The high-tariff Pennsylvania Society hired Friedrich List, a German immigrant, as its propagandist. List came up with an interesting idea. He proposed that "the friends of domestic industry should meet annually to prepare the necessary legislation for Congress after discussing the measures and gathering the facts."⁶ This forward-looking idea was the precursor of the comprehensive legislative programs now prepared every year or two by the large business associations and labor organizations.

In the 1850s the value of manufactured goods reached a level of one billion dollars a year and for the first time exceeded the value of farm products. The nation had begun the great change-over from an agricultural to an industrial economy. The stage was set for the classic period of lobbying, the flamboyant era of lavish entertaining, lavish spending, and raids on the national treasury.

By 1852 things were so bad that James Buchanan was moved to write to Franklin Pierce: "The host of contractors, specula-tors, stockjobbers, and lobby members which haunt the halls of Congress, all desirous . . . to get their arm into the public treasury, are sufficient to alarm every friend of his country. Their progress must be arrested."

Madison's dictum had run into trouble. The weak Chief Exec-utives of the 1850s, Pierce and Buchanan among them, were unable to cope with such strong-willed industrialists as Samuel Colt, Cyrus McCormick, Edward M. Chaffe and Erastus Corning. Colt was revealed to have paid one member of Congress a $10,000 "contingent fee" to refrain from opposing a patent extension bill. His chief lobbyist, high-living Alexander Hay, passed out expen-sive revolvers to deserving politicians. McCormick, the reaper baron, was equally active in other ways, and so were the railroad kings, the steamship kings and the cotton kings.

Among the swarms of lobbyists that infested Washington in the 1850s the most powerful was generally acknowledged to be the redoubtable Thurlow Weed. A self-made gentleman of parts, Weed was far from an ordinary lobbyist. He was the embodiment of a close blending of politics, business and lobbying that has been with us ever since. The elements were mixed in this extra-ordinary man: a leader of men, he was a generous public bene-factor (he was noted for his assistance to immigrants), and a talented political organizer.

Weed was also one of the pre-eminent legislative manipulators and political spoilsmen of his day. In Washington and at the New York state capitol in Albany his influence on legislation was vast. His biographer, Glyndon G. Van Deusen, has said: "There is no evidence that he put this influence up for sale to the highest bidder, but it is certain that he was perfectly com-

plaisant about taking pay for his services in legislative matters." '
To his contemporaries he was known as "the wizard of the lobby,"
"the Lucifer of the lobby," and "the father of the lobby." His
friends and enemies alike referred to him as "the dictator." He
was one of the first of the great fixers.

A tall, broad-shouldered, impressive man, Weed was born in
a log cabin, a political asset easier to arrange in those days.
From these humble beginnings, he set about resolutely providing
material for Horatio Alger. In his youth he knocked about the
country as a printer, finally landing in Albany, where he became
editor of the Evening Journal and a member of the state legislature. His editorials championing the cause of immigrants and
renters, advocating extension of the suffrage, opposing slavery
and warning against government subsidization of vested interests
made him anethema to conservatives.

But Weed's youthful zeal for reform did not last. By the
middle of the century, with his political influence at its peak,
Weed was a high-priced instrument for the same vested interests
against which he had inveighed in the 1830s and '40s.

When the Bay State Mills of Lawrence, Massachusetts, decided to spend $70,000 in an effort to lower the duties on wool,
$5,000 went to Weed through an intermediary, John W. Wolcott,
a professional lobbyist. Robert W. Lowber, who swindled New
York City out of some thousands of dollars, transferred 7,500
shares of Minnesota and Northwestern Railroad stock, par value
$100 a share, to Weed for his assistance in pushing a land grant
bill through Congress. Weed paid Lowber a grand total of $1
for the stock. Erastus Corning, president of the New York Central Railroad, got Weed to help him in seeking extra compensation from Congress for a construction company in which Corning
was interested.

"Corning's letters," Van Deusen has written, "said nothing
about emoluments, simply giving polite orders as to how to
proceed. Others were not so delicate. 'You will say nothing to
the Erie Railroad people,' wrote A. S. Diven, 'about the service
you rendered me in gitting (sic) their bill through the (New
York state) legislature. But draw on me at Elmira for five hundred dollars.'" The pay scale for lobbying at the state level
apparently was lower.

In his prime, Weed was a national leader of the "Log Cabin

Whigs," and later he rendered valuable service in organizing the
Republican Party. He was a friend and confidant of Commodore
Cornelius Vanderbilt, William H. Seward (later Lincoln's Secretary of State), Horace Greeley, William Marcy (Boss) Tweed,
bank presidents, railroad tycoons, wealthy merchants, literally
everyone worth knowing.

Weed lived to be 85 years old, a man whose conduct accorded
with his lights and the lights of the period: that business and
economic growth was the chief goal of American society, justifying a multitude of sins.

In his wake came a remarkable, attractive man, "one of the
most dazzling and puzzling personalities in American history,"
as Beverly Smith has remarked.[3] His name was Samuel Ward;
for 15 years after the Civil War he reigned in Washington as the
acknowledged "King of the Lobbyists." It's a pity Sam Ward
is not much remembered these days. His lineage was impressive,
his accomplishments and interests equally so.

His great-great-grandfather, Richard Ward, was a colonial governor of Rhode Island. His great-grandfather, Samuel Ward, was
one of the framers of the Constitution. On his mother's side, his
great-uncle was Gen. Francis Marion, the famous "Swamp Fox"
of the Revolutionary War. Sam's father headed the New York
banking firm of Prime, Ward and King. The elder Ward once
pledged his personal fortune to save the credit of the state of
New York.

Two of Sam's relatives left more enduring monuments. His
sister, Julia Ward Howe, wrote "The Battle Hymn of the Republic" (and doted on brother Sam although she highly dis-
approved of his activities), and his cousin, Ward McAllister,
coined the term "the Four Hundred" to describe New York's
society.

Sam's intellectual abilities and range were vast. He was a
mathematical prodigy, a Latin scholar, a poet, a gourmet, an
accomplished pianist and guitarist, a wit and a bon vivant. He
graduated from Columbia University at 17 and soon thereafter
began writing learned articles for the American Quarterly Review.
He updated a standard algebra text and later wrote an essay
on the science of probabilities. At 18 he was invited to West
Point as the mathematical member of the board that conducted

the annual examination of cadets. While still a young man he lectured before academic societies on mathematics, history and European philosophy, and was elected an honorary member of the Phi Beta Kappa chapter at Harvard.

A doting father sent Sam to Europe for a year's postgraduate work in mathematics. But Sam had other ideas. He applied himself assiduously to the boulevards and bistros. "His original fine scholarship," Beverly Smith has written, "faded toward dilettantism." Although he resolved periodically to buckle down to serious work, fine food, fine clothes, bright conversation and camaraderie somehow kept getting in the way.

When his father died in 1839 he left Sam several million dollars, which he frittered away with speed terrific. He was exceedingly generous. "If he liked you — and he liked almost everybody — he would give you a black sapphire, or a dozen cases of Bernkasteler Doktor, or a watch, or a horse, or a house," according to Smith.

Although the elder Ward tried to train him in the banking business, Sam never grasped the intricacies of finance. When he took his father's place in the firm, he drove his conservative partners into a tizzy; in self-defense, they dissolved the partnership in 1846. Sam decided to show them. He set up his own banking house. It went broke in a year.

Sam headed west. He joined the Forty-Niners in the Gold Rush to California, made a quarter of a million in real estate and mining shares, went broke again, lived adventurously among the Indians and then, in 1854, went to Mexico to negotiate with President Santa Anna for the life of a friend, Count Raousset-Boulbon, who had been captured leading a filibustering foray south of the border. Too late. The count had been executed before Sam arrived.

After that he kicked around Latin America for some years, conducting dancing classes for the senoras and charming everyone. "Apparently he became something between a semi-official diplomat and a secret agent, working sometimes for the State Department, sometimes for private corporations," Smith says. Financiers had spotted him as a useful agent in the turbulent Latin American situation, a handy man in wars, revolutions, filibustering, and in arranging mining and railroad concessions.

Sam had money again, but sister Julia was distressed. "Come

back to the old Puritan morals," she urged him in a letter. "Shake yourself loose from this nightmare. Wake up, and find yourself all that you ever were — the honest son of an honest man." Sam took her advice. He headed for Washington, arrived just before the guns boomed at Fort Sumter, and came into his own.

"The way to a man's Aye," Sam Ward once said, "is through his stomach." When Sam entertained at Chamberlain's or other fashionable restaurants, the stomach was the winner, regardless of what happened to the legislation. As host, Sam often prepared the main dish himself. He was an expert with soft shelled crabs, canvasback duck, stewed terrapin and Virginia ham. He cooked the ham in champagne, adding "just a wisp of new-mown hay" for an extra soupcon of flavor.

"Dined with old Buchanan [President James Buchanan] last night . . . Last Sunday General [Winfield] Scott, Senators Crittenden, Gwin, Latham and John Van Buren dined with me and sat at table until 11 o'clock." So went one of Sam's letters to Julia.

Although he was the wittiest of conversationalists, Sam Ward was usually discreet about his work; there are few specifics in his letters. It is known that when he first came to Washington he hoped to promote peace between the North and South, but he changed his tactics, if not his convictions, when Hugh McCulloch, later Lincoln's Secretary of the Treasury, offered him $12,000 a year "plus dinner expenses" to "court, woo and charm Congressmen, especially Democrats prone to oppose the war."

The size of Sam's fees, except on a few occasions, was not a matter of record. He was reported to have received $50,000 for one tariff job, and his fee in connection with one mail subsidy case was almost certainly impressive; an estimated $1,000,000 was spent on this lobbying operation. Yet Sam boasted that he had never paid a bribe to anyone to influence legislation. A Congressional investigating committee asked him what he had done, then, to earn his fee in the mail case and why he had been retained. "I suppose," he answered modestly, "because I am called King of the Lobby, but I am not Treasurer of the Lobby, that is certain."

The committee inquired about his famous dinners for Senators and Representatives. "Talleyrand," replied the learned lobbyist with a smile, "says that diplomacy is assisted by good dinners. At good dinners people do not talk shop, but they give people a right, perhaps, to ask a gentleman a civil question and get a civil answer." A good description of the Washington lobbyist at work over the dinner table then and now.

On one occasion, Sam's discretion failed him. Elated by a victory, he wrote to his close friend Henry Wadsworth Longfellow: "When I see you again I will tell you how a client, eager to prevent the arrival at a committee of a certain member before it should adjourn, offered me $5,000 to accomplish his purpose, which I did, by having his [the Congressman's] boots mislaid while I smoked a cigar and condoled with him until they would be found at 11:45! I had the satisfaction of a good laugh, a good fee in my pocket, and of having prevented a conspiracy." The allusion to a conspiracy is unclear; Sam was certainly the conspirator in this case.

Perhaps he meant that the legislation involved was, at least in his opinion, without merit. For Sam had certain principles about lobbying. "I quite agree," he once wrote, "that the profession of lobbying is not commendable. But I have endeavored to make it respectable by avoiding all measures without merit." This convenient rationalization has been invoked by some lobbyists since. The trouble is, who decides whether a bill is good or bad?

In 1879 the North American Review published a series of articles entitled "The Diary of a Public Man." This purported to be a diary kept by an anonymous resident of Washington during the critical winter of 1860-61, when the union was breaking up. It contained several accounts, apparently by an eyewitness, of previously unrevealed incidents involving Abraham Lincoln. As such, it was considered to have great historical significance, and it was accepted as authentic by many Lincoln biographers, including Carl Sandburg and Ida M. Tarbell.

But in 1949, after years of academic sleuthing, Frank M. Anderson, professor of history at the University of Minnesota, published "The Mystery of a Public Man," which Beverly Smith calls "a piece of history as fascinating as a detective story." Anderson's conclusions were that most of the diary, especially the parts referring to Lincoln, was a monumental hoax and that it had been written by Sam Ward, possibly with help from a friend, William Henry Hurlbert.

Sam Ward died in Italy in 1884 at the age of 70, with a copy of Horace under his pillow and the Rubaiyat of Omar Khayyam beside him. Three of his closest friends, the Earl of Rosebery (later Prime Minister of Britain), Hurlbert and F. Marion Crawford, the novelist, placed over his grave a tombstone with this inscription: "In loving remembrance of Samuel Ward . . . and God gave him largeness of heart even as the sands of the seashore."

The financial panic of 1857 illustrates a fundamental point about lobbying: there is just as much of it, if not more, in times of economic distress as in prosperous periods. Private interests expect the government, that is, the people of the United States, to protect them in bad times as well as good.

Karl Schriftgiesser offers a vivid picture of the scene in 1857:

"Railroads, manufacturers, bankers and brokers had been ruined by the scores, and thousands of people were unemployed as a result of the October crash of that year, a collapse that, as as we now know, had been caused by overproduction at home, overbuying abroad, the overbuilding of railroads, real estate speculation, and a completely unregulated banking system.

"There seemed to be only one place from which these victims could recoup their losses — the Treasury. And so businessmen, financiers, plungers, speculators and their agents rushed to the capital to beleaguer Congress for help . . . They flooded Congress with plans and schemes for the appropriation of public lands; they poured forth bills for the subsidization of railroads . . . there was a 'homestead proposal' to give a farm to every asker; there were proposals to strip the Indians of their remaining lands; practically every state wanted a federally subsidized agricultural college . . .

"The steamship and railroad lobbyists jostled shoulders with the huge crowd of lesser lobbyists who milled in the corridors demanding funds to widen rivers, deepen harbors, build light-houses, docks and custom houses, post offices, barracks, hospitals, and subtreasury buildings. The pressures for government-supported 'pump-priming' after the Panic of 1857 put into the shade any similar efforts during the early days of the New Deal."

The panic had only begun to subside when Congress had to turn its attention to the contracts for carrying mail to California by steamer. At this point Commodore Cornelius Vanderbilt enters the chronicle.

No account of rapacity in the nineteenth century is complete without mention of Vanderbilt, the semi-literate Staten Island ferryman who bulled and bludgeoned his way to fantastic power, the self-made autocrat who accumulated $94,000,000 in one 10-year period, the manipulator who watered stock and ruined small and large investors.

Vanderbilt bribed legislators on a grand scale, sold rotten ships to the government during the Civil War — and carved a big niche for himself in the history of the United States as a builder and creator. (Among other things he created 13 children, and when he offered to finance a joint monument to himself and George Washington, contemporary wits speculated on who was the real father of the country.)

The lucrative mail contracts between the federal government and private steamship companies were to expire in 1858 and 1859 unless renewed by Congress. The railroad lobbyists were feverishly at work trying to persuade the government to help out with the building of a transcontinental railroad. If rails were laid across the continent, they would be a powerful argument for taking the mail contracts away from the steamship lines.

Vanderbilt, the steamship king, personally directed the lobbying campaign against the transcontinental railroad. His prime intent was to kill the railroad bill and persuade Congress to renew the mail-by-boat contracts. The result was unrestrained warfare between the commodore and the "strikers" (lobbyists) for the Pacific Railroad.

Vanderbilt won. The transcontinental railroad was not completed until after the Civil War. And by that time the canny commodore had decided that railroads were the coming thing anyway, had sold his ships at high wartime prices and had gone into the railroad business.

A Congressional debate on the expensive mail contracts, and later an investigation, produced some interesting sidelights on Vanderbilt's operations.

The Pacific Mail Company, a steamship line threatened with competition from other lines, had been receiving $900,000 an-

nually from the government to carry mail to California. Officers
of the company testified that for several years they had turned
over more than half of this sum to Vanderbilt each year to prevent others from entering the field. "The terror of his name,"
one witness said, "would be effectual upon others who might be
disposed to establish steamship lines." Vanderbilt did nothing
for the taxpayers to earn almost a half million dollars annually
from the government. As Meade Minnigerode has commented,
the Pacific Mail Company was "plundering the government, but
'Old Vanderbilt' was the Kingfish [who was] robbing the small
plunderers." [9]

Another Congressional investigation dealt with Vanderbilt's
sale of rotten ships to the government during the Civil War.
Said Senator Grimes of Iowa, chairman of the investigating committee: "The whole transaction shows a chapter of fraud from
beginning to end." The commodore nearly was censured by the
Senate, but he couldn't have cared less. To the end he remained
a fearsome figure who took what he wanted in a grand, brutal,
and often ungrammatical manner. Once, when his lawyers
warned him that a certain move was illegal, he exploded: "Law!
What do I care about the law? Hain't I got the power?"

Speaking of one of the commodore's lobbyists, Senator Roscoe
Conkling commented that he was "the man that Vanderbilt sends
up to Albany every winter to say 'haw' and 'gee' to his cattle
up there." The legislators of the sovereign state of New York
were supposed to be the cattle.

Washington in the mid-nineteenth century was wide open.
Gambling dens and bawdy houses lined Pennsylvania Avenue
a stone's throw from the White House and spilled over into the
genteel residential neighborhoods, outraging respectable citizens.

"There was a hush of secrecy about the large [gambling] estab-
lishments," Margaret Leech tells us. "At the door, the applicant
for admission was scrutinized though a grated window before
he was permitted to enter 'the carpeted, elegant jungles of the
modern tiger.' The rooms were dazzlingly lighted, richly cur-
tained and hung with 'voluptuous paintings.' A buffet held de-
canters and cigars, and champagne and sherry and claret flowed
freely. There was a supper of boned turkey, ham, chicken salad
and other delicacies . . . all refreshment was free." [10]

The houses of prostitution had picturesque names — the Wolf's

Den (operated by a Mrs. Wolf), the Band Box. Patrons downed gin cocktails at eight cents each while they looked over the girls.

In the years just before the Civil War, Pendleton's gambling establishment on Pennsylvania Avenue "became the recognized clearing house for purchasable votes," Kenneth Crawford has written.[11] The business was handled in two ways. Either the Congressman was permitted to win at poker or faro, in which case Pendleton would put in a good word for a bill while the happy legislator counted his chips, or things were arranged so that he would lose.

Vanderbilt dined regularly at Pendleton's. According to Schriftgiesser it was more than mere friendship that caused the commodore to present a team of horses to Pendleton after a visit which happened to coincide with a vote on a mail contracts bill.

Whatever else it did the Civil War did not raise the moral level of politicians, lobbyists or businessmen. The chronicles of the Blue and Gray alike are filled with instances of shoddy shoes, paper uniforms, faulty rifles and moldy bread delivered to the troops under both Grant and Lee. Collusion between shady contractors and War Department officials was exposed by a Congressional investigation early in the war. The lobbyists, Sam Ward among them, were everywhere, arranging contracts, importuning Congress, entertaining influential legislators and cabinet members. The hordes of state and local politicians seeking commissions in the Army constituted a lobby of their own.

In the 20 years between 1865 and 1885 the concept of government by all the people, so movingly reaffirmed by Abraham Lincoln, almost went into eclipse. Special interest pressure and corruption in government mounted to dizzy heights. Popular democracy was threatened as never before in this country. The succession of mediocre Presidents — hapless Andrew Johnson, unfit Ulysses S. Grant, bland Rutherford B. Hayes, circumspect James A. Garfield and uneasy Chester A. Arthur — points up the truism that excessive lobbying for vested interests flourishes under a weak executive.

Grant's administration was flawed by big and little scandals, including two of the worst in the history of the republic: Credit Mobilier and Black Friday. The first involved some of the most prominent members of Congress, including Speaker of the House Schuyler Colfax (later Vice President) and Representative Garfield of Ohio (later President). The second reached into the White House itself, in the person of Abel Rathbone Corbin, a small-time Wall Street speculator who happened to be President Grant's brother-in-law.

Credit Mobilier of America was a joint stock company which, as David Loth has pointed out, "owned nothing except a charter drawn in the widest possible terms." But it served a highly functional purpose for the directors and incorporators of the Union Pacific Railroad. With the aid of generous federal grants, the Union Pacific was engaged in building part of the first transcontinental railroad. The railroad promoters took over Credit Mobilier and used it as the agency to pay themselves $93,000,000, most of it from the American taxpayer via the Union Pacific treasury. Their profit reportedly was $43,000,000. To protect this profit, it was necessary to insure that the federal subsidies kept coming. Washington was growing increasingly suspicious about the high cost of building the railroad. A good inside lobbyist was needed.

One was found. He was Congressman Oakes Ames of Massachusetts, who was given 200 unrecorded shares of Credit Mobilier stock. Within a month, according to Loth, Ames had entered in a small pocket book "the names of 12 of the most influential members of the House to whom he had given stock, and be it noted that this was the Credit Mobilier stock of the 'insiders' which carried the profits, not the Union Pacific stock which anyone could buy and would be sorry for later."

Among the 12 Representatives were Speaker Colfax, Blaine, Garfield, Boutwell of Massachusetts (later Secretary of the Treasury), and "Pig Iron" Kelley of Pennsylvania. Other Credit Mobilier shares went to Representative Brooks of New York, Democratic leader of the House. "I placed it where it would do the most good," Congressman Ames later explained.

Once he had the stock distributed strategically, Ames relaxed, secure in the knowledge that there would be no embarrassing questions from Congress, "for I have found that there is no difficulty in inducing men to look after their own property." Speaker Colfax obligingly blocked a Congressional investigation.

The public, which had bought millions of dollars worth of Union Pacific stock, "was royally bilked," as Loth tells us, "for the company could never hope to earn a return on the amount paid to the Credit Mobilier." Ames and Brooks were censured by the House but not unseated.

A few years later two of the great operators of the age, Jay Gould and Jim Fisk, growing a trifle bored with the mundane business of watering railroad stock, hit on an enterprising idea. They would corner all the gold on the New York market (which meant virtually all the gold in circulation in the country), drive the price up and make a killing.

It almost worked. From the beginning the only cloud on the horizon for Fisk and Gould was the United States Treasury, which had $100,000,000 in gold. The Treasury must be prevented from selling gold on the open market. Corbin was the inside man at the White House to make sure this did not happen. As added insurance, Gould purchased substantial amounts of gold for General Horace Porter, President Grant's secretary, and General Butterfield, head of the New York subtreasury.

At the height of the conspiracy, Corbin sent a message to Grant on the gold situation. When the message had been handed to the President, a telegram was dispatched to Fisk. As written the telegram read: "Delivered all right." But in transmission a period was inserted; when the telegram reached Fisk it read: "Delivered. All right." Believing that Grant would hold on to the Treasury's reserves, Fisk rushed into Wall Street, buying up gold. The price skyrocketed.

But Grant, belatedly, had decided to act. A few days before, he had instructed his wife to write to her sister, Mrs. Corbin. "Tell Mr. Corbin that the President is much distressed by your speculations and you must close them out as quickly as possible," wrote Mrs. Grant.

Gould dropped in on Corbin while the latter was perusing these alarming words. Corbin testified later that Gould could have learned the contents of the note only by peeking over his shoulder. "But I think him too much of a gentleman to do that," said Corbin. The best evidence, however, is that Gould did find out what was in the letter and knew that the game was up. He neglected to tell Fisk.

On September 24, 1869, while Fisk was buying gold as fast as he could, General Butterfield received a telegram instructing him to sell the subtreasury's gold on the open market. This was

Black Friday. Everybody who was anybody was ruined in the crashing fall of gold prices. Everybody but Jay Gould, who had secretly instructed his brokers to sell — early.

Fisk, fat, florid and foppish, took it in stride. When a Congressional investigating committee (throughout much of the last 35 years of the nineteenth century a Congressional investigating committee was angrily trying to find out what went wrong) asked him what happened to the money he spent trying to capture the nation's financial system, Fisk replied poetically: "Gone where the woodbine twineth."

The lackluster line of Presidents ended with Grover Cleveland's first inauguration in 1885. The civil service reforms he instituted were a long-needed first step toward clean government. But the years between Lincoln and Cleveland were a sorry chapter in American political history. Congress often was reduced to the status of errand boy for private interests.

The situation once moved Senator Justin S. Morrill, a Vermont Republican, to a memorable bit of sarcasm. Noting that the president of the Pennsylvania Railroad was in the outer lobby, Morrill rose in the Senate and offered a motion to appoint a committee to wait on him and find out if there was any further legislation he desired before adjournment.

The flagrant lobbying and boodling of the nineteenth century aroused little indignation on the part of the public, but in 1874 the Supreme Court took judicial note of the danger of unrestrained pressure tactics

The case which evoked the court's admonition was a minor one involving a long-standing claim against the United States by one N. P. Trist. Trist hired a lobbyist, Linus Child, who persuaded — or took credit for persuading — Congress to award Trist several thousand dollars. Trist failed to pay Child his 25 percent fee, and the lobbyist's son (Child had died), took the matter to court. Eventually it reached the Supreme Court, which turned down Child's claim. Justice Noah H. Swayne, a Republican, wrote a slashing decision.

"The agreement," he said, "was for the sale of the influence and exertion of the lobby agent to bring about the passage of a law for the payment of a private claim, without reference to its merits, by means which, if not corrupt, were illegitimate, and considered in connection with the pecuniary interest of the agent at stake, contrary to the plainest principles of public policy.

"If any of the great corporations of the country were to hire adventurers who make market of themselves in this way, to procure the passage of a general law with a view to the promotion of their private interests, the moral sense of every right-minded man would instinctively denounce the employer and employed as steeped in corruption and the employment as infamous. If the instances were numerous, open and tolerated, they would be regarded as a measure of the decay of public morals and degeneracy of the time . . .

"If the agent is truthful, and conceals nothing, all is well. If he uses nefarious means with success, the spring-head and the stream of legislation are polluted. To legalize the traffic of such service would open a door at which fraud and falsehood would not fail to enter and make themselves felt at every point. It would invite their presence and offer them a premium . . ."

There was no contention that Child and his son had bribed members of Congress, but the evidence was clear that they had tried to influence Congressmen on behalf of Trist's claim. Child's lawyers in effect acknowledged the attempts at influence. All that was involved, in other words, was the normal practice of lobbying.

Nevertheless, the Supreme Court refused to uphold the payment to the lobbyist on the ground that this would be contrary to "sound policy and good morals." The court, in short, rejected the normal fee-for-service arrangement that was and still is the accepted relationship between the lobbyist and his client. If the court's dictum had been enacted into law, there would be no professional lobbyists today. Needless to say, it was not.

In the following year, however, the House of Representatives did try to bring some order out of the lobbying chaos. The chairman of the Judiciary Committee, Representative George F. Hoar of Massachusetts, put through a resolution that remained in effect for one session: "Resolved that all persons or corporations employing counsel or agents to represent their interests in regard to any measure pending at any time before this House or any committee thereof, shall cause the name and authority of such counsel to be filed with the clerk of the House; and no person whose name and authority are not so filed shall appear as counsel or agent before any committee of the House."

This 1875 action was a direct ancestor of the lobbying law that finally was enacted in 1946. It made no attempt to restrict or curb lobbying. The only requirement was identification of the lobbyist and his employer so that Congress would know the sources of the pressures that beset it. Add to that the requirement in the 1946 law that lobbyists report their income and expenditures, and that is just about all that Congress has ever done to cope with special interest pressure.

The basis for the unrestrained lobbying of the nineteeth century, as we have seen, was the belief that anything business (meaning the rich) did was quite all right, simply because it was business that was doing it. The government of the United States, in effect, existed solely to serve private enterprise and to advance its interests. As the century drew to a close, Bishop Lawrence helpfully provided an even deeper rationale.

"In the long run," he wrote, "it is only to the man of morality that wealth comes. We believe in the harmony of God's universe. We believe that it is only by working along His laws, natural and spiritual, that we can work with efficiency. Only by working along the lines of right thinking and right living can the secrets and wealth of nature be revealed . . . Godliness is in league with riches . . . Material prosperity is helping to make the national character sweeter, more joyous, more unselfish, more Christlike. That is my answer to the question as to the relation of material prosperity to morality."

The eight-year-old children in the sweatshop, the women working 15 and 18 hours a day at sewing, the coal miners with tuberculosis, had difficulty achieving the requisite sweetness of character to agree with these uplifting sentiments, but they were, of course, benighted. Fortunately some improvement was on the way.

In the first years of the twentieth century a small group of American writers popularly known as "the muckrakers" spearheaded one of the greatest social, political and economic reform movements in history. Upton Sinclair's novel, "The Jungle" (1906), exposed the unbelievable conditions in the meatpacking and canning industries, especially in the Chicago stockyards.

Lincoln Steffens bared the corruption of America's cities in "The
Shame of the Cities" (1904). Ida M. Tarbell shocked the nation's conscience with a wide-ranging series of crusading articles
in McClure's Magazine between 1894 and 1906, together with
a thoroughly documented book on the monopolistic practices of
the gigantic Standard Oil Company. David Graham Phillips
(later murdered by a lunatic) exposed the sham debates and
the concentration of wealth in the Senate. Others — including
Ray Stannard Baker, Mark Sullivan, George Creel, T. W. Lawson
and Samuel Hopkins Adams — doggedly traced the powerful
pressures exerted on Congress by special interests, demonstrated
the untold ways in which the public was being victimized, misled
and mistreated, and campaigned for an end to political corruption, economic monopoly and social injustice.

In this monumental effort the muckrakers were joined by
reform groups such as the National Consumers League, by historians and political scientists such as A. F. Bentley, Charles and
Mary Beard, James Harvey Robinson and W. B. Munro, and
by a hard-driving President, Theodore Roosevelt. (The term
muckrakers was first used by T. R. in a 1906 speech attacking
corruption; it referred to a character in Pilgrim's Progress who
spent his time raking slime.) Roosevelt moved against the
trusts, against high railroad rates and against the patent medicine and drug scandals. He had some notable successes, but the
lobbyists for the vested interests fought him every step of the
way and won temporary victories against reforms in the fields
of child labor, arbitrary labor injunctions, a graduated income
tax, inheritance taxes and others.

The efforts of the reformers got a boost when Joseph Pulitzer's
New York World, in 1905, published a series of stories on the
corrupt practices of then-unregulated life insurance companies,
notably Equitable Life Assurance, Mutual Life, Prudential and
New York Life. An investigating committee of the New York
state legislature went to work. Its thorough probe was primarily
the work of a 43-year-old lawyer, Charles Evans Hughes, later
Chief Justice of the United States.

The insurance companies were shown to have spent millions
of dollars to influence legislation. Equitable and Mutual, it was
revealed, maintained a "House of Mirth" in Albany, where legislators relaxed in sensuous surroundings. Andrew C. Fields, chief

lobbyist for the two companies, presided over the House of Mirth but was listed on company books as head of Mutual's "supply department." He disappeared when the committee sought to question him about how he managed to spend almost $3,000,000 for "printing, stationery and postage."

With disclosures such as these the stage was set for Theodore Roosevelt's successor as the scourge of the lobbyists and vested interests — Woodrow Wilson. In his first campaign for the presidency, the scholarly Wilson laid it on the line in non-academic terms:

"The masters of the government of the United States are the combined capitalists and manufacturers of the United States. It is written over every intimate page of the records of Congress; it is written all through the history of conferences at the White House: that the suggestions of economic policy have come from one source, not many sources. Suppose you go to Washington. You will always find that while you are politely listened to, the men really consulted are the big men who have the biggest stake — the big bankers, the big manufacturers, the big masters of commerce, the heads of railroad corporations, and of steamship corporations . . . Every time it has come to a critical question, these gentlemen have been yielded to and their demands treated as the demands that should be followed as a matter of course. The government of the United States is a foster child of the special interests. It is not allowed to have a will of its own."

Wilson wasted no time after his election. He gathered a fistful of facts on lobbying activities and then, on May 26, 1913, he declared war on the pressure groups. The lobbyists, he charged in a press statement, were so thick that you couldn't throw a brick in Washington without hitting one. Wilson bluntly ordered the pressure gentry to get out of town. Rather surprisingly, a large number of them did — although they soon came back.

On June 29, 1913, the New York World printed a front-page story by "Colonel" Martin M. Mulhall, former chief lobbyist for the National Association of Manufacturers. Mulhall, who was paid $10,000 for the article, made some sensational revelations which, if true, indicted the integrity of a swarm of public officials and Congressmen. Among them was an assertion that he, as the agent of the N.A.M., had paid "between $1,500 and

$2,000" to Representative James T. McDermott, a Chicago Democrat, in return for legislative favors.

A four-month inquiry showed that some of Mulhall's statements were exaggerated, but it was proved conclusively that the colonel had his own private office in the Capitol, that he paid the chief House page $50 a month for inside information from the cloakrooms, that he obtained advance information on legislation from McDermott and from Representative John Dwight, the Republican leader in the House, and that he influenced appointments to House committees and subcommittees, placing members friendly to the N.A.M.

The N.A.M. was not embarrassed by these disclosures. Quite the contrary. Its general manager at the time, Philip J. Bird, was asked by the investigating committee whether his organization considered Mulhall's activities compatible with the legitimate work of the N.A.M. Yes indeed, replied Bird, and then added: "I think, sir, that these investigations . . . will be a great enlightening incident to manufacturers of this country. I believe that it will impress upon them . . . the necessity of manufacturers standing together to preserve rights that they hope to enjoy in this country of ours . . ."

Although the Mulhall disclosures cast doubt on Congress's ability to act as a free agent and sullied the reputations of several members, they produced nothing in the way of lasting reform. Six of the seven members allegedly "reached" by the N.A.M. were exonerated completely by the investigating committee. The seventh, McDermott, was censured but not expelled; he retired from Congress shortly thereafter.

(In one other instance Congress censured one of its members for conniving with a lobbyist. On November 4, 1929, the Senate voted, 54 to 22, to censure Senator Hiram Bingham, a Connecticut Republican, for conduct "contrary to good morals and Senatorial ethics." The resolution stated, however, that Bingham had not acted from "corrupt motives." What he had done was to bring one Charles L. Byanson, a paid employee of the Manufacturers Association of Connecticut, into a closed meeting of a Senate finance subcommittee writing a tariff bill. Bingham, a tall, imposing man of talent and charm, later became an aviation lobbyist.)

Out of the Mulhall inquiry did come the second effort to place lobbying under some form of regulation. A bill passed by the House in 1913 would have required all agents and lobbyists operating in Washington on behalf of individuals, corporations or associations to register with the Clerk of the House. The measure died in the Senate.

In 1927 the Senate in turn experienced a spasm of concern about lobbying abuses and set up a committee to investigate the subject. A caustic legislator, Senator Thaddeus H. Caraway of Arkansas, headed the inquiry. Caraway's bill regulating lobbying was approved by the Senate but died a quiet death in the House. Despite this setback, the Arkansas Senator performed one lasting service. He brought to light, with relish, one of the most enterprising lobbying operations in history. This involved, as Kenneth Crawford has reported, a bright young man who collected $60,000 in one year from unsuspecting businessmen by the simple expedient of writing to them every time a law favorable to business was passed and claiming sole credit for its passage. The essence of his message was, "Don't applaud, just send money."

In 1936 Senator Hugo L. Black of Alabama took up the fight against lobbying excesses. Black, now an Associate Justice of the Supreme Court, introduced a bill requiring lobbyists to register and disclose the sources of their income. It passed both houses, but in a conference committee, Representative Howard W. Smith, the wily old economic royalist from Virginia, knifed it. Smith, now chairman of the House Rules Committee, used an ancient trick that he has honed to perfection over the years. Posing as the most virtuous of the virtuous, he insisted on a spate of amendments that would have put such harsh restrictions on lobbying that they were rejected outright — and the bill with them.

Black believed that private pressure on government had grown to such proportions that it might overwhelm the democratic system. In a 1935 radio speech he warned that lobbying "has reached such a position of power that it threatens the government itself. Its size, its power, its capacity for evil; its greed, trickery, deception and fraud condemn it to the death it deserves."

Congress did not put lobbying to death. Despite Black's deeply-felt concern, this would not have been a good idea even if it had been possible. But the lobbying law that Congress did enact 11 years later was not the answer either. The solution, the proper relationship between private interests and government, remains to be found.

BATTLEGROUND

"A government is not made representative . . . by mechanical expedient of electing its members by universal suffrage. It becomes representative only by embodying in its policy, whether by instinct or high intelligence, the people's conscious and unconscious interests." —*Santayana, "The Life of Reason."*

"You can't use tact with a Congressman. A Congressman is a hog. You must take a stick and hit him on the snout." —*A member of the Grant cabinet quoted by Henry Adams in "The Education of Henry Adams."*

We may be through with the past, Bergen Evans has remarked, but the past is not through with us. This is a good description of the United States Congress. The situation in Congress is made to order for the private interest lobbyists, the lobbyists of profit and the status quo. It is one of the strongest weapons in their arsenal.

Congress, the 535 men and women elected by the people of the United States to make their laws, remains the chief battleground of the lobbyists. In this cold war era the Defense Department and the space establishment rival the national legislature as centers of lobbying pressure, but Congress's power of the purse means that even military and space lobbying starts on Capitol Hill.

Congress decides whether a President who takes his national constituency seriously shall have the legislative grants of authority and the money to cope with the tremendous social and economic needs of 190,000,000 people, the majority of whom live in overburdened cities and sprawling, disorganized suburbs. What Congress does about domestic imperatives—education, health, economic growth, civil rights and the rest—has a direct bearing on whether the United States will survive and prosper as a democracy in one of history's greatest revolutionary periods.

But the legislative branch of government, confronted by these great problems and challenges, is ill-equipped, ruled by the procedures of the past, unable to match the expertise and bureaucratic weight of the executive branch, a Prometheus that has bound itself with the chains of seniority and outmoded rules. Not even the impressive legislative accomplishments under Lyndon Johnson can paper over Congress's serious institutional frailties. The shortcomings of the national legislature have receded somewhat from public view as a result of its achievements in the past few years, but the disease has not been cured, only temporarily arrested.

Today, as in the past, Congress is riddled with conflicts of interest, obsessed with secrecy about its own finances and operations, and beset by absenteeism to the point where the usual legislative work week is three days.

It wastes precious time on investigations into such burning questions as the fate of the boiled peanut. Only under the duress of extreme social upheaval does it place the national interest above local, regional or private considerations.

Its ablest members—of both parties—are prevented from making a full contribution to the legislative process because disproportionate power is given to a handful of old men who do not believe in enacting laws to which they are personally opposed. Indeed the national legislative body of the United States is still to an unwarranted extent influenced by those who resist all efforts to legislate. Senator Richard B. Russell of Georgia, for instance, has advanced the statesmanlike idea that it's better to judge Congress by what it does not pass, rather than by the measures it does enact. "A conservative bias . . . is built into the Congress," Professor Daniel M. Berman has commented.[1] Congress's machinery— its rules and procedures—is set up in such a way that it is far easier to defeat legislation than to enact it.

A substantial advantage is thereby conferred on the private interest lobbyist. His job, fundamentally, is to prevent or delay increased allocations of the nation's resources to the public sector at the expense of the private sector. Since the conservatives who control the Congressional machinery are out to accomplish precisely the same thing, the status quo lobbyist has a significant head start. With the conservative committee chairmen and senior members, he forms an alliance against social progress.

Quaint rules give the committee chairman tremendous power. He decides the order in which bills will be called up for consideration by his group. Simply by refusing to call up a measure, he often can condemn it to death. While he can be forced to act if the other members muster enough votes, this seldom happens. A committee member who votes to overrule the chairman may find his own pet bill buried in its turn.

The chairman's power over the scheduling and timing of hearings can be used to drag out the proceedings so long that a bill dies in committee. Chairman James O. Eastland of Senate Judiciary, for example, permits other southern members of his committee to conduct little filibusters in their questioning of witnesses on civil rights bills, with the result that the committee has rarely reported out a civil rights measure.

The chairman has virtually complete authority in appointing the committee staff. With this power, he can set the whole tone of the committee, including such things as the selection of witnesses to testify at hearings, the direction of research and the wording of reports.

The committee chairman usually is floor manager for measures reported out by his unit. In the hands of a skillful parliamentary strategist, this power can be used to weaken legislation favored by a majority of the committee but opposed by the chairman. Adroitly-worded amendments are offered on the floor to gut the bill—and are accepted by the floor manager-chairman.

In consultation with the House and Senate leaders, the committee chairmen decide who shall serve on conference committees to iron out differences in bills passed by the two chambers. A chairman who opposes a bill approved by a majority of his committee gets another whack at it in conference. He usually serves as a conferee himself and can appoint other members who were opposed to the measure, although supporters of the bill are represented on the conference committee as well.

Several chairmen retain the power to decide when their committees meet, although the LaFollette-Monroney Legislative Reorganization Act of 1946 requires all standing committees to meet at least once a month. In the Senate, the Appropriations and Space Committees have no regular meeting day, and in the House, the Appropriations, Banking, Public Works, Veterans,

Ways and Means and Rules Committees convene only on the call of the chairman.

In 1962 President Kennedy submitted 298 legislative proposals to Congress. Ninety-one of these were killed in committee, according to Congressional Quarterly. The committees, in other words, prevented Congress as a whole from considering fully 30 percent of New Frontier measures. If all these recommendations were bad and deserved to be rejected, Congress was duty-bound to reject them. But all 535 legislators should have had the right to make that determination.

Some proposals by the chief executive are not as important as others and presumably can be held over without serious harm. Consider, then, the fate of the four most important bills submitted by Kennedy in 1963 — the tax reduction bill, the civil rights bill, health care for the elderly through Social Security, and federal aid to elementary and secondary education. Not one of these measures was enacted in 1963.

Unquestionably, the more important the legislation, the more time Congress should devote to considering it. But the tax reduction bill was first proposed in mid-1962. Eighteen months later it was still pending. Federal health insurance for the aged dated back to the Truman administration and had been the subject of innumerable hearings and studies, and federal aid to education had similarly been studied to death. The civil rights measure, with its public accommodations section, could fairly be said to have contained legislative approaches justifying *de novo* analysis by Congress, but it was not analysis and examination that held up this bill.

If delays in acting on Presidential legislative programs were occasioned by sincere deliberation in every instance, or even in most instances, who could quibble? The opposite, however, usually is the case. The generally prevailing pattern is procrastination for its own sake. The evidence is incontestible that the Congressional establishment is far less interested in deliberation than in furthering what Walter Lippmann has called "a conspiracy to suspend representative government."

Most of Kennedy's major proposals subsequently were enacted when Johnson became President and began weaving his legislative magic. Were they bad and unnecessary when Kennedy proposed them, and then, by some mysterious transmutation, vitally in the public interest when Johnson resubmitted them?

Two points should be borne in mind when considering the state
of affairs on Capitol Hill. One is that Congress actually does
itself a disservice in countenancing legislative paralysis. Its institutional weaknesses have contributed in substantial measure
to its decline from co-equal status with the executive branch.
Congress no longer initiates much major legislation; it has permitted itself to be reduced to the subordinate and unenviable
function of approving, delaying or vetoing a program prepared
by the executive branch.

The second point to be borne in mind is that the merits or
shortcomings of administration proposals are rarely the issue in
the legislative breakdown, however much partisan debate is used
to obfuscate. If a Presidential recommendation is unwise, it
should be defeated. But this is not what happens. Instead,
a small group of men skillfully manipulates a set of archaic rules,
and frequently prevents the representatives of the majority from
expressing the will of the majority by voting an administration
bill up or down.

In some instances urgent measures recommended to Congress
by the President of the United States, the official elected by
the whole nation, the chief lobbyist for the public interest, "are
not assured of even a hearing, much less a vote," Sam Zagoria,
former administrative assistant to Senator Clifford P. Case, has
pointed out.[2] Representative Morris K. Udall, Arizona Democrat, has commented that he knows of no other legislative body
in the world that operates on the strange principle that the majority should give the minority control over what subjects will
be debated and voted on.

While the President must lobby the entire Congress, the private interest lobbyists concentrate on the committee chairmen
and a few other key members. In their direct lobbying of Congress, they operate on the cardinal principle that the committee
is more important than the whole. The place to get what you
want — whether it is to get a bill approved, killed, watered down
or changed in your favor — is the committee.

It is in the committee that the dirty work is done. It is in
committee, away from the many-eyed scrutiny of the rest of Congress and the public, that "joker" amendments and trick clauses

are added. The "private as murder" conditions under which special interest legislation usually originates flourish in the committee room.

This means that there are two kinds of legislation in Congress.

The first is the big, general interest bill on which the attention of the nation is focused and which usually involves indirect, grassroots lobbying campaigns as well as direct contacts between lobbyists and members of Congress. Contemporary examples of the general interest bill include health care for the elderly, federal aid to education, civil rights, interest and dividend withholding, assistance for economically depressed areas and legislation dealing with urban problems. Public opinion, if it can be mobilized in the form of grassroots lobbying, usually is more decisive in determining the ultimate fate of the general interest bill than direct work by individual lobbyists on Capitol Hill.

The second type of legislation is the special interest measure pure and simple. Often highly technical, these bills attract comparatively little public attention, although they dip deeply into the taxpayer's pocket. Direct-contact lobbying by itself normally is more effective here.

The prime example is tax legislation. When tax advantages are handed out, the individual lobbyist working for a special interest group comes into his own. Nowhere else is direct lobbying so concentrated and intense. Nowhere else is the competition more fierce. The tax loopholes for which the lobbyists fight so hard — the $27\frac{1}{2}$ percent oil depletion allowance and the multitude of other mineral depletion allowances, the "structural changes" benefitting utilities, the lower capital gains rate, the dividend exclusion and all the rest — cost the taxpayer 40 billion dollars a year. This loss is borne by citizens who do not retain lobbyists.

In one recent year, the top lobbying spender was the National Committee for Insurance Taxation, which listed a total outlay of $181,667. Despite its high-sounding name, this organization made an interesting statement in its report: "Membership roster — none." It further developed that the only contributor to this "national committee" was the Allstate Insurance Company of Skokie, Illinois. The bulk of the committee's expenditures went to pay the salaries and travel expenses of 13 lobbyists. The committee stated that its purpose was "revision of the Revenue

Act of 1962 to tax mutual and reciprocal fire and casualty insurance companies on the same basis as stock fire and casualty insurance companies are now taxed."

Because it is hard to arouse public concern about special interest give-aways and privileges, this kind of legislation remains the peculiar province of the Congressional committee. When this is related back to the seniority system and to the power and background of the committee chairmen, the built-in advantage enjoyed by the special interest lobbyist is clear.

The country was treated to a public display of the intimate relationship between the committee system and private interest lobbying in 1962. The frantic lobbying over United States sugar quotas for foreign countries put the spotlight on Chairman Harold D. Cooley of the House Agriculture Committee.

Cooley, a Democrat from North Carolina, has been in Congress since 1934 and has headed the Agriculture Committee since 1949. Sugar legislation is his personal fiefdom. He has been referred to as "a second Secretary of State" on sugar matters. As the House's acknowledged expert in the intricate and complicated field of sugar legislation, he doles out the lucrative sugar quotas to foreign nations pretty much as he pleases. Under the present quota system the United States buys guaranteed amounts of sugar from foreign producers at a price higher than that paid in the world market.

According to an article by Douglass Cater and Walter Pincus in The Reporter magazine, Cooley "has allowed himself remarkable discretion, receiving the sugar lobbyists one by one to make their presentations [for quotas], then summoning them later to announce what each one has been awarded." [3] "Cooley," they added, "has little difficulty deciding among the rival claimants for sugar quotas, although, as he revealed in a recent interview, some of the lesser quotas are 'pulled from a hat.' In the main, he has felt that the rewards should be based on 'who are our friends and who are not.'

"Obviously, this rule of thumb has special meanings for a Congressman from the North Carolina tobacco country. During the 1955 sugar hearings, for example, Cooley made it quite plain to the Philippine lobbyist that his country's fate hinged on whether the Philippines could find a way to restore purchases of United States tobacco."

Some surprising documents from the files of the late, unlamented dictator of the Dominican Republic, Generalissimo Dr. Rafael Leonidas Trujillo, known as the Benefactor of the Fatherland and the Illustrious Superiority until his devoted countrymen shot him, were brought to light by the New York Times in 1962. In a series of stories based on these documents Tad Szulc traced the earlier efforts of Trujillo's agents to gain Cooley's favor, including a suggestion that he be invited to visit the Dominican Republic as the all-expenses-paid guest of the government. Cooley did not go, but his sister, daughter and son-in-law went along with other members of the Agriculture Committee when they visited the Caribbean nation in 1955. Cooley's sister at that time was clerk of the committee. The trip was paid for by Dominican sugar interests.

Cooley's name, according to Szulc, was mentioned repeatedly in the reports of the Trujillo lobbyists. While he acknowledged that he had conferred with some Dominican diplomats in his office, he insisted this was only because Trujillo had no Washington lawyers at the time. On June 22, 1960, Cooley attended a meeting at the home of Marco A. de Pena, head of the Dominican Sugar Office in Washington, and told de Pena about some amendments that were going to be added to the Sugar Act. Cooley denied that his conduct had been improper in any way, saying that he gave the Dominicans no special advice about sugar legislation and could not be held accountable for what Trujillo's men wrote about him in their reports.

There was "no evidence to support any charge of specific wrongdoing" by Cooley, the Times pointed out. Nevertheless, the sugar lobbyists were clawing their way to the chairman's door, and the story wasn't over.

A Washington lawyer told Jack Steele of the Scripps-Howard newspapers that he had been hired by the National Association of Sugar Producers of Panama on the recommendation of Mrs. Christine S. Gallagher, clerk of the House Agriculture Committee. The lawyer, Wesley E. McDonald Sr., represented the association in its effort to obtain an increased sugar quota for Panama. Mrs. Gallagher categorically denied that she had recommended the lawyer to Roberto Motta, the Panamanian sugar producer who hired McDonald. She did say that she had known McDonald for years; both are from North Carolina. Before she became clerk of the Agriculture Committee, Mrs. Gallagher was Cooley's executive secretary.

Later, McDonald submitted some of his correspondence with Motta to the Senate Finance Committee, which was considering the sugar bill.

"I hope that you have kept in touch with some of the Congressmen, and possibly spoken to Chris from time to time to see how things are coming," Motta wrote on June 18, 1962, adding: "In fact, I have put in a call for her right now, as I have not heard from Washington since I returned."

"I spoke to Chris Gallagher from Salvador and she told me that she had called you (McDonald) requesting that you write me and inform us of the latest developments," Motta wrote on July 5. And in the same letter: "Chris dropped me a line enclosing a brief summary of the committee sugar bill . . ."

Mrs. Gallagher declared that she had "steadfastly refused" to suggest or recommend lobbyists to foreign sugar interests seeking new or increased quotas under the sugar bill because "somebody might regard this as favoritism." She said that Chairman Cooley had done likewise.

When this writer asked McDonald whether Mrs. Gallagher had recommended him to Motta, he replied: "It might very well be that Chris Gallagher recommended me, but I don't know that she did, and she denied that she did . . . I've known Harold Cooley for 25 years and I think that he thinks enough of me to recommend me as a lawyer, but I know he didn't recommend me." McDonald added that when Motta first came to see him, "he said that friends of mine on the Hill had recommended me."

McDonald wasn't the only North Carolinian on hand when Cooley's committee began working on the sugar bill. Ralph W. Gardner, son of a former governor of North Carolina and a close friend of Cooley, represented the Mauritius Sugar Syndicate in its efforts to obtain a sugar quota for the island of Mauritius, a speck in the Indian Ocean. Gardner's law firm, Gardner, Morrison and Rogers, received a fee of $22,343 from the sugar syndicate. The House version of the sugar bill gave Mauritius a 110,000-ton quota. When irate Senators asked Gardner later how he justified a quota of this size for a small island (Mauritius is about 25 miles wide), he allowed as how "we'd just like to be treated like the rest of the folks."

As written by Cooley's committee (which meant, in effect, by Cooley himself), the sugar bill created a lobbyist's paradise. Under the bill, the quota formerly allocated to Cuba, some 1,500,000 tons a year, was put up for grabs. Other sugar-producing nations desiring a piece of this manna hired Washington lobbyists to get them a share, and the scramble was on. "The lobbyists were clamoring all over the Agriculture Committee," recalled one Congressional staff member.

In addition to their fixed retainers, many of the lobbyists had contingent-fee arrangements with their foreign employers. The larger the quota they obtained, the larger their fee. The result was a lobbying orgy so excessive that it produced a wave of revulsion even in a case-hardened Congress.

The fees payable in this connection were handsome. The law firm of Dawson, Griffin, Pickens and Riddell was to receive a basic fee of $50,000 and a maximum of $5,000 in expenses under its agreement with the Indian Sugar Mills Association. If Congress approved a two-year sugar law, the Dawson firm would receive $66,000 and up to $10,000 in expenses. If Congress voted a three-year sugar law, the fee was to be $99,000 and a maximum of $15,000 in expenses, for a possible total of $114,000. The law as enacted was for three years. One of the partners in this law firm is Donald S. Dawson, a White House aide in the Truman administration.

The law firm of Chapman and Friedman — in which former Secretary of the Interior Oscar L. Chapman is a partner — received $50,000 a year for four years under its agreement with Mexican sugar interests. In addition, the Mexican producers agreed to pay the Chapman firm an additional 25 cents a ton for any increase in Mexico's quota. The new sugar law gave Mexico a hefty increase, adding up to $18,000 more for Chapman, but because of a technicality in the complex quota formula he did not get it.

The law firm of Cleary, Gottlieb and Steen received $23,150 in fees from the Colonial Sugar Refining Company of Australia in a 15-month period. Under Secretary of State George W. Ball formerly was a member of this law firm, but he opposed the

House version of the sugar bill, which gave Australia a United States sugar quota for the first time.

A. S. Nemir Associates, a firm of international consultants, received a "minimum fee" of $24,000 a year — later raised to $35,000 — from the Brazilian Sugar and Alcohol Institute, an agency of the Brazilian government. Brazil got its first formal United States quota — 340,000 tons — under the House bill, but this was reduced in the final version to about 190,000 tons. Nemir told this writer that the intent of his complicated contract with the Brazilian agency was that he would receive a total of about $100,000 a year. He explained that his organization performed many other functions for the Brazilians, in addition to legislative work. Among them he listed technical and marketing research, legal counsel and sales service. Several other foreign agents, including Cleary, Gottlieb and Steen, said their activities on behalf of their clients were not confined to legislation.

Charles H. Brown, a former Democratic Congressman from Missouri, represented sugar producers on the island of Fiji for $24,000 a year. Fiji was given a 10,000-ton quota under the House bill. Brown is an active lobbyist who moves back and forth easily from lobbying to public relations. Among his other lobbying clients are the National Education Association, the American Society of Composers, Authors and Publishers (ASCAP) and the Associated Cooperage Industries. His public relations clients include Ozark Airlines, Fairchild Stratos Company and the Kellogg American Company.

James H. Rowe Jr. and Richard C. O'Hare represented the Haitian-American Sugar Company for a $15,000-a-year fee. Haiti's sugar quota was increased substantially under the House bill. Rowe, a former administrative assistant to President Franklin Roosevelt and later an Assistant Attorney General, is a member of the law firm of Corcoran, Foley, Youngman and Rowe. Another partner in this firm is Thomas G. (Tommy the Cork) Corcoran of New Deal fame.

Other agents of sugar interests included Ganson Purcell, a former member of the Securities and Exchange Commission, who represented the Nicaragua Sugar Estates, Ltd.; Robert L. Farrington, chief counsel of the Agriculture Department in the Eisenhower administration, who represented Nationalist China; Walter S. Surrey, brother of Assistant Secretary of the Treasury Stanley

S. Surrey, who represented Guadeloupe, Martinique and the South Puerto Rico Sugar Corp., and Rocco C. Siciliano, an Assistant Secretary of Labor in the Eisenhower administration, who represented the Sugar Producers Association of El Salvador.

When the House bill reached the Senate Finance Committee, its chairman, Harry F. Byrd, was moved to unusual criticism of the work of a southern colleague. "This is the worst sugar bill I have ever seen," Senator Byrd declared.

The Senate Finance Committee proceeded to abolish the country-by-country quota system altogether, except for domestic producers and Philippine sugar growers. The Senators substituted a global quota system favored by the Kennedy administration, under which foreign producers would bid openly for the United States market. The final version of the bill, agreed on by both houses and accepted by the President, was a compromise. It retained existing country quotas, increased them in some cases by siphoning off some of the old Cuban allotment, and put the rest of the Cuban quota into a global quota.

Everybody but Castro got a little something, and nothing could be fairer than that, especially since so much time, effort and money had gone into the situation. So much, in fact, that the Federal Bureau of Investigation developed an interest in the matter. It conducted a quiet little inquiry, questioning many of the foreign agents and their employers, but nothing came of this.

The chairman of the Senate Foreign Relations Committee, Senator J. William Fulbright, also became interested in the activities of the foreign lobbyists as a result of the sugar imbroglio. "Where the sugar is, there you will find the flies," he observed. Fulbright was particularly concerned about the extent to which foreign agents were influencing foreign policy, the impression they might give other nations about the way in which governmental decisions were reached in the United States, and the effect of their operations on programs costing the taxpayers hundreds of millions of dollars a year.

The extensive investigation by the Foreign Relations Committee developed a mountain of further information about the activities of the lobbyists and public relations men who, in Murray Kempton's caustic phrase, are hired by foreign interests "to

stand in the corridors of power and importune each passerby
on his way to the washroom."⁴ More big fees came to light —
$300,000 to the Hamilton Wright Organization, a New York
public relations firm, to burnish the lackluster image of Chiang
Kai-shek and his exile regime (discussing this propaganda campaign in a letter to a Nationalist Chinese official, Wright said:
"Money is the 'oil' that will make it work smoothly"); a $500,000
campaign by the public relations firm of Selvage and Lee on
behalf of the Overseas Companies of Portugal, including a $90,000
fee; an earlier sugar fee of $95,000 from the Dominican Republic
to Walter Surrey's law firm.

In more than 1,400 pages of testimony, the Fulbright committee spread out a record of high-powered propaganda operations — propaganda masking as "documentary" films, news releases and newsletters, television interviews, magazine stories, as
anything but what it was; front groups set up to evade the registration and disclosure requirements of the Foreign Agents Act;
canned speeches for cooperative Congressmen, with the speeches
then mailed out free under the Congressional franking privilege;
expense-paid junkets to exotic way-stations for friendly newspapermen who reciprocated with friendly articles — and money.
The record was full of money. The fees had a habit of esca-
lating; the contracts refused to die.

To the public at large one lesson from the Fulbright hearings
might have an interest transcending all the other lessons: the
American taxpayer is paying for the privilege of being propagandized. A certain amount of each year's foreign aid appropriation is sent right back to the United States to hire lobbyists to
make sure that next year's foreign aid appropriation is forthcoming or to insure other American financial assistance.

Early in the hearings Fulbright drew the attention of Under
Secretary of State Ball to the $99,000 lobbying fee paid by the
Indian Sugar Mills Association. In view of India's economic
condition, he asked, "don't you think this is a case where they
could ill afford to pay that kind of money for a lobbyist?"

Ball agreed that it was a "highly unfortunate" situation. "In
effect," Fulbright then commented, "we find ourselves in the
strange position of paying to India large sums of United States
dollars and then having large sums of those dollars paid to
American citizens to influence the action of Congress, don't we?

Doesn't this strike you as rather unusual?" Replied Ball: "I don't think it is a very attractive picture, Mr. Chairman, and I think it is an accurate description in many cases."

The Fulbright hearings produced much information about another facet of lobbying: some lobbyists spend almost as much time lobbying their clients as they do lobbying Congress. The lobbyist does this by name-dropping. He boasts and puffs about his putative connections with the great and near-great. He implies that these connections will lead to all kinds of nice things. If he attends a large luncheon meeting at which Secretary So-and-so is the speaker, his next letter to his client is likely to mention casually that "I had lunch with Secretary So-and-so the other day, and he let it be known that . . ."

At one point in its hearings the Foreign Relations Committee delved into a 1954 agreement between the Dominican Republic's sugar commission and the Washington law firm of Surrey, Karasik, Gould and Efron. The Dominicans were attempting to increase their exports of sugar and hired Walter Surrey's law firm for $95,000 to help out.

Fulbright put into the record a memorandum dated Jan. 28, 1956, from Monroe Karasik, a partner in the law firm, to Jesus Maria Troncoso, then president of the Dominican sugar commission.

"Through channels of personal obligation," the memorandum read, "we have made contact with a powerful law firm in the Senator's home state. The senior member of the firm is the executive officer of the Senator's political machine. The second partner is the son of the Senator's first campaign manager; there are very close family connections between this man and the Senator. The third partner is the private confidential attorney of the Senator; he handles important confidential matters for the Senator's machine.

"All three propose to call upon the Senator on Monday, January 30, to engage his sympathy for the position of the Dominican Republic, with respect to sugar legislation. They will represent themselves as being interested purely because of their very close ties of friendship and business with my (Karasik's) firm. Each of the three will adopt a different approach to arouse the Senator's sympathy.

"They ask for a retainer fee of $2,500. In addition to this, they ask a fee of $5,000 if the Dominican allocation under the legislation as finally enacted is no less than that under the present House version . . .

"We believe that these lawyers can be effective in advancing the interests of the Dominican Republic and we accordingly recommend that the retainer fee be paid, and the contingent fee be agreed, all as outlined."

Who was the Senator? To the amazement of Fulbright and the other committee members, Walter Surrey said he didn't know. So they called in Monroe Karasik, author of the memorandum. And lo and behold, he said he didn't know, either. Astonishment deepened into incredulity. "We were relying on you to know," Fulbright said a little plaintively.

In response to unbelieving questions from Senator Bourke B. Hickenlooper, Karasik stated under oath that he knew nothing about the memorandum. He didn't know anything about the "powerful law firm in the Senator's home state." He didn't know the names of the partners. He didn't know anything about the $2,500 fee. All that he knew was that he wrote the memorandum. As to the rest, "the fact is that I don't recollect it," said Karasik.

"My disgust is complete," Hickenlooper finally declared, "and my contempt is utter in this case, because it is beyond my belief that a man of this background and experience, in writing a detailed letter of the intimate detail which this contains, cannot remember a single thing about any of these people . . ."

Well, it was all cleared up later. Samuel Efron, a former partner in the Surrey firm, came on from New York and disclosed that the memorandum referred to former Senator Harry F. Byrd Sr. of Virginia, then chairman of the Senate Finance Committee, which handles sugar legislation.

All hands agreed that Byrd never knew anything about the matter. Efron said he didn't. The law firm of Bendheim, Fagelson, Bragg and Giammittorio, located in Alexandria, Virginia, which was the "powerful law firm in the Senator's home state," said it had been approached by Efron about approaching Byrd but had decided not to do it.

Said Efron: "I suppose Mr. Fagelson had told me certain things [about the Virginia firm], and, perhaps, as is normal with lawyers, he may have puffed a bit. I may have puffed a bit to

Mr. Karasik, he may have puffed a bit to Troncoso, and Troncoso may have puffed a bit to his government."

Fulbright: "By 'puffed,' you mean misrepresented the facts?"

Efron: "No, sir, I do not mean that."

The Surrey firm's code name for Senator Byrd, in its cablegrams, was "Petrol Boy." The code name for former Senator Edward Martin of Pennsylvania, a Republican who served on the Finance Committee, was "Bloom."

In his sworn testimony Efron said that Karasik did know the name of the Senator mentioned in the memorandum and that it was Karasik's idea to retain a Virginia law firm close to Senator Byrd. The F.B.I. investigated the Karasik-Byrd memorandum, too, but there were no further developments.

The Fulbright committee heard some more testimony about name-dropping when it summoned another Washington lobbyist, Michael B. Deane. In opening the Deane hearings, Fulbright declared:

"We are particularly concerned with Mr. Deane's apparent use of the commercial technique of 'puffing' the effects of his activities in Washington for his Dominican clients, in an area in which the use of such a technique may have had serious political ramifications for the policies of the United States government. Obviously, the exaggeration by a lobbyist of his ability to control the processes of government in this country, when conveyed to a foreign client, can lead not only to an increase in the lobbyist's remuneration but also to contempt on the part of the foreign client for United States institutions."

When Deane, who represented the Dominican sugar commission in 1960 and 1961, wrote his client that "I received an invitation from the President to attend a reception . . . at the White House," it turned out to be a routine invitation from the Democratic National Committee. When Deane wrote to the Dominicans that "I also talked to Secretary of Agriculture Freeman" and described Freeman as "a friend of mine of long standing," it turned out he did not have an appointment with Freeman at all. He just spoke with someone in the Secretary's office.

After the committee had filled the record full of a great deal more of this kind of stuff, Deane explained how it was: "Well, Mr. Chairman, in your relationship with a client, I don't intend to misrepresent, but like everybody else, you don't underplay

your part. You try to overplay your part in what you are doing
for them . . . In these communications you tend to exaggerate
a little."

Deane's testimony apparently did not hurt his standing with
the new administration of President Lyndon Johnson. Early
in 1964 Johnson appointed the lobbyist to a Presidential emer-
gency board to investigate a railroad labor dispute.

The most sensational disclosure to come out of the Fulbright
hearings dealt with the generosity of John A. O'Donnell, a lobbyist for Philippine war damage claimants. The committee revealed that O'Donnell, whose nickname among his colleagues is
"Windy," contributed more than $9,000 to the 1960 campaigns
of 24 members of Congress and two other persons. Some accounts put the total at $9,100, others at $9,300 — O'Donnell's
financial path was tortuous.

The largest single contribution — $2,000 — went to Represen-
tative Clement J. Zablocki, a Wisconsin Democrat. Zablocki,
who heads a House Foreign Affairs subcommittee on the Far
East, introduced the Philippine bill in 1959 and again in 1961.
His subcommittee approved it both times, and it was finally
passed and signed by President Kennedy in 1962. The measure
authorized the payment of an additional $73,000,000 by the
United States to Philippine citizens and corporations in settle-
ment of World War II damage claims.

The bill provided for direct payments to individuals rather
than a lump sum to the Philippine government. O'Donnell came
in here. He proposed to represent the individuals in pressing
their claims, and he had the necessary background as a member of the Philippine War Damage Commission in the Truman
administration. The staff of the Senate Foreign Relations Committee said O'Donnell already had made $250,000 to $300,000
representing previous Philippine claimants and stood to garner
another $150,000 if the new bill passed.

O'Donnell's letters to his associates in the Philippines were
full of the familiar pats on the back: "I prevailed upon" Zablocki
to introduce the bill; "I hurriedly changed Zablocki's introductory speech," and "I had today in the Senate introduced a similar
bill by Senator (Hubert H.) Humphrey." Shocking syntax, but

the meaning was clear. O'Donnell, according to O'Donnell, was running the show.

Zablocki saw things in a different light. O'Donnell, he said, "exaggerated his influence" on the war claims legislation, which Zablocki said he would have introduced "whether or not John O'Donnell had ever been born." The lobbyist, he added, "in no way influenced me." Humphrey, who introduced the bill in the Senate, said he did not know O'Donnell and knew nothing about a $500 campaign contribution from the lobbyist.

The contributions came from an $18,000 fund channeled to O'Donnell by the then-Philippine ambassador, Carlos P. Romulo. Others who received donations from the fund were: Senator Pat McNamara, Michigan Democrat, $100; Senator E. L. Bartlett, Alaska Democrat, $100; Senator Jennings Randolph, West Virginia Democrat, $500; Senator Paul H. Douglas, Illinois Democrat, $100, and former Senator J. Allen Frear, Delaware Democrat who was defeated in 1960, $500.

And the following Representatives were beneficiaries: James J. Delaney, New York Democrat, $100; John D. Dingell, Michigan Democrat, $300; Daniel J. Flood, Pennsylvania Democrat, $200; Earl Hogan, Indiana Democrat who was defeated in 1960, $200; W. Pat Jennings, Virginia Democrat, $200; former Representative Walter H. Judd, Minnesota Republican, $500; Eugene J. Keogh, New York Democrat, $200; Robert W. Levering, Ohio Democrat who was defeated, $300; Joseph W. Martin Jr., Massachusetts Republican and former Speaker of the House, $100; George McGovern, South Dakota Democrat who ran unsuccessfully for the Senate in 1960 and was elected in 1962, $100; Clifford G. McIntire, Maine Republican, $400; George P. Miller, California Democrat, $500; William E. Miller, New York Republican who became the GOP vice presidential candidate in 1964, $500 (which he accepted on behalf of the Republican National Committee); Thomas P. (Tip) O'Neill Jr., Massachusetts Democrat, $100; W. R. Poage, Texas Democrat, $300; Stanley A. Prokop, Pennsylvania Democrat who was defeated, $100; Albert H. Quie, Minnesota Republican, $200.

A $1,000 contribution went to Edward McCormack, nephew of Speaker John W. McCormack. At that time the young McCormack was running for attorney general of Massachusetts. A $200 contribution went to John O'Keefe, legislative assistant to Senator George A. Smathers, Florida Democrat. O'Donnell testified that this money was for the purchase of two tickets to a Democratic dinner.

Of the 18 Representatives who received contributions from O'Donnell. nine voted for the war claims bill when it came up in 1962. Four— Representatives Jennings, Poage, Miller of New York and Quie — voted against it. One — Representative Flood — was not recorded on the vote, and four were defeated in 1960. Since the Senate passed the bill by voice vote, the positions of individual Senators are not a matter of record.

A good many Washington lobbyists are frequent contributors to party committees and individual members of Congress. When they give, of course, it is "in the interests of good government" or "because Congressman So-and-So is an old and dear friend of mine." If it happens that the Congressman is on a committee that handles legislation in which the lobbyist is deeply interested, that, they say, is like so much of life — pure coincidence.

A spot check of campaign contributions by lobbyists in 1962 showed, for instance, that Michael B. Deane gave $200 to Representative Emanuel Celler, New York Democrat who heads the House Judiciary Committee; $50 to former Representative Thomas J. Lane, Massachusetts Democrat who was on the Judiciary Committee until he was redistricted out of Congress, and $73 to Representative George H. Fallon, Maryland Democrat. An "M. B. Dean" of Washington gave $100 to Representative John Dowdy, Texas Democrat who is a member of the Judiciary Committee. Deane also gave $2,000 to the Democratic National Committee in 1962, and a "Michael B. Deane" was listed as having given $2,000 to the Philadelphia Democratic Campaign Committee. Repeated efforts to reach Deane to ask him about his campaign donations were unsuccessful.

Charles Patrick Clark, who represents Franco Spain in Washington and is registered as a lobbyist for domestic clients, gave $1,000 to Representative Michael J. Kirwan, Ohio Democrat who is one of the powerhouses of Congress, and $1,000 to Senator Vance Hartke, Indiana Democrat. Clark also gave $3,000 to the Democratic National Committee.

Irvin A. Hoff, executive director of the United States Cane Sugar Refiners' Association and a registered lobbyist, gave $1,000 to the 1962 campaign of Representative W. R. Poage,

Texas Democrat who ranks next to Chairman Cooley on the House Agriculture Committee. Hoff acknowledged that the contribution came from him, although the report listed it as given by "Irving Hoff of Houston, Tex." He said this was an error. Poage had no opponent in the 1962 election but said he would keep the contribution and use it, if necessary, in his next campaign. He also received $1,500 from William Louvia, owner of a cane sugar refinery in Sugarland, Texas, and $300 from Philippine lobbyist John O'Donnell.

Arthur L. Quinn, a lobbyist for the British West Indies Sugar Association, gave $500 to Representative Clifford G. McIntire, Maine Republican, then a member of the House Agriculture Committee. McIntire also received $400 from O'Donnell. J. Paul Marshall, a lobbyist for the Association of American Railroads, gave $750 to the campaign of Representative Harold T. Johnson, California Democrat. Lobbyist Dale Miller gave $100 to Representative Homer Thornberry, now a Federal judge. Lobbyist Scott W. Lucas gave $250 to Representative Oren Harris, now a Federal judge and former head of the House Commerce Committee, as well as $200 to the Democratic National Committee. Lobbyist Donald S. Dawson gave $500 to Senator Daniel B. Brewster, Maryland Democrat, and $2,700 to the Democratic National Committee. Harold Lovre, a lobbyist for the American Trucking Associations, gave $100 to Representative Charles R. Jonas, North Carolina Republican; lobbyist Oscar Chapman gave $100 to Representative Ralph R. Harding, Idaho Democrat, and $3,750 to the Democratic National Committee. Lobbyist Hyman B. Raskin gave $500 to Representative Dante B. Fascell, Florida Democrat, and $1,000 to the Democratic National Committee.

Representative Eugene Keogh, New York Democrat who is a member of the tax-writing House Ways and Means Committee, received a $500 campaign contribution in 1962 from a group of trucking operators. The contribution was transmitted by John V. Lawrence, a lobbyist for the American Trucking Associations. Keogh received another $500 campaign donation from Robert E. Lee Hall, treasurer of the Committee on American Leadership. Hall also is vice president of the National Coal Association, a registered lobbying group; he said the Committee on American Leadership "operates out of my house." H. Vernon

Scott, a public relations man whose clients include several lobbying organizations, contributed $500 to Keogh's 1962 campaign. Eugene F. Bogan, a registered lobbyist, gave $100 to Keogh's campaign, and Leonard Silverstein, another registered lobbyist, gave $100. Keogh received $200 from Philippine lobbyist John O'Donnell.

Monroe Butler, a lobbyist for the Superior Oil Company of California, gave $500 to the 1962 campaign of Representative Charles M. Teague, California Republican. In 1956 Superior Oil was fined $10,000 and two of its attorneys, Elmer Patman and John Neff, were fined $2,500 each and given suspended one-year jail sentences after the oil company and the two lawyers pleaded guilty of violating the Lobbying Act. The charge against Patman and Neff was that they had failed to register as lobbyists. Superior Oil was accused of "aiding and abetting" their failure to register. The charges stemmed from a $2,500 campaign contribution which Neff tried to give to the late Senator Francis Case of South Dakota while the Senate was considering the Harris-Fulbright natural gas bill. It was the one and only time in 20 years that anyone has been convicted of violating the lobbying law.

When is a campaign contribution a legitimate donation to a legislator and when is it an inducement for the purpose of influencing his vote on legislation? No question is more central to the ethics of lobbying than this one, and none is more puzzling to the average citizen—or to the legislator himself.

In a day when it often costs several million dollars to run for the Senate from a populous state and sometimes as much as $50,000 or $100,000 to get elected from a House district, the campaign contribution is an immensely important lobbying weapon. But its propriety as a technique of modern lobbying is one of the most arguable points in the American political dialogue.

The late Senator Richard L. Neuberger once summed up the dilemma that confronts the lawmaker by pointing out that if he accepted $100 from a lobbyist to vote for or against a particular bill, he would be guilty of accepting a bribe, a criminal act. The lobbyist, similarly, would be guilty of offering a bribe. But if the lobbyist donated $100 — or $5,000 — to Neuberger's campaign for re-election and the contribution was publicly reported, the action would be entirely legal — even though the intent was the same, to influence Neuberger's vote. Thus can the law operate to make hypocrites of the lawmakers.

After looking into the $2,500 campaign offer to Case, a Senate committee set about deciding what had happened. Had it been intended as a bona fide contribution to aid Case's campaign for re-election? The Senators quickly found themselves bogged down in a slough of indecision. As Mr. Samuel Goldwyn once remarked: "I can give you a definite maybe."

The committee started out bravely enough. On the seventh page of its report it stated: "The . . . committee finds and concludes that there was neither a bribe nor an attempt to bribe. The evidence is clear that the contribution which Mr. Neff attempted to make to Senator Case's campaign fund was not conditioned upon the Senator's agreeing to vote for the natural gas bill or to take any other specific action."

On page eight, however, the native hue of resolution began to be sicklied o'er with the pale cast of thought: "The next issue confronting the . . . committee was whether there had been an improper attempt to influence the vote of Senator Case on the natural gas bill. To state it differently, this contribution was something other than a bribe or an attempted bribe; its exact character, however, and its significance presents a most complicated problem. In essence, this can be reduced to the question of whether this was a bona fide campaign contribution as distinguished from a gift to a member of the Senate in connection with pending legislation, the relationship of the gift to the campaign being only incidental."

On page nine: "The circumstances here [make] almost inexorable the conclusion that the paramount motivation for this contribution was interest in the natural gas bill, as contrasted with aiding Senator Case's campaign. It thus follows that the offer of the contribution was for the purpose of influencing the Senator's vote."

The committee had wrestled with, but not resolved, one of the thorniest questions in lobbying.

A federal law makes it a criminal offense to promise, offer or give money or anything of value to a member of Congress "with intent to influence his action, vote or decision on any question,

matter, cause or proceeding which may at any time be pending
in either house of Congress or before any committee thereof."
It is, however, perfectly legal — and salutary to the democratic
process — to contribute money to the election campaign of any
member of Congress or any candidate for Congress. The investigating committees and the courts are left to deal with the questions of intent and motivation as best they can.

As to the effectiveness of the campaign contribution as a
lobbying device, opinion varies.

One cynical Capitol Hill veteran, asked what he considered
the surest way of getting laws passed or defeated — the most
effective lobbying technique in other words — replied bluntly:
"The little black bag." This is still a prevalent school of thought.

Philip M. Stern, in his book, "The Great Treasury Raid,"
dealing with the nation's soak-the-poor tax laws, noted that
"there is little talk in Washington of personal venality among the
Senators and Congressmen who sponsor special tax amendments, but campaign contributions are another matter. One
high-ranking Senate Finance Committee member, asked by a
newsman about his uncharacteristic sponsorship of several pro-
insurance company amendments, explained, in an unguarded
moment: 'This is the way we finance our campaigns. Hell, I wish
there was a tax bill up every year.' "[5]

The hue and cry over the Case episode did not end the
practice of offering campaign contributions with strings attached.
In 1958 Frank E. Moss, a Democrat running for the Senate
from Utah, heard from a man who said he thought he could
"find" $5,000 for Moss's campaign. There was just one little
hitch. The candidate would be expected to declare himself publicly in favor of continuing the $27\frac{1}{2}$ percent oil depletion allowance. Moss could have used the money, but he rejected the
offer — and was elected anyway.

Despite the prevailing cynicism, the little black bag (a phrase
that gained currency in the Teapot Dome scandal) is not a comprehensive explanation for legislative phenomena. It is a convenient, easily-understood whipping boy and for that reason is
much favored by those for whom analysis of more subtle forces
is arduous. But it is only one of many explanations, and it ignores
the manifold other pressures at work on the legislator.

Without minimizing the impact of campaign contributions on

legislation, the fact is that in the politics of a pluralistic society the campaign donation is not the only monetary weapon. And money itself is not the only factor carrying weight with the lawmaker when he casts his vote.

If the campaign contribution were the only effective way in which cash was used to influence legislation, the hundreds of millions of dollars spent on grassroots lobbying would be money wasted — and this is not the case. As the results of grassroots lobbying campaigns show, the voice of the voter, when orchestrated by the lobbyist into a mighty symphony of pressure, can sound as loud in the ear of the legislator as the purring tones of the campaign contributor.

When the lobbyists themselves are asked to define the chief value of campaign contributions in their work, they frequently reply with one word: access. The campaign donation, they say, helps them obtain access to the legislator so they can present their case. The reasoning is that the other fellow is contributing to the campaign of Congressman Doe and therefore is likely to get a cordial reception when he visits Doe's office, so we had better do the same. This, according to many lobbyists, is all that is gained from a campaign donation — a chance to present facts, figures and arguments to the lawmaker in the privacy of his office.

The lobbyist, of course, can do this in the committee hearing, on the public record. But perhaps Congressman Doe wasn't there that day. Or perhaps it is felt that a more extensive and intimate conversation is needed. At any rate, lobbyists seem to share a common passion for privacy.

Since it would be unrealistic to expect the lobbyist to describe his campaign contributions as attempts at influence, the "access" explanation may be, in some cases, a cover story. In the majority of instances, however, it is probably the truth or close to it. Senators and Representatives are busy men, and the competition for their attention is keen. The lobbyist who makes a campaign donation — or arranges for one to be made by his client — frequently is doing nothing more than meeting the competition and creating good will, to insure that he, too, will be heard.

When the lobbyist gives a campaign donation directly to a member of Congress, it shows up in the required reports filed with the clerk of the House and the secretary of the Senate and is a matter of public record. Not surprisingly, many of these

contributions are relatively small, as a look at the list earlier
in this chapter will show.

The public record, however, is frosting. The cake underneath
is something else. The lobbyist or company representative often
has the more important function of channeling money from his
employer to the Congressman. These amounts tend to be larger,
and the larger they are, the more coyly they are sheltered from
view.

In arranging this largess, the role of the lobbyist or company
rep is advisory. He may mention this or that legislator to his
client as deserving a campaign donation. He may suggest that
the client throw some business to the Congressman's law firm.
Or he may point out that Senator Roe, by virtue of his committee position, would be an ideal choice to address the trade
association's annual convention, for a sizable fee.

One lawyer-lobbyist whose law firm represents large insurance
companies and corporations told this writer that some of his
Republican clients "occasionally" ask his advice about campaign
contributions. "I advise them to give to Democrats," he said
with a chuckle. "A lot of these Democratic Senators are more
reasonable men than the closed-minded Republicans, if the businessmen only knew it, and they've been in power longer — and
they're likely to be in power longer."

If the campaign contribution from his employer is a large one,
the lobbyist often channels it through the Democratic or Republican campaign committee in the House or Senate. Contributions so arranged have a singular advantage: they can be, in one
important respect, secret. Money contributed to the House and
Senate campaign committees can be earmarked for a specific
candidate, but this does not show up on the public record. All
that is disclosed is a contribution to the committee, but the candidate knows where the money came from.

This was one of the wellsprings of Bobby Baker's power in his
Senate salad days. In addition to his job as secretary to the
Democratic majority, he was secretary of the Senate Democratic
campaign committee, which doles out the elixir of life.

BUSINESS

"The business of America is business." — *Calvin Coolidge.*

"Eisenhower asked him [Secretary of the Treasury George M. Humphrey] if it were not possible for American businessmen to make some sacrifices in . . . the interests of world peace.

" 'No,' Humphrey replied candidly. 'The American businessman believes in getting as much as he can while the getting is good.'

" 'Maybe that's the trouble with businessmen, George,' Eisenhower said seriously." — *Sherman Adams in "Firsthand Report."* [1]

Ten men were gathered for lunch at the Pentagon in the private dining room of Secretary of Defense Robert S. Mc-Namara. The Defense Secretary was at the head of the table. With him were four top aides: Roswell L. Gilpatric, then Deputy Secretary of Defense; Assistant Secretary of Defense Thomas D. Morris, in charge of military installations and logistics; Cyrus R. Vance, then general counsel of the Defense Department, who later succeeded Gilpatric, and Adam Yarmolinsky, a special assistant to McNamara.

The other five men were from the Chamber of Commerce of the United States. They were: Robert S. Ingersoll, president of the Borg-Warner Corporation; John F. Rudy, assistant to the executive vice president of the Goodyear Tire and Rubber Company; George F. Metcalf, a regional vice president of the General Electric Company; Charles E. Hastings, president of Hastings-Raydist, Inc., of Hampton, Virginia; and Theron J. (Terry) Rice, then manager of the national defense department of the Chamber of Commerce and later the Chamber's chief lobbyist. All but Rice were members of the Chamber's national defense committee, one of about 30 committees of business leaders appointed each year to study trends and problems in various fields and propose policy declarations for consideration at the Cham-

103

ber's annual meetings. Ingersoll was chairman of the national defense committee.

In the course of a cordial lunch the ten men discussed various defense issues likely to come up in the next session of Congress. These included the military assistance part of the foreign aid program, civil defense and fallout shelters, the Renegotiation Act, government patent policy on inventions resulting from government-financed research, conflict of interest legislation, and the Defense Production Act.

All these were matters of the greatest interest to the business community. Under the Defense Production Act, mining and metals companies hold billions of dollars in government stockpiling contracts. The administration's legislative recommendations with respect to this law could vitally affect many of these companies. The White House's proposals in the field of military assistance abroad would mean hundreds of millions of dollars in orders placed with American business firms by foreign governments. The patent legislation would involve untold millions in future profits resulting from government research and development contracts with private companies.

When the luncheon was over the Chamber of Commerce representatives had what one of them called "a good advance idea" of what was to be recommended to Congress in all these fields. In effect the Chamber had a "lead time" of two months in which to consider and pass on to its members knowledge of the matters that had been discussed and to decide what its policy would be on each of them. It also had two months' advance notice in which to prepare its lobbying campaigns in Congress.

At about the same time other Chamber committees were holding similar meetings with other members of the President's cabinet. At each of these sessions, usually over the luncheon table, the businessmen got a preview of the government's legislative program in agriculture, economic and tax policy, commerce, labor relations, education, and foreign affairs, among others. The lone cabinet holdout was Secretary of the Interior Stewart L. Udall. After postponing two meetings with the businessmen, he finally sent a subordinate.

The Chamber calls these sessions "executive conferences." They are part of one of the best organized and most comprehensive lobbying and political activity programs in the nation's capital. The purpose is to get American businessmen into national affairs in a big way and to keep them there. When every businessman in the country becomes a grassroots lobbyist for the business point of view, the national Chamber of Commerce will have achieved one of its main goals.

Organized labor — the AFL-CIO — has had no comparable advance access to a broad spectrum of governmental legislative plans.

Lobbying is big business for business in the United States. Defense contracts account for about 10 percent of all business volume in this country. Expenditures for space exploration are in the billions. The federal government is a multi-billion-dollar customer for civilian goods and services. Whether he likes it or not, the American businessman is in a partnership with Washington. He has to be to stay alive competitively.

The last 20 years have seen a phenomenal increase in the number of company "reps" in Washington. Hundreds of corporations now have their own permanent representatives in the capital to handle their business dealings with federal agencies and to look after their legislative interests.

A great wave of business "reps" hit town in World War II and swelled to flood tide during the Korean conflict, when President Truman and Congress were considering whether to reimpose wartime price ceilings and wage controls. "The impact of war solidly established lobbying as a major industry," the Buchanan committee concluded. "Our national effort, entailing as it did far-reaching controls over the entire economy, prompted a hitherto-unequaled mobilization of group interests of every conceivable kind."

Another factor contributing to the influx of company "reps" has been the growth of federal regulation of many business activities. The degree to which businessmen have accepted such regulation as inevitable in a mixed economy is a measure of their maturity, but it has curious variations. When a Republican occupies the White House, business criticism of regulation is muted. Under a Democratic chief executive, resistance to regulation becomes more apparent. With this pattern in mind, President Johnson has wooed business — especially big business — assiduously and so far successfully.

At any rate, the government's "balance-wheel" role in the economy has provided large corporations with a personal incentive to send their own men to Washington to keep an eye on things, to bring pressure on the regulatory agencies, and, if possible, to capture them.

In its investigation of lobbying, the Buchanan committee made this observation: "So far as reported expenditures for lobbying are concerned, organized business far outspends other interests." The situation has not changed since the committee made its findings public. Business still spends substantially more money than any other segment of the economy to put pressure on government.

In a representative year, Congressional Quarterly's tabulations show that business groups reported spending a total of $1,598,091 for lobbying, compared with $857,789 reported by labor unions and employee groups. In another typical year, business outlays for lobbying totaled $1,836,126, compared with $945,206 spent by unions and employee groups. In both years the business category topped the spending list, with unions and employee organizations second.

Because of the Supreme Court decision in U.S. v. Harriss, the "principal purpose" clause in the Lobbying Act and the resulting practice of reporting only a fraction of the amount spent on lobbying, existing figures do not begin to give an accurate picture of the actual lobbying outlays .

Nor do they take into account the money contributed to political campaigns by businessmen and members of labor unions in their efforts to influence the conduct of government. In this area, too, studies have shown that business spending far exceeds that of labor. A Senate subcommittee found that officers and directors of the 225 largest corporations in the country contributed just under $2,000,000 to candidates and party committees in the 1956 election, while labor leaders contributed $19,000. In that election various labor contributions accounted for less than 10 percent of the total of $22,000,000 reported. In the 1960 election 60 large labor organizations with a combined membership in the millions listed contributions totaling $2,154,000 while 334 wealthy individuals accounted for $2,700,000 in campaign donations.

Fragmentary as they are, the formally reported lobbying expenditures do indicate the financial advantage enjoyed by business in the expensive contest for the favors of government. Congressional Quarterly's figures show that business groups spend roughly twice as much as labor organizations and three times more than citizens' groups, the two segments which most often lobby for the over-all public interest.

Registered business lobbyists in Washington outnumber labor and citizens' lobbyists by a topheavy margin. Reports filed with Congress show a total of 523 individual lobbyists working for corporations, trade associations and other organizations clearly identifiable as business interests, compared with 83 lobbyists for labor unions and 22 lobbyists for citizens' groups.

The relationship between Congress and the American businessman is intimate, inevitable and often constructive. Some aspects of the business-legislative relationship have changed over the years — and changed for the better — but Congress still needs to do a great deal of ethical repair work in this area, as the Bobby Baker case shows.

Describing the Senate in the nineteenth century — the era of the business barons who paid their way in Congress — William Allen White pointed out that "one Senator represented the Union Pacific Railway System, another the New York Central, still another the insurance interests . . . coal and iron owned a coterie . . . cotton had half a dozen Senators. And so it went . . . the collar of any great financial interest was worn in pride."

Since then a spate of laws — the Corrupt Practices Act, the conflict of interest statutes, the penalties for bribery, the Hatch Act, the law against conspiring to deprive the government of the impartial services of Congressmen and other federal officials, the statute prohibiting political contributions by government contractors — have been placed on the books to protect the public interest.

In some important respects, modern government undoubtedly is much cleaner. The days when a Daniel Webster could accept a direct cash payment for his Senatorial services have passed. There is no twentieth century counterpart for Simon Cameron, who robbed the Winnebago Indians blind and then became a United States Senator and Lincoln's Secretary of War. Dr. George B. Galloway of the Library of Congress has concluded that "there are few deliberately dishonest men and women in

Congress; fewer in proportion, certainly, than in the population at large." [2]

But the outside business and financial dealings of some members of Congress and Congressional employees continue to pose a problem when related to their responsibility to act in the national interest.

The close social relationships between Robert G. Baker and a number of lobbyists and company reps are a case in point. Many of these friendships began with a drink at the Quorum Club, but not all of them stopped there. Baker had business dealings with several powerful lobbyists.

One of his many outside interests while he was serving as secretary to the Democratic majority in the Senate involved a Capitol Hill travel agency known as Go Travel, Inc. Baker was a director and, for a time, secretary of this firm, which does about 35 percent of its business with Congressmen and Congressional employees. The president of the travel agency is Cyrus T. Anderson, a registered lobbyist for three labor unions — the International Union of Operating Engineers, the International Hod Carriers, Building and Common Laborers Union and the Hotel and Restaurant Employees and Bartenders International Union. Anderson also is secretary-treasurer of Railway Labor's Political League and was once secretary to Representative Melvin Price, Illinois Democrat.

Anderson acknowledged that Baker was associated with the travel agency but said he owned no stock, received no income from the firm and brought in no business. The lobbyist said he had known Baker for 20 years — their friendship began when the budding entrepreneur was a Senate page boy — and he retained Baker's law firm to handle the incorporation papers for the travel agency. Baker was appointed a director, Anderson explained, to meet a requirement that at least one director of corporations located in the District of Columbia be a District resident.

Another business venture that attracted the attention of the Senate Rules Committee when it began an investigation of Baker's labyrinthine financial affairs concerned a company known as Wertco. This firm was set up to handle a Florida real estate project that later fell through. The proposed development, a

motel in Jacksonville Beach and some housing units, was to have
been financed with a $400,000 loan from the Teamsters Union
pension fund, and $105,000 was advanced by the fund before the
project ran into difficulties and had to be abandoned. One of
Wertco's backers was Thomas D. Webb Jr., Washington representative for the Murchison interests of Texas and a registered
lobbyist for D.C. Transit System, Inc. Martin G. Williams Jr.,
president of Wertco, admitted that Webb negotiated the loan
from the Teamster pension fund and bought 520 of Wertco's
1,000 shares of stock himself. Later, Williams said, he was told
by another Wertco executive that Baker and Scott I. Peek had
purchased some of Webb's shares. Peek formerly was administrative assistant to Senator George A. Smathers of Florida.

Baker's relations with the Murchison oil barons were cordial.
In May, 1963, the Senate official called on Governor Edmund G.
(Pat) Brown of California, accompanied by Clint Murchison Jr.,
to discuss the Del Mar race track in San Diego County. The
Murchison interests held the lease on the race track, but a bill
was pending in the California legislature to open the lease to
competitive bidding when it expired. Baker told Brown that the
Murchisons' share of the track proceeds went to Murchison chari-
ties, especially boys' clubs in Texas, but the Governor replied that
he would continue to support the bill. It later passed, and the
lease was opened to bidding when it ran out several years later
on. Baker was reported to have told friends that the appointment with Governor Brown was arranged by Lyndon Johnson.

The first darkling omen on Baker's horizon was a $300,000 suit
filed on September 9, 1963, by Ralph L. Hill, president of Capitol
Vending Company of Washington. In the suit and later in sworn
testimony before the Rules Committee, Hill stated that he paid
Baker a total of $5,600 in cash between April 1962 and August
1963 "for his services in securing and retaining a contract" with
Melpar, Inc., of Falls Church, Virgina. Under the contract,
Capitol was permitted to place its vending machines in plants
operated by Melpar, a manfacturer of aerospace components.

Later, the suit alleged, Baker became a stockholder in another
vending machine firm, the Serv-U Corporation of Washington,
and then tried to persuade Capitol to sell out to Serv-U. When
Capitol refused to do so, the suit charged, Baker "conspired
maliciously to interfere with the outstanding contract between

Melpar and Capitol," in an attempt to influence Melpar to cancel its contract with Hill's company.

Melpar, whose president, Edward M. Bostick, was a member of the Quorum Club, subsequently canceled the agreement with Capitol and gave its vending machine business to a third company, not Serv-U. Baker denied all the charges in Capitol's suit, including the allegation that he was a stockholder in Serv-U. Subsequently, however, a financial statement by Baker which came to light listed among his assets 2,850 shares of Serv-U stock which he valued at $1,000,000.

Named as co-defendants in Capitol's suit were Ernest C. Tucker, Baker's law partner, and Fred B. Black Jr., a Washington consultant and government contact man for the North American Aviation Corporation. In February 1962, North American Aviation gave Serv-U the vending machine concession at its California headquarters, where 15,000 persons are employed. The following August, North American granted Serv-U the concession at its space division and in October 1963 the vending machine contract at its Rocketdyne division. Eugene Hancock, former president of Serv-U, told the Rules Committee that Black arranged the meeting with North American officials at which the first Serv-U contract was negotiated. At that time, Hancock said, Serv-U had no equipment and no employees.

Black's name cropped up again when the Senate Rules Committee disclosed that Baker, Black and two Nevada gamblers borrowed $175,000 in March 1962 and used the money to buy a substantial amount of stock in the Farmers and Merchants State Bank of Tulsa, Oklahoma. The committee counsel, L. P. McLendon, identified the two gamblers as Edward Levinson and Benny Siegelbaum, who operate casinos in Las Vegas. McLendon also revealed that Levinson and Siegelbaum were stockholders in Serv-U.

Baker, Black and the two gamblers borrowed the $175,000 from the Fidelity National Bank and Trust Company of Oklahoma City. The late Senator Robert S. Kerr, Oklahoma Democrat, was associated with this bank, and his son, Robert S. Kerr Jr., is a director. Not too long after the loan was made to Baker, Black and the others, Senator Kerr acquired stock in the same Tulsa bank.

Black, a member of the Quorum Club, is not registered as

a lobbyist. In May 1964, he was convicted of fraudulently evading $91,000 in federal income taxes after executives of several business firms testified that they paid him to help them obtain government contracts. Black, according to his accountant, spent thousands of dollars on hotels, transportation, lavish parties and other entertainment in Washington and at night spots around the country. After he was indicted for income tax evasion, Black was fired from his $160,000-a-year job with North American Aviation.

"Magic" is the nickname for another firm in which Bobby Baker was interested, the Mortgage Guaranty Insurance Corporation of Milwaukee, and magic it proved for the boy from Pickens.

Baker and his associates bought their first Mortgage Guaranty stock in 1959. They paid $25,000 for 200 shares — $125 a share. But Max H. Karl, president of the company, told the Senate Rules Committee that three weeks before Baker sent in his check, MGIC's board of directors had voted to split the company's stock on an eight-for-one basis. Karl said that Baker knew of this when he made his purchase. As a result of the split, Baker's holdings immediately increased to 1,600 shares, meaning that he actually had paid only $15.62 a share. A year later the stock was split again, this time ten for one. This gave the Baker group 16,000 shares, for which they had paid $25,000, or $1.56 a share. A stock dividend further reduced the price to $1.49 a share, Karl testified.

When the Securities and Exchange Commission approved Mortgage Guaranty's first public stock offering on February 21, 1960, the price was set at $25 a share, making the Baker holdings worth $400,000 after the second stock split. At one point, MGIC stock went to $54 a share.

Although Baker bought his stock in August 1959, Karl acknowledged that the shares were not issued to the Senate official until March 1960, after the SEC had approved the stock offering. He said this delay in listing the stock in Baker's name was due to the fact that Baker did not furnish a list of the others in his group until that time. Then Karl admitted that Mortgage Guaranty had informed the SEC in its registration application that some of the company's stock had "inadvertently" been sold in possible violation of the Securities and Exchange Act. He said that $1,070,000 worth of MGIC stock was sold to persons other than officers, directors and promoters of the company before the stock registration was approved by the SEC.

The Senate Rules Committee put in evidence a partial list of other Mortgage Guaranty stockholders. One of them was Maywood Boggs, a registered lobbyist for the International Brotherhood of Boilermakers. Boggs said he bought his stock through Baker in 1959 for $2,300 and sold it back to Baker a year later for $4,000. "Being a lobbyist," he explained under oath, "I had to know Bobby Baker. I knew him as a business connection for some years." He added, however, that Baker did not approach him about the MGIC stock. "I knew that he knew something about it, and I asked him if some was available," Boggs said.

Senator John Williams of Delaware saw the Boggs-Baker transaction in a different light. According to him, the lobbyist sold his stock to Baker two months after it had split ten for one. This made the value of Boggs' shares about $31,600, or $27,000 more than Baker paid him for the stock. "What service was Mr. Baker expected to render, or what service had he rendered . . . in return for this $27,000?" the Delaware Republican asked. The Senate, obsessed with secrecy about its affairs, returned no answer. Williams pointed out that in the Rules Committee investigation the alleged $27,000 profit "was not even mentioned, nor were any questions asked about this phase."

Mortgage Guaranty is in the business of insuring home loans, a sort of "little FHA." For a time it struggled along with indifferent success. The company lost $63,677 in its first year, 1957, and $7,567 in 1958. Then in 1959 MGIC asked the Internal Revenue Service for a ruling that would exempt half the money paid to it in premiums from federal income taxes for 15 years. Since Wisconsin law required the company to put half its premiums into a contingency reserve for 15 years, preventing MGIC from using the funds except to cover extraordinary losses, the company argued that it should not have to pay federal income taxes on these funds until the 15 years were up and it had the full use of the money.

After the Internal Revenue Service twice denied the request, Karl and one of his associates went to Representative John W. Byrnes, a Wisconsin Republican and a member of the tax-writing House Ways and Means Committee. They asked Byrnes to introduce a bill giving the company the tax break desired. Byrnes introduced the legislation; a few months later the IRS reversed itself and gave Mortgage Guaranty the ruling it wanted. The company's fortunes thereupon underwent a dramatic improvement. In 1960 it made a profit of $234,241 and in 1962, $974,428. The price of its stock soared.

In September 1960, four months after the favorable IRS ruling, Representative Byrnes purchased $2,300 worth of Mortgage Guaranty stock, paying $2.50 a share. When the transaction came to light, Byrnes took the floor of the House and, in an emotional speech, insisted he had done nothing wrong. He acknowledged that the company had "extended a preference to me," but he said he knew nothing about this at the time he bought the stock. "I swear, before my God and this House, that had I known of these facts, I would not have purchased this stock," he declared. Then he announced that he would donate the stock, which had risen in value to about $26,000, to a non-profit foundation. That made everything all right. The House rose and gave him an ovation.

In his testimony, Karl denied that Baker had anything to do with the favorable tax ruling. He said he never asked the Senate aide to "use his influence in behalf of the company," and he added: "Nor did I authorize him to do anything, if he did."

How did Bobby Baker come by his confidence that Mortgage Guaranty stock was about to do an Horatio Alger and provide one of the foundation stones for the Baker family fortune?

Karl first told reporters that he was introduced to Baker by Glen Troop, a lobbyist for the United States Savings and Loan League. "Glen told Bobby to get Mortgage Guaranty stock because MGIC was going places," Karl recalled. Later, however, he told the Rules Committee that he was not sure whether Troop had introduced him to Baker. Asked about Karl's account of the meeting, Troop said he did not recall the exact circumstances, "but I'm sure that either directly or indirectly, Karl met Baker through me. I don't recall it, but I don't dispute the facts. It's well known that Baker is one of my good friends. I've known him since 1955." In 1963 no less than eight members of Mortgage Guaranty's board of directors, including the board chairman, were executives of savings and loan associations, for which Troop is a Washington lobbyist.

Another matter that came to the attention of the Rules Committee involved Baker's dealings with Myron (Mickey) Weiner, a Washington public relations man, who testified that he paid Baker $5,000 in "legal fees" two days after Congress enacted a bill in which Weiner was interested.

A swarthy man in a pinstripe suit, Weiner told the Senate committee that he was retained by an association of freight forwarders who were seeking legislation permitting them to collect brokerage fees. Weiner said he was paid $50,000 for four months' work, adding that the work consisted of "watching and evaluating" the progress of the bill. Two days after the bill was passed he decided to retain Baker for a year's legal service and paid him a retainer of $5,000. Weiner acknowledged under questioning that he never called on the Senate official for legal advice during the period covered by the retainer and did not renew it when the year expired.

"For a reasonable man, this is a tough story to swallow," observed Senator Claiborne Pell, Rhode Island Democrat, after listening to the testimony.

Weiner insisted that he did not ask Baker's help in obtaining passage of the freight forwarding bill. He said the understanding was that Baker would not do any legislative work for him because that would have been a conflict of interest. However, Weiner's client, Henry A. Barr, chairman of the Association of Freight Forwarders, told the Rules unit that Weiner boasted several times that he was "a friend of Baker." Weiner himself said that he was told by Wayne L. Bromley, a lobbyist for the coal industry, that it would be "an excellent idea" to hire Baker as his attorney. Later, a federal grand jury was to have more to say about Bromley.

The freight forwarders were seeking legislation that would license them with the Federal Maritime Commission so that they could receive brokerage fees from steamship companies. The forwarders act as middlemen between small shippers and steamship lines, assembling cargoes from many small companies so that the shippers can take advantage of bulk rates. The forwarders, Barr testified, were desperate because of a Maritime Commission ruling that would have prohibited payment of fees to the middlemen. Barr said that the association hired Weiner because "he made a very impressive presentation. He said he

knew people here [in Washington]. We weren't particularly interested in knowing their names."

Weiner, however, insisted to the Rules Committee that he had
no experience in promoting legislation through Congress, that he
did not testify on legislation and that he did not register as
a lobbyist.

"Exactly what did you do for the $50,000 fee?" asked Senator
John Sherman Cooper, Kentucky Republican.

"I was able to convince these people that I had the ability
to perform," Weiner replied. "I guess I'm a good salesman."

As part of its inquiry into the Baker-Weiner dealings, the Rules
Committee put into the record a notation that Weiner had made
a $1,000 contribution to a dinner honoring former Representative
Victor Anfuso, a New York Democrat. While in the House,
Anfuso had introduced and supported the legislation sought by
the freight forwarders, saying that "I certainly will exert every
effort to have this beneficial legislation passed." The Rules Committee did not question Barr or Weiner about the contribution.

Early in 1966, after a 15-month investigation of Baker's tan-
gled financial web, a federal grand jury indicted the former Senate
wheeler-dealer on nine counts charging tax evasion, conspiracy,
fraud and felonious theft. In the conspiracy count, longest in the
indictment, lobbyist Bromley and Clifford A. Jones, former
lieutenant governor of Nevada, were named as co-conspirators
but not as defendants. There were indications that Bromley,
who had known Baker ever since they both served as Senate
pages years ago, had been a cooperative witness before the grand
jury and would be a key witness in Baker's trial.

The conspiracy count charged that Baker concealed large
amounts of income in 1963 and 1964 by arranging for Bromley
to be the conduit through which payments were channeled to
Baker. The grand jury listed a series of payments, ostensibly to
Bromley, from the First Western Financial Corporation of Las
Vegas; United States Freight Company of New York, a freight
forwarding firm; the Redwood National Bank of San Rafael,
California; Harvey Aluminum Sales, Inc. and Harvey Aluminum,
Inc. of Torrance, California, and International Marketing Associates, Inc. of Los Altos, California. In each case, the grand jury
said, Bromley received the payments, purportedly for legal serv-

ices, reported them as his own income on his tax returns and then gave the money to Baker. The amounts were substantial — $14,000 from First Western, $7,500 from United States Freight, $10,000 from the Harvey firm — according to the indictment. The grand jury did not say what the alleged payments were for; that ostensibly was to be brought out at Baker's trial.

Another count in the indictment charged that Baker committed felonious conversion, or theft, by taking approximately $50,000 from Stuart Davis, about $17,000 from John F. Martin and $33,000 from Sidney Taper, and failed to report a substantial part of each sum on his 1962 income tax return. All three men are executives of savings and loan firms in Los Angeles. Baker was accused of taking the $50,000 and $17,000 payments for the use and benefit of the donors and "other persons, said other persons not including Robert G. Baker" and then fraudulently converting it to his own use. The indictment did not identify the "other persons" to whom the money was supposed to have gone.

The grand jury action has presumably halted the career of Bobby Baker, who rose from Senate page boy to majority secretary under the auspices of Lyndon Johnson. As majority leader, Johnson described Baker as "my strong right arm" and "one of my most trusted, most loyal and most competent friends."

Of late, the relationship between Johnson and Baker has undergone dramatic change. When White House Press Secretary Bill D. Moyers was asked about the indictment, he replied curtly: "I have not seen the indictment. There would be no comment on a grand jury action." And when Moyers' predecessor, George E. Reedy, was asked by a reporter what was the real relationship between the President and Baker, Reedy replied solemnly: "I'm going to be completely frank with you. They hardly knew each other.'"

Bobby Baker's circle of business cronies was not confined to lobbyists. Another witness told the Rules Committee that Baker was associated with Senator Smathers and Scott Peek, Smathers' former aide, in a profitable Florida land deal. The venture involved the purchase of about 143 acres of land in Maitland, Florida, just north of Orlando. The land was developed as Dommerich Estates and Dommerich Woods. Nearby is a huge Martin Company missile plant, and many Martin executives bought homes in the Dommerich subdivisions. Smathers said he was invited to invest in the land early in 1957. The Martin plant was completed late in that year.

Because his assistant, Peek, was trying "to raise a large young family on a limited salary" and because of "the similar circumstances of Robert G. Baker, who, too, had a growing family," Smathers said, he offered each of them a one-eighth share of his investment. At that time, Baker was making $19,600 a year in his Senate job, Peek about $16,000.

Smathers put up $12,000 for his share. Baker and Peek gave him $1,500 each for their sub-shares, making the Senator's net investment $9,000. According to Smathers' figures, he made about $42,000 when the land was resold for building lots, and Baker and Peek made $7,000 each. Reporters for the Miami Herald who checked into court records came up with different totals. They said Smathers made $75,488 on his $9,000 investment and Baker and Peek ran their $1,500 up to $12,580 each.

When the Smathers-Baker-Peek venture came to light, newsmen asked Senator B. Everett Jordan, the 67-year-old chairman of the Rules Committee, whether Smathers would be invited to testify. "We don't need him," replied Jordan. "We're not investigating Senators."

Jordan's old-world courtesy notwithstanding, Smathers' outside interests continue to attract the attention of the press and public. The Florida Senator is a member of a law firm whose clients include Pan American World Airways, Gulf Oil Corporation, Standard Oil Company, Western Union Telegraph Company, McKesson and Robbins, Inc., Anheuser-Busch, Inc. and the Seaboard Air Line Railroad. All these clients except Pan American have been added since Smathers entered the Senate in 1951. The handsome Senator has said that his law firm "scrupulously avoids" accepting any legal work involving the federal government and that he himself has not practiced law since entering Congress.

Smathers has served as chairman of a special railroad subcommittee of the Senate Commerce Committee. In 1958 he pushed through a bill to aid the railroads. His law firm also represents an airline in Nicaragua and a Dominican steamship line, and Smathers is one of the Senate's chief spokesmen on Latin American affairs. In 1963 he acknowledged that he talked with top

State Department and foreign aid officials in an effort to expedite a government loan guarantee for a housing project in Panama. The project was being promoted by Eugene McGrath, a Panama insurance man who is a close friend of Smathers. The Senator has said that he has had no business dealings with McGrath; he insisted that he supported the project because improved housing is needed in Latin America "as an essential element in fighting Communism."

Smathers is far from being the only member of Congress whose outside business interests have aroused interest. Senator Thomas J. Dodd, Connecticut Democrat, while a member of the House, led a move to increase United States foreign aid to Guatemala by $5,000,000. Less than a year later, after being defeated for re-election, he went to work as legal counsel to Guatemala's government for a fee of $100,000. He served in that capacity from the spring of 1957 until he was elected to the Senate in November 1958. In his successful effort to obtain more foreign aid money for Guatemala, Dodd was assisted by Sheldon Z. Kaplan, then a staff member of the House Foreign Affairs Committee. Later, Kaplan showed up as lobbyist for the Guatemalan Sugar Producers Association.

The list goes on and on:

Senator Kerr, Oklahoma Democrat, had multimillion-dollar oil, natural gas and uranium interests.

Senator Jordan, chairman of the committee that investigated Bobby Baker, owns a large textile mill.

Senator Wallace F. Bennett, Utah Republican and a former president of the National Association of Manufacturers, heads an insurance company and automobile agency.

Senator Clinton P. Anderson, New Mexico Democrat, is president of an insurance company.

Senator Edward V. Long, Missouri Democrat, has extensive banking, insurance and small loan interests.

Representative Emanuel Celler, New York Democrat and chairman of the House Judiciary Committee, maintains an active law practice while serving in Congress, as do many other members.

Representative James Roosevelt, California Democrat, served as board chairman of a savings and loan firm in his spare time.

Representative Abraham J. Multer, New York Democrat, was associated with lobbyist Thomas D. Webb Jr. in a romantically-named Florida land venture, the Honeymoon Isle Development Corporation.

The business involvements of some members of Congress are

matters of abiding interest to lobbyists for corporations and trade associations. Some lobbyists are reported to keep lists of Congressmen who have financial connections with savings and loan firms, banks and insurance companies. And lobbyists are generally well informed about the client lists of Congressional law firms.

Although the veteran professional lobbyist usually is too wise a bird to engage in patently illegal transactions with members of Congress, the Bobby Baker investigation showed that profitable business and financial dealings between lobbyists and legislators or Congressional employees are not uncommon.

Like the campaign contribution, the business deal is susceptible of various interpretations. The more charitable view holds that the underpaid Congressman can hardly be blamed if he seeks to supplement an inadequate salary through outside activities, so long as they do not influence his official actions. This interpretation might be more persuasive if the business dealings between lobbyists and legislators were not so consistently clandestine and if Congress did not resist so stubbornly all efforts to enact a law requiring its members to disclose their sources of outside income and their assets.

It is interesting to note that some business lobbyists do not have a high regard for the political acumen of their employers. A lawyer-lobbyist who represents several large corporations told this writer that he considers the American businessman "almost a primitive" when it comes to knowledge of government and the realities of Washington. "I travel around the country a lot to confer with clients," he explained, "and they will say to me: 'You tell Senator X that he had better do thus-and-so, or else.' I tell them if that's what you want, you'd better get another law firm."

The chief Washington lobbyist for a large business association observed that one of the hardest things about his job was "the fact that our board of directors turns over every three years." He added that "it takes about three years for me to educate these fellows in what can and what can't be done in this town, and just when they begin to have some understanding, their terms expire, and I have to start all over."

The Brookings Institution's study of business representatives in Washington found that many of the company "reps" complained that it was hard to get their firms interested in governmental affairs.

"The reluctance of companies to adopt a policy on a bill . . . appeared to stem primarily from the pressure of other business," the Brookings report said. "There was a definite tendency not to participate, especially on legislation that would affect the company only indirectly . . . Several of the (company) representatives reported that members of their top management believe that 'the business of business is business' . . . This leaves little or no time for getting embroiled in legislative programs, except when the interests of the company are directly and immediately threatened or can be aided. The majority of the representatives tended to deplore this 'provincial' point of view, and a few believe that in the past few years their managements have begun to consider their political and legislative interests and responsibilities from a somewhat broader point of view."

Another reason for the reluctance of business firms to interest themselves in government "is apparently that top executives view such activity as barely respectable," the Brookings report said. "They do not want their representatives to be registered lobbyists."

The Brookings study included quotes such as these from the company reps:

"For five years I have been trying to get the company to say to me: 'This is our legislative program. We want to get from here to here in antitrust, in tax, in all these other fields in which we are interested. These are our long-range objectives.' "

"Until now our [company's] fight has been defensive. We have been fighting brush fires as they have occurred. I contend that we must have a long-range program in, for example, the antitrust field. What changes do we want in the antitrust law?"

"I go back [to the company's home town] and sit down with the staff people with a working paper, saying: 'This is where we have been, this is the situation today, this is where we want to go. These are the positions we should take with regard to this legislation.' Not one of them has matured today."

Business lobbying in Washington does not fall into one set pattern. Many companies maintain their own full-time representatives in the capital. Others retain lawyer-lobbyists who work for many clients. Some send lobbyists from the home office as required. Still others rely primarily on a trade association to look after their governmental interests. Many firms use two or more of these arrangements.

Many of the Washington representatives working full-time for one company register as lobbyists, but since many others do not, there is no way to determine precisely how many company reps there are in Washington. The figure certainly is in the thousands. Often the company rep devotes primary attention to the Pentagon and gets up to Capitol Hill only occasionally. There is no legal requirement that defense lobbyists seeking military contracts register as lobbyists.

How much actual lobbying the company reps do — under the legal definition or otherwise — is hard to pinpoint; it varies with the individual. Most of them, however, perform at least one key function of the lobbyist — reporting to their home offices on the status of legislation affecting their company.

Although individual arrangements vary widely, the set-up used by the General Electric Company is reasonably typical of the Washington operations of large companies. Its Washington office is headed by Laurence I. Wood, whose title is vice president in charge of government-corporate affairs. Wood is not registered as a lobbyist, but three of the other five men in the office are. Two of them handle General Electric's legislative work; the other, F. Gerald Toye, is the company's full-time Washington counsel.

General Electric also has a regular retainer arrangement with the influential Washington law firm of Clifford and Miller, in which Clark M. Clifford, special counsel to President Truman, personal adviser to President Johnson, and chairman of the C.I.A.'s Foreign Intelligence Advisory Board, is a partner. The company retains other Washington law firms as needed; it hired Covington and Burling to defend it in an antitrust proceeding several years ago. Former Secretary of State Dean Acheson, a partner in Covington and Burling, has been a White House adviser intermittently since 1961.

General Electric also has a defense programs division in Washington. Under the direction of Richard L. Shetler, this office coordinates the company's defense contracts work.

Altogether, G.E. has about 600 people in Washington. Most of these are in the sales operation and have no connection with the government-corporate affairs office. But some of the sales personnel occasionally get into the government picture. G.E.'s Washington regional manager of electric utility sales, for example, has had government experience and keeps an eye on utility regulation matters at the Federal Power Commission.

With some fluctuations, the lobbying reports show that:

Standard Oil Company of California has six registered lobbyists.

Standard Oil of Indiana, four, including a law firm in which Gerald D. Morgan, an aide to former President Eisenhower, is a partner.

The American Telephone and Telegraph Company, five.

The Pennsylvania Railroad, three.

The Pacific Gas and Electric Company, three.

The Atchison, Topeka and Santa Fe Railway, three.

The Ford Motor Company, three, including the law firm in which Civil Aeronautics Board member Charles S. Murphy formerly was a partner.

General Motors Corporation, three.

The Superior Oil Company, four.

Standard Oil Company of New Jersey, three, and its subsidiary, Humble Oil and Refining Company, four.

The American Can Company, two.

The International Telephone and Telegraph Corporation, five.

Sears, Roebuck, two.

The Marathon Oil Company, three.

The trade association representing a particular industry — automobiles, steel, chemicals, oil, metals, consumer goods, food, machinery, aircraft, electronics and so on — is another form of business lobbying.

The trade association, of course, performs a variety of functions having no direct relation to government or lobbying. It provides its members with information about developments in the industry, serves as a clearing house for industry statistics, conducts educational programs, sometimes engages in technical research, arranges conventions and generally promotes the interests of its industry.

But to an ever-increasing degree, the actions of the federal government affect industry. So the trade association sets up a Washington office or in some cases moves its national headquarters bag and baggage to the shores of the Potomac, and settles in to see to it that the Congressmen and the bureaucrats do right by the worthy and deserving member companies of the National Wholesale Widget Association or the Institute of Gizmo Manufacturers.

As noted earlier, the Washington telephone directory lists some 1,200 trade, business and professional associations. An idea of the kaleidoscopic variety can be gained from a look at another list, the membership directory of the Washington Trade Association Executives.

More than 350 associations are represented by the individual members of this organization, according to its directory. Membership is open to any individual "who has managerial, executive, or administrative responsibilities in a local, state, regional or national trade association or professional society. " Washington reporters refer to the WTAE membership list as "the lobbyists' directory."

In it are listed officials of the Advertising Federation of America and the American Bakers Association, the Calcium Chloride Institute and the Conveyor Equipment Manufacturers Association, the National Machine Tool Builders' Association and the National Terrazzo and Mosaic Association, the United States Beet Sugar Association, the Upholstery and Drapery Fabric Manufacturing Association, the Bituminous Coal Institute, the Grain and Feed Dealers National Association, and a host of others.

Some trade associations disavow any lobbying function, but many of them are active, registered lobbyists. The National Association of Electric Companies, for example, reported $547,-000 in lobbying spending in one year, the American Trucking Associations, $105,000.

The American Petroleum Institute, the American Medical Association, the National Lumber Maunfacturers Association, the American Gas Association, the National Association of Food Chains and the National Association of Real Estate Boards are all registered lobbying groups.

The American Medical Association has six registered lobbyists; the American Gas Association, three; the United States Savings and Loan League, seven; the Life Insurance Association of America, eight; the National Association of Home Builders, five; the Association of Oil Pipe Lines, two; the American Farm Bureau Federation, ten; the Mid-Continent Oil and Gas Association, three, and the International Association of Ice Cream Manufacturers, three.

Finally, there is the general business association. In this cat-

egory are the two business groups with which Americans are
most familiar: the Chamber of Commerce of the United States
and the National Association of Manufacturers.

Together, these two mammoth organizations speak for American business in the councils of government. Usually they speak
with one voice. But not always. There are stresses and strains
in the relationship between the Chamber of Commerce and the
N.A.M.

The differences between them are not primarily matters of
basic philosophy. Both organizations are fundamentally opposed
to the concept of a national government "constantly impelled to
increase the strength and scope of its authority in order to maintain the necessary minimum of cohesion in the social fabric," in
E. H. Carr's words.[3]

Both the Chamber and the N.A.M. are opposed to those federal
activities which they construe as being in competition with private business (this is a very long list). Both are against increased government regulation of business through strengthened
antitrust and merger legislation and the like. Both oppose almost
all proposals to expand the federal role in providing social services. They oppose hospital insurance for the elderly through
Social Security, federal aid to education, federal assistance to
economically depressed areas, and so on. Ignoring the diminished
tax bases of the central cities, they insist that all such activities
are properly matters of state, local or private concern.

The Chamber and the N.A.M. bring two bedrock views to any
proposed legislation in the domestic economic and social fields:
they are fundamentally opposed to any increase in the federal
role, and they are just as fundamentally against increased allocations of the nation's resources to the public sector at the expense of the private sector. In these "gut" respects, there is no
appreciable variation in their philosophy.

A study of their policy statements, however, discloses some
subtle differences. They are differences of emphasis, approach
and tone rather than basic outlook. The N.A.M.'s language tends
to be flat, the Chamber's a little more flexible. Non-military
(economic and technical) aid to foreign nations, says the N.A.M.,
should be curtailed. The Chamber's wording has a different ring:
it recommends "development of the economic resources . . . of
the peoples of the free world through cooperation and self help."

A word like "cooperation" provides a lot of leeway.

A tenuous thing called "image" is involved here. The Chamber is not at all eager to be lumped together with the N.A.M. in the mind of the public and the Congress. It grumbles, for instance, when Congressional committees schedule N.A.M. and Chamber witnesses for the same day in hearings on proposed legislation.

Current Washington opinion tends to downgrade the influence of the N.A.M. compared with its *fin de siecle* days of glory in the late nineteenth and early twentieth centuries, the era in which Col. Martin Mulhall was riding high as chief N.A.M. lobbyist. The N.A.M., in this opinion, has proved too rigid and resistant to changing social and economic conditions in a day when some flexibility is necessary all around. A little forlornly, it stands out there alone in right field after dusk has halted the game. It is enveloped in a faintly fusty aura of dignity, lavender and the Union League.

There are those Congressmen who, when they learn that the N.A.M. favors or opposes a bill, have a knee-jerk reaction the other way. Even when they agree that the N.A.M.'s stand has merit, as inevitably happens from time to time, they tend to respond like the Boston lady who was told about man's descent from the apes. They hope it doesn't become generally known. This is image at work, negatively.

The middle-of-the-road or moderately liberal Congressman feels less unhappy when he finds himself in the same camp with the Chamber of Commerce on a particular piece of legislation. He is less furtive about it. This is image in action, positively. To the Washington community, the permanent corps of government officials, longtime legislators, lawyers and newspapermen, the Chamber has a more modern image. And although image is a hard thing to define, it is one source of power. The Chamber works hard at cultivating a more up-to-date, "of this world" image.

An experienced Senator, a liberal Democrat, put it this way: "You may not agree with the Chamber on this or that issue — I usually don't — but you can *talk* to them. You can work something out."

"We believe that lobbying is the art of the possible," said Terry Rice, until recently the Chamber's chief lobbyist. "We don't throw principle out the window, but we realize that you

don't get everything you want every time. You get part of it."
With image and maneuverability going for it, the Chamber is
an immensely influential organization.

A few years ago, the White House was preparing to issue an
executive order establishing a government-wide policy reserving
for the federal government all patent rights on inventions and
developments resulting from government-financed research work
performed by private industry. The idea was strongly backed by
Assistant Attorney General Lee Loevinger, in charge of the Justice Department's antitrust division.

The Chamber opposes a single, government-wide policy on
such patents, believing that each federal agency is a different
case. When it learned that the executive order was in the works,
it moved fast. Chamber officials informed Representative Emilio
Q. Daddario, a Connecticut Democrat who heads a House science
and astronautics subcommittee on patents. Daddario went to
the White House and talked with Myer (Mike) Feldman, deputy
special counsel to the President, and Presidential Science Advisor
Jerome B. Wiesner. He pointed out that his subcommittee had
recently held hearings on this subject but had not yet issued its
report. The executive order was laid aside.

At another point the Chamber learned that Senator John L.
McClellan's subcommittee on patents was about to promote to
the important post of chief counsel a man whose views coincided
with Loevinger's. "We knew it wouldn't be enough just to oppose
this appointment," said Terry Rice. "We had to come up with
a positive alternative of our own, a man who was equally well
qualified." The Chamber went to the Aerospace Industries Association and some individual companies. It got the names of two
or three men qualified in the patent field and willing to accept
the subcommittee job, and submitted them. These were men,
of course, whose views on patent matters were in line with the
Chamber's stand. The appointment unwelcome to the Chamber
was blocked.

The significance of these two power plays is best understood
when it is realized that about 14 billion dollars is spent annually
on research and development in the United States — with the
federal government putting up about nine billion dollars of this.
As by-products of this research come great numbers of new products and techniques for the civilian market. Who should get

the profits? The public, which put up much of the research
money, or the companies that did the research? The Chamber
argues that if industry is expected to undertake the research,
it must have the incentive of future profits.

The United States Chamber of Commerce is a business and
professional federation. It has more than 3,900 organization
members — local and state chambers of commerce, trade associations and professional organizations — and over 30,000 business members — that is, individual companies and businessmen.
It was founded in 1912 with the encouragement of President
William Howard Taft, who believed there should be a national
organization to bring business's views to the attention of the
federal government.

The Chamber's national headquarters are located at 1615 H
Street N.W. in a four-story marble building that sits solidly on
the north side of Lafayette Square. Directly across the square
is the White House. About 350 people are employed here and
another 450 outside Washington. Heading the Washington operation is Arch N. Booth, executive vice president of the Chamber
and its highest-ranking full-time staff member.

In one way or another, about three-fourths of the work of the
Chamber's national office bears on the business of influencing
government. From 1615 H Street pours a ceaseless flood of testimony, statements, research studies, news releases, publications,
reports to members, speeches and reprints. "We're in the publishing business in a big way," said Terry Rice.

This avalanche of printed material has two prime purposes:
to inform Congress of the business community's opinion on pending legislation, and to tell businessmen, in turn, what the President and Congress are up to, "in the hope that they will exert
their influence" on the course of government, as Rice put it.

The Chamber's principal publications are "Nation's Business,"
a monthly general business magazine with a circulation of about
750,000; "Washington Report," a weekly report on pending legislation and other governmental matters, which has a circulation
of about 130,000, and "Congressional Action," a weekly bulletin
on legislation, with a circulation of some 30,000.

The Chamber does not consider "Nation's Business," a general
circulation magazine, as having any lobbying aspects at all.

"Washington Report" and "Congressional Action" are specifically and closely identified with the organization's governmental aims, but since they do not involve direct contacts with members of Congress, the Chamber does not consider that they come under the purview of the lobbying law either.

"Washington Report," a four-page, letter-size bulletin, provides capsule summaries of proposed legislation, together with news about public affairs and the Chamber's activities. The first page usually discusses a matter of general interest — health care for the elderly under Social Security, the trade expansion bill, unemployment, transportation and the like. The inside pages are headed "departmental report" and deal with more specific governmental and economic matters. "Washington Report" frequently exhorts businessmen to get in touch with their Congressmen about legislation. Occassionally, the exhortation is left to a special one-page insert.

The Chamber's Washington staff prides itself on a factual approach to lobbying, but the calm, factual approach is noticeably absent from these supplements. They are often straight propaganda. "The King-Anderson Bill," one insert declared, "is just one more step down the road certain Pied Pipers would have us take while humming, 'May Uncle Sam Bless You and Keep You from the Cradle to the Grave.'" The supplement wound up with an appeal: "Now is the time for you to let your Senators and Congressmen know how you feel about this vital issue. Your views will count most while the King-Anderson Bill is being studied by the House Ways and Means Committee. You may get some ideas for your letters and discussions from the summary of principal arguments against the King-Anderson Bill printed on the reverse side of this sheet." The reverse side listed arguments against the bill (none for) under such headings as "It's not necessary," "It's unfair" and "It's discriminatory." [4]

Here we have a national organization:

1. Urging its members to get in touch with members of Congress on a specific issue.

2. Suggesting the exact time when they should do this and the exact Congressional committee to lobby ("Your views will count most while the King-Anderson Bill is being studied by the House Ways and Means Committee").

3. Listing canned arguments against the bill. The business-man, if he chose, could lift the Chamber's language verbatim to use in his letter to a Senator or Representative.

But in the never-never world of lobbying, none of this is lobbying. The organization that appeals to its members to com-municate with Congress, and helpfully provides the arguments, is not required under the Supreme Court ruling in U.S. v. Harriss to report the amount of money it spends in publishing the appeals.

"Congressional Action," another of the Chamber's regular pub-lications, makes similar appeals for businessmen to communicate with Congress. Consider this example from "Congressional Ac-tion": "The continued delay by the House Rules Committee in acting on higher education bills passed by the House and Senate provides a timely opportunity for expressions of personal views to members of Congress on controversial provisions in the bills. Provisions on which back-home sentiment is most meaningful are: the proposal in the Senate-passed bill to spend $920 million for college scholarship grants; and the proposal in the House-passed bill to spend $900 million in subsidies for building class-rooms in church and private colleges, as well as public colleges. Continued evidence of strong, back-home opposition to these pro-posals may have an important bearing on the final outcome of the drive to push through such precedent-setting subsidies in this session of Congress."

Lest the legislators miss the deeper significance of all this, "Congressional Action" pointed out that "expressions of informed views on these highly controversial provisions *by citizens who indicate an understanding of election-year pressures and problems will be especially meaningful to many Congressmen and Senators who are candidates for re-election.*" (Emphasis supplied.)[5]

It is always helpful, in other words, to remind a legislator when he is up for re-election. It may have slipped his mind. But none of this is lobbying.

Another Chamber publication is "Here's the Issue," a bulletin sent to employers for distribution to their employees. "Here's the Issue" is billed as an entirely factual summary of the pros and cons of controversial legislative issues. When it discusses some-thing like health care for the aged, however, adroit use of such phrases as "revolutionary step," and "huge system of Social Security financing" creates those old nagging doubts.

Vast amounts of material flow unceasingly from the Chamber's Washington headquarters to businessmen across the country, and in particular to the Congressional Action Committees of local chambers of commerce.

These committees are the Chamber's principal mechanism for mobilizing grassroots pressure on Congress. There are more than 1,100 of them. They are set up by the local chambers of commerce to bring the views of local businessmen to the attention of Congress. The Chamber's "Congressional Action" bulletin is aimed at these local committees particularly.

The Chamber's 450 field employees work out of six divisional offices across the country. Many of them work for "Nation's Business," but others, as part of their duties, help local chambers set up Congressional Action committees. A substantial number of the field men, in other words, assist in installing the machinery for grassroots lobbying.

The Chamber also encourages its trade association members to set up legislative committees similar to the Congressional Action groups. It publishes a "Legislative Handbook for Associations" outlining the most effective ways of communicating with Congress.

"To facilitate 'grassroots action,' " the handbook says, "many [trade] associations maintain a card file listing members who have personal relationships with their elected representatives. When specific action is needed, these members are requested to present their views and the views of their industry to their legislators. If appropriate, they are requested to personally contact their legislators . . . Experience has taught that personal letters are much more effective than form letters." [6]

The Chamber strives without letup to organize an unending torrent of letters, telegrams, telephone calls and personal visits from businessmen to Senators and Representatives. It is a gigantic catalyst stimulating grassroots pressure on Congress.

Another of the Chamber's prime techniques for whipping up the businessman's interest in governmental affairs is the "Aircade for Citizenship Action." These have been held annually since 1957, usually just before Congress convenes. The Chamber charters an airplane and loads it with a team of specialists on legislation and public affairs led by the incumbent national president of the Chamber and Arch Booth.

The experts crisscross the country, holding a series of one-day meetings. They answer questions from the floor on major issues expected to come up in the new Congressional session. Audience participation is emphasized; speech-making by the visiting specialists is held to a minimum. In the first six years, an estimated 60,000 businessmen attended the Aircade meetings.

The list of ways in which the Chamber seeks to get businessmen interested in government goes on and on. In connection with its annual meeting in Washington each spring, Congressional dinners are held, at which businessmen get together with the Senators and Representatives from their states. Each January, the Chamber sponsors an Association Public Affairs Conference for members of its affiliated trade associations. Members of Congress participate in panel discussions at these conferences.

The Chamber blends this gigantic grassroots lobbying effort with a certain amount of direct lobbying by its Washington staff. But direct lobbying plays a subordinate role in its operation. This is not accidental. The Chamber considers indirect lobbying by its members more effective. Only a rare Congressman will ignore personal letters or visits from the substantial businessmen of his home state or district. And, of course, the money spent in stimulating indirect lobbying, under the Supreme Court's definition, does not have to be reported as a lobbying expenditure.

Nor does the money spent on research, and the Chamber has an impressive research setup. This is the basis for the statement that about three-fourths of the work of the Chamber's Washington staff bears in one way or another on the business of influencing government, for as Terry Rice said: "About 75 percent of the Washington office's time is spent in research." Among other things, this research enables the Chamber to present Congress with extensively documented arguments, and it provides the basis for the formulation of policy. The research and the policy stands are then funneled to the businessman to keep him informed and interested. Research is a fundamental part of the Chamber's grassroots approach to lobbying.

With this emphasis on research and indirect lobbying, the Chamber's chief lobbyist is primarily a coordinator. As legislative action general manager, his formal title, he spends more time in his fourth-floor office directing an elaborate battle plan than in the halls of Congress buttonholing legislators.

The legislative department comprises 12 persons out of the Chamber's 350 Washington employees, but that does not begin to tell the story. The legislative office is the conduit through which flows the work of the Chamber's other departments on its way to Capitol Hill.

To illustrate how this complex lobbying juggernaut works, let us suppose that the President has proposed an education program to Congress. The Chamber's education department goes to work on research. The White House education message is dissected and analyzed. The results are transmitted to the news and legislative departments, to be sent out to the Chamber's businessman members in "Washington Report," "Congressional Action" and other Chamber publications. When the House and Senate education subcommittees hold hearings on the education bill, the legislative department works with the education department in lining up the witnesses who will testify for the Chamber, writing their testimony and briefing them on the questions to expect from the Congressmen.

The scope of the Chamber's legislative interests is illustrated by the 13 staff departments concerned with governmental matters: agriculture-natural resources; construction and community development; economic research; economic security; education; finance, government expenditures and taxes; foreign policy-foreign commerce; insurance; labor relations and legal department; manufacture-domestic distribution department; national defense, and transportation and communications. These staff departments carry on a year-round research program, assembling information for the Chamber's committees. The committees in turn develop policy recommendations on a wide range of subjects. Their recommendations go to the board of directors and the annual meeting for the formulation of general Chamber policy.

The work of these 30 committees is not confined to legislation. They study and discuss the entire spectrum of problems in their fields, but the development of Chamber policy on forthcoming legislation is a major concern of most of them. And, as was shown at the beginning of this chapter, the committees have another important function. Through the "executive conferences" with cabinet members, they get an advance idea of the legislation that the President is likely to propose.

In general, the lobbying activities of the United States Chamber of Commerce are descriptive of most large lobbying groups. There are variations, but the Chamber is the personification of the large institutionalized lobbying organization. What the Chamber does to influence the course of government — and how it does it — is pretty much the standard operating procedure for the other big business and professional associations.

The Washington office of the National Association of Manufacturers is located on the seventh floor of the World Center Building at 918 Sixteenth Street, near one of the capital's busiest corners (the Statler Hilton and Sheraton Carlton hotels are its neighbors) and three blocks from the Chamber of Commerce building. Unlike the Chamber, the N.A.M. has its principal headquarters in New York.

Founded in 1895 as the spiritual descendant of the Pennsylvania Society for the Encouragement of Manufactures and the Mechanic Arts, the N.A.M. has about 15,000 "active" members — companies directly engaged in manufacturing — and some 2,000 "cooperating" members — those which have a direct interest in or close relationship to manufacturing. This category includes banks, insurance companies, railroads and the like. Several hundred state manufacturers associations, local, state and national industrial organizations and manufacturing trade associations are affiliated with the N.A.M. through its National Industrial Council.

There is some reason to believe that the N.A.M. speaks for a smaller segment of American business than the Chamber of Commerce — smaller but not necessarily less wealthy. Professor V. O. Key Jr. has said of the N.A.M.: "A small number of large concerns has assumed a greater and greater importance in the management of its affairs . . . Like many other groups, the [N.A.M.] appears to be fairly rigidly controlled by a comparatively small number of its members." Key cited a study which showed that 125 corporations held 63 percent of all directorships, 88 percent of executive committee memberships, 79 percent of finance committee members and 52 percent of the major executive offices in the N.A.M.[7]

From a comfortable but not elaborate corner office overlooking
Sixteenth Street, Ralph Theodore (Ted) Compton, vice president in charge of the N.A.M.'s government relations division,
directs an operation similar to that of the Chamber in its emphasis on indirect lobbying. The N.A.M. expends a great deal of
time, money and effort exhorting its members to make their
views known to Congress. Its principal publication, the weekly,
four-page "N.A.M. News," is packed with appeals for grassroots
communications to the legislators. The business of influencing legislation, Compton explains, is left to the N.A.M.'s member businessmen. His division's primary job is to obtain the information
on which the members base N.A.M. policy and decide what legislation to support and oppose.

Much of the N.A.M.'s legislative research is done in the New
York office. Experts from New York, together with businessmen
members of the N.A.M., present testimony before Congressional
committees. The government relations division does no testifying; its lobbyists confine themselves principally to keeping tabs
on the status and prospects of pending legislation.

"Given current standards of judgment," Professor Key has
written, "it is not unfair to characterize the N.A.M. in its lobbying
work as one of the most reactionary business associations."
Since 1934, Key says, a major objective of the N.A.M.'s "public
education" program has been "to create antilabor sentiment."
This effort continues to the present day. Recently there came
to light a 37-page document marked "Not for distribution —
Confidential." It was headed "Initial Meeting — N.A.M. Center
for the Study of Union Monopoly Power," and it summarized
a discussion by 21 N.A.M. officers and staff members, business
leaders, lawyers and professors on how to curb the power of labor
unions. Later, Charles A. Kothe, head of the N.A.M.'s industrial
relations division, confirmed that the N.A.M. had decided to set
up such a center. Its objective, he said, would be to collect and
disseminate information on the subject and then draft remedial
legislation for introduction in Congress.

One of the participants in the N.A.M. meeting on union monopoly power was Horace B. Clay, legislative assistant to Senator
John G. Tower, Texas Republican. Another was Denison Kitchel,
a Phoenix, Arizona, lawyer who is a political associate of Barry
Goldwater.

LABOR

"Clear everything with Sidney." — *Attributed to Franklin D. Roosevelt at the 1944 Democratic national convention.*

"Labor, like Israel, has many sorrows." — *John L. Lewis.*

The lobbyists for organized labor could hardly believe it. As they were preparing for the fight to repeal Section 14 (b) of the Taft-Hartley Act, word came from the White House that the chief administration lobbyist for the repeal bill would be W. Marvin Watson, one of President Johnson's special assistants. Watson, rated as probably the most conservative member of Johnson's staff, is a former executive of the Lone Star Steel Company of Texas, whose antiunion attitude is a byword in labor circles. The labor strategists reacted with stunned disbelief. A slow curve had floated across the plate, and the ball game, they suspected, was over in the first inning. They were right.

Looking at it one way, the unions have had legislative troubles in recent years. They have been notably unsuccessful in persuading Congress to rescind Section 14 (b), a top item on labor's priority list of legislation. Senate Republican Leader Everett McKinley Dirksen of Illinois, the orotund terror of the plains, blocked repeal of 14 (b) in 1965 with a filibuster for which labor's leaders and lobbyists were not fully prepared. A Dirksen-led filibuster stalled the repeal measure again in 1966. Labor was unwilling to meet what was widely assumed to be Dirksen's condition — Senate approval of a Constitutional amendment to overturn the Supreme Court's one-man, one-vote decision requiring reapportionment of state legislatures. Majority Leader Mike Mansfield could not muster the votes to invoke cloture in the Senate and bring 14 (b) to a vote. A key ingredient was missing: Lyndon Johnson.

Viewed another way, organized labor's legislative efforts in recent years have been an immense success. Hard-working labor lobbyists have helped significantly to enact two landmark civil rights bills, massive federal aid to education, assistance to economically depressed areas, the war on poverty, tax reduction, manpower retraining, Medicare and a host of others.

The unions have long since ceased to concentrate on narrow legislative goals directly affecting the working man's right to organize and bargain collectively with his employer. Labor lobbying has become broad-based. The unions press untiringly for a wide spectrum of economic and social improvement. So effective have they been that the AFL-CIO has clear title to being the foremost non-governmental lobbyist for the general public interest. With much justification, the AFL-CIO calls itself the people's lobby. If labor's legislative record is judged in the light of its broad goals, its lobbyists get high marks.

It is ironic, therefore, that labor suffered two successive defeats on a piece of legislation — repeal of 14 (b) — that was of major importance to every union member.

With 14 (b) as a symbol of discontent, relations between organized labor and the Johnson administration have deteriorated sharply. For all its hard-won middle-class respectability, the AFL-CIO has been finding that living in the bland land of political consensus is not all roses. Many labor leaders are angry at President Johnson's lackadaisical performance on the repeal bill, at his wage-price guidelines and at an administration proposal that labor contends would lead to compulsory wage settlements. Increasingly the unions are coming to believe that Great Society consensus is a one-way street in which labor gives but does not get. Like a lover scorned, the AFL-CIO has watched with growing perturbation Johnson's courtship of business. Union leaders realize that the President is, of course, playing standard politics when he takes advantage of semi-prevalent prosperity to try to lure businessmen away from their traditional Republican allegiance, but that makes it no easier for labor to contemplate its diminishing influence in the councils of government.

The Taft-Hartley Act, enacted over President Truman's veto, prohibits the closed shop, under which a worker must belong to a union before he can be hired. The law permits other forms of union security — the union shop, in which workers, to keep their jobs, must join a union within a certain time after being hired; the agency shop, in which workers must join the union after being hired or pay an amount equal to union dues, and maintenance-of-membership arrangements, in which workers who are union members when the contract is signed, and those who join later, must remain in the union while the contract is in force. In Section 14 (b), however, Taft-Hartley allows the states to enact more restrictive laws on union security. Nineteen states, most of them in the South and Middle West, have statutes prohibiting the other forms of union security. They are known, euphemistically, as right-to-work laws.

In 1965, for the first time, the AFL-CIO decided on a frontal attack on 14 (b). There was no thought of going after the closed shop prohibition, since many people in the labor movement itself do not believe in the closed shop. But Section 14 (b), the unions feel, is the most restrictive provision of Taft-Hartley and blatantly hostile toward the concept of collective bargaining. To the unions, moreover, it is a singular kind of law, since the federal government, having asserted jurisdiction in a field, has ceded part of that jurisdiction back to the states. Lastly, 14 (b) has cost the unions dearly in time and money. As right-to-work laws have been proposed in various states, labor has had to fight a series of expensive brush-fire wars to defeat them. Sometimes it has been successful; often not.

With the 1964 Democratic platform pledging repeal of 14 (b), the unions delivered handsomely for Lyndon Johnson at the polls. Party chieftains acknowledge that union votes were a major element in the defeat of Barry Goldwater. Implicit in labor's support was the belief that the President would move swiftly for repeal of Section 14 (b).

Even so, the unions did not press for repeal in the early stages of the 1965 Congressional session. They agreed with the White House that a fight over 14 (b) should not be allowed to delay the Great Society legislative program, especially Medicare and the voting rights bill. With the help of the AFL-CIO, the bulk of the administration's priority legislation was approved before the repeal measure was brought up in the Senate.

But the AFL-CIO was slow in changing gears. Its earlier planning had been based on the assumption that the chief battle over 14 (b) would come in the House. The 1964 election results,

which gave the Democrats a huge majority in the House, transformed the picture. There were now plenty of votes in the House,
which passed the bill in July. With its eye on the House, however, the AFL-CIO paid less attention to the Senate in the early
stages of the game. As it mapped its lobbying campaign in the
spring of 1965, the idea that Dirksen might lead a filibuster to
prevent the bill coming to a vote "did not loom as a real possibility in our thinking," a labor official said. Not believing that
a filibuster was likely, the AFL-CIO did not mount a grassroots
lobbying campaign at that point to bring pressure on the Senate.
Its head counts showed that there were enough votes to pass the
bill in the Senate, assuming that it were brought to a roll call.
This would have required only a simple majority. What labor
did not have — and did not think it needed — was the two-thirds
majority needed to break a filibuster.

The failure to launch a grassroots campaign in 1965 was a
costly miscalculation, as it turned out. Labor confined its lobbying to Washington, and even there, as one strategist explained,
"We put on no great pressure, since we had the votes to repeal
14 (b) in the Senate." It was the second time in recent years
that a delay in starting a grassroots lobbying effort has hurt the
AFL-CIO. A similar miscalculation, as will be seen later, was
a factor in labor's defeat on the Landrum-Griffin Act.

When Mansfield brought up the repeal bill in October 1965,
time and circumstances were running out. Congress had been
in session almost ten months and had worked hard. Adjournment fever was epidemic. At this point the President was hospitalized for a gall bladder operation, and Dirksen mustered the
Republicans and southern Democrats for a filibuster. Knowing
that the votes were not at hand to invoke cloture, the AFL-CIO
accepted the inevitable. Repeal of 14 (b) was laid over.

Between sessions, the labor federation did undertake a grassroots lobbying campaign. Its purpose was two-fold: to try to get
the repeal bill through in 1966 and to help the first-term House
Democrats who had voted for the bill in July. Some of these
freshman Representatives were from right-to-work states such
as Iowa, where their stand might hurt them politically, and labor
was anxious to do what it could to protect its friends. The union
strategists selected 13 parts of the country in which it was
thought that a public education campaign was necessary and

might do some good. One or two experienced men from international unions or state labor federations were sent into these areas with an impressive campaign handbook prepared by AFL-CIO headquarters in Washington. The handbook contained sample advertisements, news releases, prepared speeches, material setting forth labor's arguments for repeal of 14 (b), sample radio commercials and the like. The material was given to local unions, state labor councils, civic, religious and civil rights groups — anyone and everyone who might make a speech, buy an ad or sponsor a radio commercial advocating repeal.

As part of the lobbying campaign, an open message to Congress from AFL-CIO President George Meany was placed in several large newspapers just before the 1966 session opened. Meany also sent letters to every newspaper in the country and to editorial cartoonists, emphasizing that the immediate issue was whether the Senate would be allowed to vote or whether a filibuster would prevent the majority from expressing its will, as permitted under the Senate's quaint rules. Most newspapers ignored Meany's letter. The few that ran it edited the letter heavily, and some of them printed the AFL-CIO communication alongside one from Reed Larson, executive director of the National Right to Work Committee, a right-wing group leading the fight against repeal of 14 (b).

The issue, as far as labor was concerned, remained the first item on the Senate agenda when Congress reconvened in 1966. Mansfield agreed and brought it up early in the new session. Dirksen, as expected, resumed the filibuster. And now an interesting phenomenon was observed, something that happens every now and again on Capitol Hill. A lassitude settled over the Senate. There was a strange desultory atmosphere as the filibuster droned on routinely. Few legislators paid much attention to the proceedings. The filibuster gave the news from Viet Nam little competition. To the reporters in the galleries, and to the Senators themselves, there was no great mystery about the prevailing ennui over 14 (b). They know from long experience the electricity that stirs Congress when the White House is really pushing a bill, when the President says this is one I want and I want it now, when the opponents know that they are to be tested in the crucible and that the moment of truth is at hand. No such excitement pervaded the 14 (b) debate. Everyone was just going through routine motions. The result was predictable.

After a short filibuster, Mansfield moved to invoke cloture and bring the repeal bill to a vote. With 99 Senators present, the administration needed 66 votes to break Dirksen's stranglehold. On the first try the vote was 51 to 48 for cloture — enough to pass the repeal measure itself but 15 shy of the necessary two-thirds to cut off debate. Two days later Mansfield tried again. The vote was 50 to 49 for cloture — 16 shy. The bill, Mansfield said, would remain on the Senate calendar, but he added wryly, "with the inscription R.I.P." Repeal of Section 14 (b) would rest in peace for the remainder of the session.

The morning after found many labor men blaming Lyndon Johnson bitterly for letting them down. Some union strategists argued that even if the President had pushed hard, he still would have been able to pick up only seven or eight more votes for cloture, not enough to break the filibuster. But the general feeling was that even if the battle could not have been won, considering the Senate's reluctance to vote cloture, Johnson had dragged his feet on an issue of crucial importance to the labor movement. The selection of Watson as the White House's chief lobbyist on 14 (b) contributed to this feeling. Labor's view of the administration took a turn for the cynical.

It is probable that an intensive grassroots lobbying campaign in 1965 would not have changed the outcome either. Indirect lobbying is not omnipotent. But a point often overlooked about this kind of lobbying is that it frequently picks up additional votes even if it falls short. This in turn creates bargaining power. If the AFL-CIO had come close to cloture, a prospect particularly frightening to the southerners, it would have been in a better bargaining position.

The defeat on 14 (b), an issue vital to labor's interests, should be considered in the larger context of the trials and troubles besetting the union movement. Labor's weaknesses contribute to its legislative difficulties in a national capital where the only joy is in strength. The unions have come a long way from that stirring moment at the Democratic national convention in Chicago in 1944, when labor's pre-eminence as a political force was acknowledged in the reference to Sidney Hillman, then head of the Congress of Industrial Organizations. Whether Roosevelt actually said "clear everything with Sidney" on the nomination of a vice presidential candidate is not important; the remark was accepted as an accurate description of labor's high place in the political coalition put together by F.D.R.

Today things have changed for organized labor, and not always for the better. An estimated 16,841,000 Americans belong to labor unions, an increase of about 255,000 since 1962. But this is only 28.9 percent of the non-farm labor force, compared with 33.4 percent in 1956. The unions, in other words, are not enrolling the increasingly important white collar workers. Many of the AFL-CIO's blue collar members in such industries as steel, automobiles and coal are losing their jobs to automation. Some unions are gaining new adherents; the Retail Clerks, Meatcutters and the aggressive Teamsters are examples. But it is proving difficult to organize the growing army of salaried white collar employees — they seem to identify more with management than with labor. Solomon Barkin, research director for the Textile Workers Union, has pointed out that white collar and service workers make up 55 percent of the labor force today, but only 20 percent of them are union members.[1]

Since 1900 the percentage of white collar workers in the labor force has more than doubled, while the percentage of blue collar workers has remained almost constant. The number of white collar employees shot up from slightly more than 22,000,000 in 1950 to 31,000,000 in 1964. But the number of blue collar workers went from just under 24,000,000 in 1950 to just under 26,000,000 in 1964. In the same period the number of man hours required to produce 1,000 tons of steel dropped from 19,600 to 15,700, the number of man hours required to produce an automobile from 198.3 to 160.9, the number of man hours to produce 1,000 tons of coal from 1,200 to 600, due to automation and productivity improvements. These are the statistics behind labor's demand for an increased share of the material fruits of productivity. The same statistics underlie labor's legislative troubles and its lessened influence with an intensely, even a cruelly pragmatic President.

A grueling effort to organize the 10,000,000 non-union workers in the south, in such industries as textiles, clothing, chemicals, paper and furniture manufacturing and in the building trades,

has not been notably successful. In 1962 there were some 22,000,
000 women in the work force, but only 3,400,000 of them belonged
to unions. The restrictions in the Landrum-Griffin Act of 1959
on organizational picketing, together with other provisions of
this law, have made the task of enlisting new members even
harder. The younger generation of union officials grumbles about
the older leaders, complaining that they are rigid, unimaginative
and slow to recognize and adjust to changed conditions. A bitter
feud between the AFL-CIO's two top leaders, Meany and Walter
Reuther, has been largely healed, but their discord for a time
was deep, and it has left some scars. The Teamsters under Dave
Beck and Jimmy Hoffa have hurt labor's image. Racial segregation in many union locals has embittered the National Association for the Advancement of Colored People and similar
groups. Labor, as John L. Lewis said in another context, has
many sorrows.

The labor movement still has a great deal going for it as a
political and legislative force. Many of its hardest battles have
been fought and won. The right to bargain collectively has been
established. The minimum wage, the 40-hour week, unemployment compensation, pension plans, social security, child labor
laws—two generations of social legislation and bargaining gains
—have vastly improved the life of the working man. Union treasuries and strike funds bulge with the sinews of war. Labor can
afford able lawyers, economists and lobbyists to look out for its
interests and press for further social gains. The glittering Washington buildings that house the AFL-CIO, the Teamsters, the
Machinists, the Carpenters, the Communications Workers and
others have replaced dingy walkup offices. The modern building
housing the national headquarters of the AFL-CIO is as close to the
White House as that of the U.S. Chamber of Commerce; the two
mammoth organizations are only a block apart, physically. In
the Committee on Political Education labor has a smoothly
functioning apparatus to conduct grassroots political programs,
instill political awareness in union members and raise money for
pro-labor candidates. (The National Association of Manufacturers and the American Medical Association have paid c.o.p.e.
the compliment of imitation).

And yet the labor movement struggles against a host of
internal and external problems. Political scientists and sociolo-

gists are busy assessing the impact on trade unionism of such
trends as automation, suburbia and an expanding, affluent,
white collar middle class. Much will depend on how labor reacts,
how well it can cope with a push-button culture and the centrist
politics of consensus.

Trade unions in the United States have been involved in politics for a long time, at least since the early nineteenth century.²
In the early stages of labor's political activity, it was not unusual
for workingmen to form what amounted to political parties, supporting their own slates of candidates for public office. In 1828
the Mechanics Union of Philadelphia formed the Republican
Political Association of the Workingmen of the City of Philadelphia and ran candidates for city and county offices on a working-
man's ticket. Later the National Labor Union and the Knights
of Labor engaged in similar direct political action.

The American Federation of Labor, established in 1881 under
the leadership of Samuel Gompers, was formed in part as a reaction against this kind of direct political involvement by trade
unions. Fundamentally opposed to the creation of a labor party,
as Samuel C. Patterson has pointed out, Gompers preferred to
place "primary reliance for political success on lobbying the Congress." To the extent that the federation was active in politics,
Gompers believed it should be non-partisan, supporting its
friends and working against its enemies, regardless of party. The
AFL had a political arm, the National Non-Partisan Political
Campaign Committee (no longer in existence), but it urged
union members to vote for labor's friends without regard to
party. Most of the time this meant Democrats, but some AFL!
leaders publicly supported Republican candidates. Gompers'
influence, especially among older AFL unions, lasted far beyond
his death in 1924. Under the leadership of his successor, William
Green, labor's involvement in political action was still quite
restricted. The AFL as an organization never endorsed Franklin
Roosevelt for President, although Green personally supported
F.D.R. in 1940.

An effort was made in 1936 to unite the AFL and the newly
formed CIO in Labor's Non-Partisan League, with the initial
purpose of backing Roosevelt for a second term. The AFL co-
operated in the League for a time, but in 1938 Green's anti-

pathy to its broad political aims led him to denounce the League. In a letter to all local, state and international AFL unions, he said the League had "declared [that] the future and salvation of American workers rested upon independent political action"; he called this a "false doctrine." Finally, in 1939, Green took the AFL out of the League altogether. The AFL continued to emphasize direct lobbying in Congress as the primary way of achieving its political and legislative goals.

Until the Taft-Hartley Act came along in 1947, that is. Then the AFL realized that lobbying in Congress was not enough and that organized labor must supplement or complement direct lobbying with massive political action—raising funds for political campaigns, organizing grassroots lobbying efforts, educating its members. In 1947 the AFL convention voted to set up Labor's League for Political Education as the political arm of the federation.

The Congress of Industrial Organizations, formed in 1935 when John L. Lewis' United Mine Workers and several big industrial unions broke away from the AFL, recognized the importance of grassroots political action from the start. It set up the famous Political Action Committee, probably the first organized recognition of what has since become a basic principle of lobbying: it is not enough merely to lobby incumbent Congressmen. There may not be enough of them who see things the way you do. You have to get out and try to elect some more.

Under Gompers the AFL generally limited its lobbying to legislation closely related to unions themselves. The AFL concentrated on pushing through laws guaranteeing labor's right to organize, to bargain collectively and to strike. If Congress gave it these weapons, Gompers believed, labor could and would get what it wanted in the way of higher wages, job security and the like by bargaining with management—and without any further action by the federal government. Gompers, for instance, opposed a federal minimum wage law.

In the years after his death, however, the AFL's legislative horizons, like its political activities, gradually were broadened. A report to the final AFL national convention in 1955, just before the merger with the CIO, expressed strong interest in a long list of legislative matters. The list went far beyond strictly union legislation into programs of social and economic improvement.

Since the CIO had had a wide legislative outlook from its inception, the merger created an organization whose lobbying efforts were broad-based. Important differences remained within the new AFL-CIO, of course.

"The merger of the AFL and the CIO in 1955 . . . brought together two labor federations with different political orientations and traditions," Samuel Patterson has observed. "It is obvious even to the casual observer that the merger did not eliminate conflict in the labor movement, particularly between the craft and industrial unions, over economic questions. What is not so obvious is the fact that the merger did not resolve conflicts over political style and objectives." [3]

Patterson, who made a 10-month study of the AFL-CIO's lobbying operations, concluded that merger of Labor's League for Political Education (AFL) and the Political Action Committee (CIO) into a new organization known as the Committee on Political Education went relatively smoothly and was successful. As a result the AFL-CIO had an efficient mechanism for political action and indirect lobbying from the grassroots. But the merger of the AFL and CIO legislative departments did not go as smoothly. Patterson's observations led him to describe the AFL-CIO's lobbyists as falling into three categories: the contact man (primarily an AFL man), the campaign organizer (usually a CIO lobbyist) and the testifier-expert. When it came to lobbying methods, AFL and CIO men were still going separate ways, he found.

Patterson defined the contact man as the lobbyist who concentrates on a personal, direct approach to members of Congress, their assistants, and the staffs of Congressional committees. Generally he devotes "his time and energies to walking the legislative halls, visiting legislators, collaring them in the halls, establishing relationships with administrative assistants and others of the Congressman's staff, cultivating key legislators on a friendship basis, and developing contacts on the staffs of critical legislative committees."

The campaign organizer, Patterson observed, "conceives his job as that of organizing mass grassroots support for labor's legislative program. He believes his most important contacts are with labor leaders 'in the field' and with rank and file members. The campaign organizer does not believe that the goals of the labor movement can be achieved merely by contacting and cultivating personal friendships with legislators. He feels that the most effective lobbying for the labor movement is achieved by demonstrating mass support for that program among labor union members' 'back home' who are the legislators' constituents."

While contact men were usually lobbyists from AFL unions or legislative representatives for unions formerly affiliated with the AFL, the campaign organizers were predominantly CIO men "who believed that organized labor could only securely achieve its goals through broad political action," particularly through grassroots campaigning, Patterson concluded.

The terms contact man and campaign organizer are accurate, serviceable descriptions of the two main methods of *lobbying.* But as categories of *lobbyists,* they are too neat. Most lobbyists —labor lobbyists, lobbyists for business groups and freelancers— use both methods at one time or another, alternating them according to the situation. Lobbying is largely played by ear. If the circumstances call for direct contacts with Congresmen, that method is used. If the context seems to require an indirect lobbying campaign from the grassroots, a campaign is organized.

The trick is in knowing when to use which technique, which one will be more effective, or whether the circumstances call for a mixture of both methods, as frequently happens. Here the lobbyist's experience comes into play. He must have a sort of sixth sense that tells him when Congress has been pushed too hard or can be pushed a little more, when a member is wavering, what argument or method of persuasion is most likely to work. If the timing is wrong or the wrong method is chosen, the cause is likely to be lost. The AFL-CIO's defeat on the Landrum-Griffin Act was due in part to overemphasis on one lobbying method at the expense of another.

Many labor lobbyists do not agree with Patterson that the AFL-CIO's legislative representatives fit neatly into the category of contact man or campaign organizer. The effective lobbyists for former AFL unions are just as good at "field work" (organizing grassroots pressure) as the lobbyists for former CIO unions, one AFL-CIO lobbyist has said. "Conversely, those from the CIO are just as active on Capitol Hill as those from the AFL," he added.

Among labor lobbyists proficient in both types of lobbying are the veteran, widely-respected John Edelman of the Textile Workers Union, a CIO union before the merger; George Nelson of the

Machinists Union, a former AFL union; Evelyn Dubrow of the International Ladies Garment Workers Union, a former AFL union, and the lobbyists for the United Auto Workers and the Steelworkers, both CIO unions before the merger. These lobbyists spend a great deal of time in direct lobbying on Capitol Hill, but all of them have well-developed, functioning programs behind them to mobilize grassroots pressure campaigns when needed and to stimulate political activity and awareness by the members of their unions. Arnold Mayer of the Meatcutters Union (formerly AFL) is another labor lobbyist who regularly uses both the direct contact and grassroots lobbying methods. He combined the two techniques with notable success in a campaign to enact the Poultry Inspection Act.

Patterson's categories may not be entirely adequate but they do point up a continuing difficulty within the AFL-CIO itself. The alliance between the two big organizations remains to some extent an uneasy one, and this poses problems for labor's lobbyists. Not surprisingly, things go best when the union lobbyists have a clear mandate from headquarters, when labor is united—and stays united—on a particular piece of legislation. This is not a guarantee that the labor lobbyists will be successful but it helps. When the opposite prevails, there is likely to be chaos.

The merger of the AFL and CIO created a loosely-knit federation of some 130 international unions. These in turn have been grouped into seven semi-autonomous departments. The best known are the Industrial Union Department, (headed by Reuther and composed largely of former CIO unions plus the Machinists and the I.L.G.W.U.) and the Building Trades Department, stronghold of the old AFL unions. The others are the Metal Trades, Maritime Trades, Railroad Employees, Food and Beverage Trades and the Union Label and Service Trades Departments.

The I.U.D. and the Building Trades, in particular, often seem to pursue an independent course within the merged organization, although they are bound by AFL-CIO policy. Each has its own lobbyists, and each sponsors its own legislative conferences. The Building Trades Department, for instance, brought more than 3,000 union members to Washington to lobby for labor-backed legislation including housing, urban renewal and airport construction programs, which create jobs for building trades unions. This was part of the department's national legislative conference. On another occasion, during a two-day legislative conference sponsored by the I.U.D., some 500 union leaders visited members of Congress to lobby for minimum wage legislation, health care for the aged, federal aid to education and other programs.

In 1962 Reuther held the first of a series of annual dinners for all members of Congress. Some 200 Senators and Representatives from both parties showed up at the Mayflower Hotel in Washington for cocktails, dinner and a 40-minute speech by Reuther urging them to support the administration's legislative program. The lobbyists for the AFL-CIO itself had little to do with this important lobbying effort. "We have no idea what goes on in the Industrial Union Department," one of them said. He added that there is some communication with the I.U.D., "but not a helluva lot." However, I.U.D. and Building Trades lobbyists regularly attend meetings of an administrative committee which handles the AFL-CIO lobbying operation.

Every other year, the AFL-CIO holds its own legislative conference, usually in January or February. These meetings bring several hundred state and local union officers to Washington for three or four days to hear talks on national issues and participate in workshops. One day is set aside for a mass visit to Capitol Hill. But there is little co-ordination between this big AFL-CIO lobbying event and Reuther's lobbying efforts.

During the Landrum-Griffin debate, costly dissension arose in the AFL-CIO's executive council. After a long, damaging delay, Meany endorsed a mild labor bill introduced by Representative John F. Shelley, a California Democrat and former president of the California Federation of Labor. It was painfully obvious, however, that the Shelley bill had no chance of passing. The choice lay between the restrictive Landrum-Griffin bill and a more moderate measure sponsored by Representative Carl Elliott, Alabama Democrat. The Elliott bill had been approved by the House Education and Labor Committee and had the full support of the House Democratic leadership. A powerful southern Democratic-Republican coalition was backing the Landrum-Griffin measure.

In the executive council, several AFL-CIO vice presidents urged· support of the Elliott bill. They feared, with good reason as it

turned out, that unless the AFL-CIO threw its full weight behind
the Elliott measure, the House would approve Landrum-Griffin.
One of the union leaders who strongly urged this course of action
was Walter Reuther. Meany, however, "remained adamant, and
the council of moderation did not prevail." [4] The AFL-CIO's lobbyists on Capitol Hill continued to attack the Elliott bill as well as
Landrum-Griffin, and this apparently swung more southern Democrats to Landrum-Griffin.

Had the AFL-CIO strongly supported the Elliott measure, according to Sar Levitan, a labor relations specialist for the Library
of Congress, the southerners might have gone along with Speaker
Sam Rayburn in supporting the moderate bill. "The House
Democratic leadership put its full support behind the moderate
committee bill [the Elliott bill,] but the AFL-CIO's objection to
this bill divided the pro-labor forces within the House," Levitan
pointed out. "At first, supporters of the labor position had no
bill at all which they favored. This gave the impression that labor
would just as soon not have any legislation at all."

Labor's actions in this connection "appear to have been
crucial," Levitan added. "Until the last week prior to the House
approval of the Landrum-Griffin bill, lobbying by the AFL-CIO
representatives lacked any coordination. In some cases they even
worked at cross-purposes." On the other side, Landrum-Griffin's
backers were conducting a unified and well-co-ordinated effort.

Labor's friends in the House didn't know what labor wanted.
Reuther and James B. Carey of the Electrical Workers wanted
good reform legislation. John L. Lewis, controlling a bloc of
12 to 18 votes in the House, was opposed to any legislation regulating internal union affairs. So were the Teamsters. The building trades unions, Patterson reports, were "lukewarm to hostile
about reform legislation." Some unions were concentrating their
lobbying efforts on pushing pet provisions of this or that bill.
Meany refused to support the Kennedy-Ervin labor reform bill
passed by the Senate. Nor would he endorse the Elliott bill. All
was confusion in the house of labor.

"Our friends [in Congress] know what we wanted," a labor
lobbyist said wryly. "That was the trouble. They knew what we
wanted this week—and the week before that and the week before
that. But it was never the same thing." However, a union lobbyist who disagreed with this interpretation of events, said the idea

all along was to back the Shelley bill as a first line of defense and then if necessary fall back on the Elliott bill. But he acknowledged rather ruefully that "perhaps the message didn't get through." Apparently it didn't. As late as August 6, seven days before the crucial vote in the House, Meany was telling a nation-wide radio audience that "we must oppose and we do oppose the Elliott bill."

Meany clearly underestimated the pressure that had built up for labor reform legislation—the cumulative impact on public opinion of a long series of Congressional investigations spotlighting labor racketeering and other abuses. As a result, the AFL-CIO did little work with the public to counteract the effect of the hearings by Senator John L. McClellan and others. "In the initial stages of the lobbying operation, no all-out campaign was planned, and the actual lobbying activities were entrusted to a few experienced lobbyists working informally," Patterson reports. "The strategy involved emphasis upon direct contact by lobbyists with Congressmen . . . It hinged on Congressional understanding of the problems and complexities of organized labor, without planning for a campaign to engender widespread public support for sympathetic treatment."

At the last minute an effort was made to mobilize pro-labor grassroots sentiment. Some 2,000,000 copies of a leaflet entitled "Get Crooks, Not Unions" were distributed, and 90 union leaders were brought to Washington to aid in the fight. But that was about all, and it was too late. The AFL-CIO had concentrated too heavily on direct lobbying on Capitol Hill, neglecting the grassroots. There was little to counteract the impact of President Eisenhower's television speech to the nation on August 6, in which he praised the Landrum-Griffin bill. This speech had a significant bearing on the outcome.

The Landrum-Griffin Act was passed by the House on August 14, 1959 by a vote of 303 to 125. An AFL-CIO spokesman described it at the time as a more restrictive piece of labor legislation than the Taft-Hartley law, and House Democratic Leader John W. McCormack referred to August 14 as "Black Thursday for labor." The key vote actually had come the day before, when the House voted 229 to 201 to substitute the Landrum-Griffin language for the milder bill reported out by the Education and Labor Committee. The fight was lost on August 13. It was a

stunning defeat for organized labor, its worst in more than a
decade. Divided and confused, the AFL-CIO had failed to stop a
frontal attack striking directly at its vital interests. Every lobbyist expects to lose peripheral engagements from time to time,
but this was a battle deep in labor's home territory, and its
enemies carried the day.

In the way its lobbying activities are organized, the AFL-CIO
generally follows the standard pattern for large institutionalized
lobbying groups. Primary responsibility for lobbying is vested
in the department of legislation, headed by a former Congressman, Andrew J. Biemiller. Working under him are four legislative representatives, giving the AFL-CIO a five-man lobbying staff.
There are, in addition, approximately 100 other union lobbyists
in Washington. About half of these are active in general labor
lobbying efforts. To plan and coordinate Congressional strategy,
the AFL-CIO has a National Legislative Council headed by Meany
and consisting of the other union lobbyists and the AFL-CIO legislative staff. The day-in and day-out lobbying operation is
handled by an administrative committee headed by Biemiller.
About 20 union lobbyists, including representatives of the I.U.D.,
Building Trades and the other AFL-CIO departments, attend the
weekly meetings of this committee.

In addition to the legislative department, several other AFL-
CIO staff departments are involved in legislation. The research
department under Nathaniel Goldfinger has a staff of nine persons, including four economists and an industrial engineer. The
social security department headed by Raymond Munts, who recently succeeded Nelson Cruikshank, handles legislation dealing
with social security, unemployment compensation, workmen's
compensation and health programs. The education department under Lawrence Rogin, the civil rights department under
Donald Slaiman and the public relations department headed by
Al Zack also get into the legislative picture. The work of the
publications department, headed by Saul Miller, has an impor-
tent bearing on the AFL-CIO's efforts to keep union members
aware of legislative issues. Miller and his staff put out the weekly
AFL-CIO News, with a circulation of 100,000, and the American
Federationist, a monthly magazine with approximately the same
circulation.

Labor's informal allies play an essential role in many of the battles for social and economic improvement. Some of these groups are small in numbers; others have significant memberships, but all of them have in common a dedication to social progress. Among the organizations that frequently will be found working with the AFL-CIO on this or that domestic issue are: the American Association of University Women; the American Civil Liberties Union; the American Friends Service Committee; the American Nurses Association; the American Veterans Committee; Americans for Democratic Action; the Anti-Defamation League of B'nai B'rith; the Co-operative League of the U.S.A.; the Jewish Labor Committee; the National Association for the Advancement of Colored People (although relations between the N.A.A.C.P. and the AFL-CIO have been strained by racial discrimination in local unions); the National Catholic Welfare Conference; the National Consumers League; the National Council of Jewish Women; the National Council of Negro Women; the National Farmers Union; the National Urban League and other civil rights groups; the Unitarian Fellowship for Social Justice, and the United States Conference of Mayors.

A favorite cry of conservative orators is that labor rules the roost in Washington, that it gets anything it wants from Congress and the White House. To the realistic men of the Washington community, including labor and business lobbyists, the picture is not that simple. They know they live in a half-a-loaf town. Many factors beyond labor's control play a large part in determining the course of government and the pace of social progress.

MEN

"All legislative bodies which control important pecuniary interests are as sure to have a lobby as an army to have its camp followers. Where the body is, there will the vultures be gathered together."
— *Lord Bryce.*[1]

"Lobbying . . . is, in its proper use, a necessary and beneficial adjunct to the orderly processes of government." — *Report of the Senate committee that investigated a $2,500 campaign contribution to Senator Francis Case.*[2]

There are no college courses for lobbyists. There are no groves of Academe through which the budding pressure boys can stroll, listening respectfully to their elders discourse on the ethical implications of the campaign contribution. No college catalogue lists Introductory Lobbying, Theory and Practice of the Direct Contact or Graduate Seminar in the Metaphysics of the Grass-roots. Talk to a Washington lobbyist and you find a man who started out as something else — lawyer, politician, public relations man, businessman, union leader, newspaper reporter, economist, teacher, industrial engineer — or oboe player. For most of them, lobbying, like Topsy, just growed.

It is not easy to draw a composite picture of the Washington lobbyist. What is the very model of a modern lobbyist? Is it Charlie Clark, gaudy, gregarious, overflowing with Irish *Gemutlichkeit?* Or is it Terry Rice, solid suburbanite, Cub Scout leader, P.T.A. president? Perhaps it is Ted Compton, economist and Ph.D. from Yale; poetry-scribbling Scott Lucas, wrapped in the faded remnants of Senate glory, or former union organizer Andy Biemiller of the AFL-CIO. It is a crazy quilt, but there are some common denominators.

All lobbyists, for one thing, live by their wits. There is no routine which, once learned, can merely be repeated without variation to earn them a living. Their work is not cut and

153

dried. They must master some basic skills and techniques —
how to marshal and present facts and arguments most effectively,
for instance. But after that is done, the rest is largely improvisation. The stock in trade of the lobbyist is an intangible thing
called "feel" — adaptability and intuition honed by on-the-job
experience. Given a job to do, the lobbyist goes through an
initial routine, researching his case, presenting his testimony
or brief. From then on, he usually improvises. He selects the
approaches, techniques and combinations that intuition and experience tell him are most likely to be successful. He weighs
alternatives, compromises, deals. He plays it by ear.

Politics is another common denominator. The Washington
lobbyist is a political animal in a political town, although he
may not be actively engaged in politics per se. When political
scientist Lester Milbrath interviewed 100 Washington lobbyists,
he found that 44 of them had never been active in a political
party. Twenty-eight had been at one time but no longer, and
only 28 were still active in party work. Thirty-six of the lobbyists reported that they never attended party meetings, 27 attended fewer than one a year, 27 attended occasionally and only
10 attended regularly. Milbrath also found that 77 of the lobbyists had never held office in a political party.[3]

But active political participation aside, all lobbyists are vitally
interested in politics. They are technicians of politics who study
political and legislative developments as the doctor reads medical
journals or the horseplayer analyzes the form sheets. Politics
is an integral part, a very big part, of their livelihood. The
political situation at a given moment almost always looms large
as a factor that the lobbyist must take into consideration when
he begins his improvisation.

The educational and professional backgrounds of Washington
lobbyists provide some points of similarity. In his survey, Milbrath found that about three-fourths of the 100 lobbyists had
law degrees and that more than half had worked for the federal
government at one time or another.

A substantial number of lobbyists come from government —
from the staffs of Congressional committees, the executive departments and the regulatory agencies. Their work on Capitol
Hill or in the federal bureaucracy gives them experience that they
carry over into specific lobbying and legal fields. Examples are

Robert L. Farrington, who was chief counsel of the Agriculture Department in the Eisenhower administration; Joseph Adams, former vice chairman of the Civil Aeronautics Board and now a lobbyist for domestic airlines; Irvin A. Hoff, former administrative assistant to Senator Warren G. Magnuson of Washington, now a top sugar lobbyist as executive director of the United States Cane Sugar Refiners Association; Oscar Cox, former assistant solicitor general of the United States; Myer Feldman, a former aide to Presidents Kennedy and Johnson; H. Struve Hensel, former assistant secretary of Defense; David A. Lindsay, general counsel of the Treasury Department in 1960 and brother of New York Mayor John V. Lindsay; Everett Hutchison, a former member of the Interstate Commerce Commission, and many others.

Another trait common to the lobbyist is pragmatism. In this respect he is no different from the rest of the technicians who comprise Washington's permanent population — the faceless horde of bureaucrats, agency lawyers, Congressional staffers and military men who make the government go, sometimes well, occasionally badly, most often mechanically. There is far more activity than thought in Washington. The technicians are concerned with making government work. Few have the time or temperament to reflect on how it works, or why, or how it could be made to work better. The lobbyists share in this preoccupation with effect rather than cause. By and large, the lobbyist does not consider it part of his job to ponder the proper relationship between the organized special interest group and the general public interest. He is a technician of government and legislation, an operator and implementer, not a student or an innovator.

As a result, most Washington lobbyists, like the rest of the town, are determinedly middlebrow and consciously conformist. For a long time Washington has had the idea that it is dangerous to appear to be too far ahead of the rest of the country. This is a curious municipal state of mind which affects, in one way or another, all those who live there, as Thurber said of Columbus, Ohio. The capital lives in mortal dread that it will be found too avant garde in political attitudes, especially those concerning foreign policy. "Mr. Sam" Rayburn's famous advice to new Congressmen was: "If you want to get along, go along." The lobbyists, like the other branches of government, have taken this admonition to heart. For the most part the lobbyist works unquestioningly and uncritically within the established framework. In general, he gets the most he can for his clients without regard to the effect this will have on the general welfare or the national interest.

On the night of March 9, 1961, a convivial gathering of leading political figures took place at the Mayflower Hotel in Washington. The occasion was the twentieth anniversary of the formation of the Senate Committee to Investigate the National Defense Program, later called the Committee to Investigate the War Effort and commonly known as the Truman Committee. The valuable work of this committee brought a Missouri Senator, Harry S. Truman, to the attention of the nation and led to his nomination for Vice President at the "Clear it with Sidney" convention in 1944.

One of the guests at the anniversary dinner was the new President of the United States, John F. Kennedy. As Kennedy arrived, the toastmaster, a ruddy-faced, jovial man, stepped forward, greeted him and with practiced ease began introducing Kennedy around. The toastmaster was Charles Patrick Clark, one of Washington's best-known attorneys and lobbyists. At the head table that night, Clark was flanked by President Kennedy, former President Truman, Vice President Lyndon B. Johnson (who was one of Clark's classmates at Georgetown University School of Law in the 1930's), Speaker Rayburn and Chief Justice Earl Warren. In the toastmaster's deft hands, the evening flowed smoothly and sentimentally, like good Irish whiskey.

In a day when lobbying has lost much of its flamboyance, Charles Patrick Clark harks back to the era of Sam Ward. The son of an Irish immigrant horseshoer from County Fermanagh, Clark earns an average of $50,000 a year from Spain as its registered foreign agent in Washington, and his work as lawyer and/or lobbyist for domestic clients brings him a tidy additional income. One of his other clients is the Panhandle Eastern Pipe Line Company, a giant of the natural gas industry. Clark also represents clients in the savings and loan industry. For years his annual gross income, including the retainer from Spain, has been reputed to be upwards of $150,000 and more recently it has hit $200,000 a year.

Clark's office is in Suite 500 of the World Center Building, two floors below the Washington headquarters of the National Association of Manufacturers. The walls of his well-furnished office are adorned with autographed photographs of prominent figures, among them three Presidents — Johnson, Kennedy and Truman — and General Franco. Kennedy's picture is inscribed: "To Charles Patrick Clark, with every good wish, John F. Kennedy." Truman's picture has this phrasing: "To my good friend, Hon. Charles Patrick Clark, with kindest regards, Harry S. Truman." Franco's picture is signed: "To Mr. Charles Patrick Clark, lawyer and advisor of the Embassy of Spain in Washington. With my recognition of a great work in the service of Spain, Francisco Franco." Other photographs include those of Speaker McCormack; Speaker Rayburn; Senate Majority Leader Mansfield; Senate president pro tem Carl Hayden of Arizona; Senator Styles Bridges of New Hampshire; a photo of President Kennedy as a Senator; former Senate Majority Leader Scott Lucas; Senator John Sherman Cooper of Kentucky; Representative Michael J. Kirwan of Ohio, one of the powerhouses of Congress; King Ibn Saud of oil-rich Saudi Arabia; retired Justice Harold H. Burton of the Supreme Court; John L. Lewis; Representative William J. Green Jr. of Pennsylvania; Senator J. Glenn Beall of Maryland; Senator Stuart Symington of Missouri, and former Senator Tom Connally of Texas.

Clark, who was born in New York City in 1907, attended Fordham University and received a law degree from Georgetown University in 1933. He has experience in both the executive and legislative branches of government, having worked for Representative John J. Boylan of New York, for the United States Employee's Compensation Commission, for the General Accounting Office as a senior auditor, the Public Works Administration as an attorney and then for four Congressional committees as an attorney, investigator and counsel. His friendship with Truman dates from the last of the committee jobs. In 1941 he was the Missouri Senator's first appointment to the staff of the Senate unit set up to investigate the national defense program. Clark served for two years as associate chief counsel and acting chief counsel before resigning late in 1942 to enter the Army as an enlisted man. He prizes a letter from Truman praising his "magnificent job" for the committee. Truman added: "I am happy to say that as a public servant he has no equal."

When Clark got out of the Army in 1945 he went into private law practice in Washington. In 1949 he went to work for the Spanish Embassy at a starting retainer of $50,000 a year. Later this was raised to $100,000; it now ranges between $36,000 and $50,000. An ardent admirer of the Spanish people and their leader, General Franco, Clark felt that Spain's low standing in official Washington in the late 1940s was the result of what he calls a "vicious propaganda campaign." After a conversation with Spanish envoy Jose Felix de Lequerica, the personable attorney undertook to rectify what he considered a highly unfortunate situation.

Clark has been a notable success When he took over as the Spanish Embassy's non-diplomatic representative in Washington, Spain was not a member of the United Nations or the Inter-Parliamentary Union. Clark is given much of the credit for bringing Spain into both organizations.

Spain wasn't receiving any American aid under the Marshall Plan when Clark began what he calls his "counter-propaganda with a personal approach." Subsequently the financial picture changed rapidly. In 1949, with Clark as deus ex machina, a resolution was introduced in the Senate to give Spain a direct loan of $100,000,000. The sponsors were Senators Patrick McCarran and Owen Brewster, two of Clark's closest Congressional allies. The resolution was defeated twice, but a year later the Senate reversed itself and approved the loan with only 15 dissenting votes. The House approved $50,000,000, a conference committee settled on $62,500,000, and Spain was on the way. Between 1950 and 1962 the American taxpayer shelled out one billion, seven hundred and eleven million, three hundred thousand dollars to the dictatorship of Francisco Franco.

Much of the credit for arranging this largess goes to Charles Patrick Clark. In the years since he first went to work for Spain he has become one of Washington's best-known and most proficient practitioners of the complicated art of persuasion. In appearance and temperament he is well suited to the role

Admire him or deplore him, he is indubitably a personality — quick-witted, aggressive and articulate. He is as different from the dun-colored organization lobbyist as day from night. No conservative grays for this paycock-proud Son of Erin. Walking down Connecticut Avenue on a spring day on his way to Paul Young's, one of his favorite restaurants, he customarily sports an expensively-cut black suit with a white tie or a brown suit with a fawn-colored vest. A shock of steel gray hair and glasses with thick black rims complete an impressive ensemble, a combination of Jimmy Walker and Gaylord Ravenal.

Clark lives in a fashionable apartment house commanding one of Washington's finest views. His top-floor apartment looks out over wooded Rock Creek Park. Luxuriously furnished, the apartment reflects his varied tastes. He is a bon vivant, an amateur interior decorator, an art collector (Spanish paintings predominate). His coat hangers are made of red velvet with a gold "C" monogram. A young lady of his acquaintance once expressed the desire to have a dress made of his shower curtain. His Christmas gifts to the employees of the apartment building are fifths of fine champagne.

Of an evening, Clark may be found in the Blue Room at the Shoreham Hotel, one of the town's poshest pubs, where the head waiter gives him the visiting royalty treatment. He is noted for sending bottles of champagne to the tables of friends. "He's a very generous man," confided one lady friend. Clark seldom entertains at home, but when he does it is in lavish style. He is a non-smoker, a sparing drinker.

When Clark hosts an anniversary party for Harry Truman at the Mayflower Hotel, the invitations inform the guests that "the President" (Truman) would appreciate their attendance. At a dinner given by members of the old Truman committee in June 1963, Clark announced the establishment of a "Harry S. Truman Chair of American History" at Westminster College in Fulton, Missouri, and reported that a fund of $20,000 to endow the chair had been raised to start things off.

A man with a phenomenal memory for names and faces, a rapid-fire talker, a hard worker who keeps in trim by playing squash and handball (he won a four-wall doubles handball championship in New York some years ago, played professional basketball for a time and was a wrestler, boxer and rower in his younger days), a collector of fine old silver and china, accomplished on the piano, handy with his fists (in 1952 he punched

columnist Drew Pearson in the eye and was fined $25) and with
his hands (he designs and makes jewelry for his distaff friends),
a perennial bachelor with an appreciative eye, a man of parts,
Charles Patrick Clark.

A different breed entirely is Theron Jennings Rice, until recently chief lobbyist for the United States Chamber of Commerce. When Hollywood gets around to distorting the Washington lobbyist in a wide-screen spectacular, Terry Rice will not
be cast in the starring role. He doesn't have enough glamor.
And yet he exemplifies a new and increasingly important breed
of lobbyist, the legislative technician working for a large organization.

A brisk, business-like, friendly man in his mid-forties, Rice is
a homebody whose life centers around his family. With his wife
and son he lives the quiet life in Arlington, Virginia, where it is
almost unthinkable to live any other way. He is studiously
unflamboyant — a Cub Scout leader, president of the parent-
teacher association at his son's school. He is a lay reader at St.
Andrews Episcopal Church in Arlington and coaches a boys'
basketball team. Prior to becoming the Chamber's legislative
action general manager (chief lobbyist), he was active in Arlington County Republican politics. He left the Chamber recently
to become manager of the Washington office of the Continental
Oil Company.

"I'm not much of a joiner," says Terry Rice. "I like to go
home at the end of the day, whenever that is." He does not
belong to any of Washington's major clubs, although he says
"I suspect there are advantages in this job to belonging to clubs;
perhaps I will later."

Rice is tall, informal, likes to work in his shirt sleeves. His
office at the Chamber was spartan, functionally furnished without
a trace of show — a desk, a small conference table and a black-
board on which he outlined the next day's schedule of Congressional testimony, which Chamber witness was due to appear
before which committee, etc. Nary a picture of a politician on
the walls.

A native of Harrisonburg, Virginia, Rice attended Harrisonburg High School, graduating third in a class of 55. In 1941-42
he attended George Washington University in Washington, where

he majored in English and journalism. He graduated from junior college but did not complete a four-year course because of military service. While in college he worked for the Washington Star, and he spent three years in the Marine Corps as a combat correspondent in the Pacific. From 1945 to 1951 he worked for the Army and Navy Bulletin as a reporter, Navy editor and then managing editor. In 1951 Clarence R. (Lefty) Miles, the Chamber's veteran chief lobbyist, hired him as associate editor of the various publications put out by the legislative department. Rice began a steady climb up the Chamber's organizational ladder — assistant manager of the manufacture department, special coordinator of the Hoover Commission program, manager of the national defense department. In 1962 he succeeded Miles as chief lobbyist.

The concern — or rather, preoccupation — of the National Association of Manufacturers with taxes and government fiscal policy is reflected in its chief lobbyist, Ralph Theodore Compton, a former instructor in economics at Yale and an expert on taxes. Seated squarely and solidly behind a square and solid desk, Ted Compton gives a visitor a no-nonsense, let's-get-down-to-cases look from behind severe glasses and answers questions in a voice to match. Like Terry Rice, he is a highly competent, no-frills organization lobbyist. Compton has been with the N.A.M. for 25 years. He is a tough, resourceful old pro.

Born in Avalon, California, in 1903, he has A.B. and A.M. degrees from the University of California and a PH.D. in economics from Yale. From 1926 to 1929 he taught in the Yale economics department. After that he was on the tax staff of the National Industrial Conference Board, served as director of the Governor's Taxation Committee of Ohio, and from 1931 to 1941 was director of research for the Associated Industries of Missouri. In 1941 he joined the N.A.M. as economic security director, handling social security tax legislation. In 1950 he was named executive director of the National Industrial Council, a division of the N.A.M. Ten years later he became a N.A.M. vice president in charge of the government relations division. He has written several books on tax and fiscal matters, including "Fiscal Problems of Rural Decline" (1929), "State and Local Taxation of

Property" (1930) and "The Social Security Payroll Taxes" (1940).

Compton lives in fashionable Potomac, Maryland, in a house with eight acres of land. He admits to few hobbies outside his work but does like to putter in his garden and has a ham radio operator's license. He belongs to the popular Congressional Country Club and the Yale Club of New York. He has a son, a daughter and three grandchildren; his daughter is married to the son of William F. Schnitzler, secretary-treasurer of the AFL-CIO — the N.A.M.'s mortal legislative enemy.

The AFL-CIO's chief lobbyist is Andrew John Biemiller, a former Democratic Congressman from Wisconsin. Heavy-set, hardworking, usually a little rumpled, Andy Biemiller is one of the best-known men on Capitol Hill. He has, moreover, one of the toughest jobs in Washington. He is caught in the occasional crossfire between the AFL and the CIO, and beset by the prickly personalities of some of labor's top brass. Biemiller himself points out that, legislatively, there is no central direction in the American labor movement. "The only labor lobbyists over which I have control," he says, "are those directly employed by the AFL-CIO. There are some 95 other labor lobbyists in Washington. With these, all I can use is suasion."

In addition, some of the top lobbying for labor, as we have seen, is done by the union leaders themselves, men such as Walter Reuther, who have a wide circle of friends and allies in Congress and the executive branch. Biemiller describes his boss, George Meany, as "one of the most successful lobbyists of all time" and points out that the AFL-CIO president was once praised in a Congressional resolution for his service in providing information to Congress. Meany's lobbying motto, Biemiller likes to recall, was "don't beg, don't threaten and don't assume you're always right."

Although he does not always represent a completely united organization, Biemiller is rated as an effective advocate of labor's legislative causes. The Senators and Representatives in the committee hearings and the reporters at the press tables have no trouble hearing and understanding what he says. His deep, booming voice, trained at hundreds of raucous labor meetings in the union halls of Wisconsin, conveys an impression of great sincerity.

Biemiller was born in Sandusky, Ohio, in 1906. He graduated from Cornell University in 1926 and did graduate work at the University of Pennsylvania. From 1926 to 1931 he taught history at Syracuse University and the University of Pennsylvania. In the '30s he was an organizer for the Wisconsin State Federation of Labor (AFL). He was a member of the Wisconsin legislature from 1937 to 1941, including two years as floor leader. During World War II he was a labor specialist for the War Production Board. In 1944 he was elected to Congress from Wisconsin. Defeated in the Republican surge of 1946 — the famous Eightieth Congress — he ran again in 1948 and was elected. In 1950 he was defeated again but stayed in Washington as a public relations counselor until he went to work for the AFL-CIO.

"They never go home to Podunk" is one of Washington's favorite cliches. It is not uniformly true, but Potomac fever, once acquired, usually is hard to shake. A large number of former Congressmen do choose to stay on after leaving office, and many of them become lobbyists. One of the best known is Scott W. Lucas. Since he served as majority leader of the Senate, this noble Roman from the Illinois prairies can lay claim to being the ranking former legislator in the lobbying corps. White-haired, tall and erect in his mid-seventies, he is an impressive embodiment of the folk image of a Senator.

Lucas is a practicing attorney who says that no more than 10 percent of his time is devoted to lobbying. Nevertheless, the list of clients for whom he has registered as a lobbyist is a fairly long one. Although he walks a little slowly and stiffly these days, he gets around. He is a familiar figure at the Capitol and whenever a delegation from Illinois visits the White House, he is likely to be in the group.

Among the present or recent clients for whom Scott Lucas registered as a lobbyist are: the Illinois Bell Telephone Company, the Mobil Homes Manufacturers Association, Western Medical Corporation of Chicago, the Outdoor Advertising Association of America, the American Finance Conference, the Western National Life Insurance Company of Texas and the National Association of Chain Drug Stores.

With more than 40 years of experience in politics and Washington in-fighting, Lucas sometimes gets called in as a sort of

senior lobbying or legislative consultant. His work for Illinois
Bell brought him into the struggle over the communications satellite (Telstar) bill. Part of A.T. & T.'s lobbying strategy was
mapped out in Lucas's office, under pictures of Franklin D.
Roosevelt, Harry Truman and the late Senator Robert S. Kerr
that adorn the walls. ("If he was on your side," Lucas says of
Kerr, "you didn't have to talk to many other Senators.") At
one point in the strategy huddles, a top A.T. & T. executive decided
that he would personally visit every member of the Senate to
lobby for the Telstar bill. Lucas argued against this, saying that
the company should make its case on the record, in the public
committee hearings. The executive heeded this advice, but
others did not, and A.T. & T.'s intense ex parte lobbying outside
the committee room became a prime issue in the Telstar fight.

Lucas was born in Cass County, Illinois, in 1892, graduated
from Illinois Wesleyan University in 1914 and was admitted to
the bar the following year. A lifelong Democrat, he was elected
to his first public office, state's attorney of Mason County, in
1920. In 1934 he was elected to the first of two terms in the
House and in 1938 he was elected to the Senate, where he served
12 years. From January 1949 to January 1951 he was majority
leader. Since 1951 he has engaged in general law practice, maintaining offices in Washington, Chicago and Springfield, Illinois.

His desk is piled high with scrapbooks and files as he works
on a book about the famous men he has known in the course
of a long career. "I'm writing it mainly for my family," he says.
For his family, too, he continues to write poetry, a hobby of
many years. He used to employ a pseudonym, "Senator Sor-
ghum," for his verses, but nowadays he acknowledges the modest
creations as his own.

Ever since the New Deal, at least, bright young men have been
coming to Washington. Some of these Dick Whittingtons are
seeking their fortune, others the bubble fame, and some are
public-service motivated. A few are idea men who leave some
kind of imprint for the better on the American system, but the
vast majority are, or soon become, technicians of government.

One of the better-known of the younger lobbyists is Arnold
Mayer, public relations director and legislative representative
for the Amalgamated Meat Cutters and Butcher Workmen. Al-

though still in his thirties, Mayer has several impressive Congressional victories to his credit. Among them was a dogged campaign to put through a bill requiring federal inspection of poultry; in this successful effort he teamed up with a persistent crusader for consumer protection, Representative Leonor K. Sullivan of St. Louis.

Mayer was born in Mainz, Germany, and came to the United States with his parents when he was eight years old. The family settled in Bridgeport, Connecticut. He attended Yale on a full-tuition scholarship, majored in history, made Phi Beta Kappa and worked as a reporter for the Bridgeport Herald while in college. After graduation he was the labor reporter for the Herald and then handled public relations for the United Auto Workers during a strike against the brass industry in Connecticut. In 1952 he came to Washington as a reporter for the United States Information Agency. Later he went to work for a public relations firm, where he handled the account of the postal clerks union. He got his first taste of lobbying doing the public relations work for this union in its campaign for a pay raise in 1954. In 1955 he joined the Meat Cutters union as public relations director, with the title of legislative representative added later.

Slight of build but wiry, he is a serious individual and a very hard worker. To see him in action and talk to him is to watch a Washington personality in formation. Unlike many lobbyists, he is interested in the theoretical foundation underlying what he is doing. He is more concerned and articulate about the role of pressure groups in the governmental process than most of the older technicians, particularly the business lobbyists and free-lancers who have long since given up puzzling over such non-utilitarian questions. At the same time the necessity of getting things done, the pressure for achievement and all the things that Washington sums up as "the political realities," force Mayer into a workaday posture of intense pragmatism.

At the Interlochen music camp in 1936 and 1937, a tall, gangly North Carolina youth named Henry Hall Wilson tootled away earnestly on the oboe, blowing an ill wind good. Later he played the oboe in the Charlotte symphony orchestra and the North Carolina Symphony. But when he grew up he did not raise a beard and lead sing-alongs on television. He grew up, instead, to be a lobbyist for the White House, and he no longer has any time for the oboe. Or for much of anything else except work.

Henry Wilson is an unusual sort of lobbyist. He belongs to no clubs — no time. He practically never sees a member of Congress socially — no time. He has no expense account as such. He is President Johnson's lobbyist for the House of Representatives. Under the immediate direction of Lawrence F. O'Brien, the Postmaster General who doubles in brass as chief White House lobbyist, his job is to shepherd the Great Society program through a legislative chamber that is dominated by Democrats who are occasionally obstreperous. To this assignment he brings considerable political experience at the state level, courtly Southern manners and a fund of patience.

A soft-spoken man in his forties, Wilson is a native of Monroe, North Carolina. He took an A.B. in pre-law at Duke University in 1942, went into the Army as a private and emerged a first lieutenant, then got his law degree at Duke in 1948. He practiced law in Monroe, served three terms in North Carolina's House of Representatives, headed the state's young Democrats for two years, ran Governor Terry Sanford's state campaign in 1960 and later was named Democratic national committeeman from North Carolina. He joined the White House staff on Inauguration Day in 1961 with the official title of administrative assistant to the President and has stayed on in the same job under President Johnson.

Americans have a need, emotional and commercial, to rate people and things — the "best" actor or actress, the "top" television show, the "man of the year," the horse of the century, the outstanding this and the leading that. Not even lobbying, essentially an unglamorous business, escapes the general urge. Periodically, a journalist decides that Doaks is the current "king of the lobbyists," succeeding Smith, who succeeded Jones, who traced his lineage back to Sam Ward and Thurlow Weed.

The present "king of the lobbyists" is an unlikely title-holder. He is not especially flamboyant, represents no big names in industry, commands respectable but not gigantic fees and has never hit the headlines and television cameras as the subject of a Congressional investigation. His popularity with the journalistic kingmakers is due largely to the fact that he is one of Lyndon

Johnson's oldest and closest friends, an intimate of the Johnson family and "Uncle Dale" to the President's daughters. That is enough to elevate him to lobbying's transitory royalty.

Dale Miller is a gregarious, hard-working lobbyist who has been spectacularly successful in a quiet way for a group of Texas clients. He is a regional, not national lobbyist. With the exception of one year in which he registered for General Motors, "to look after some of their interests," as he puts it, he represents no corporate giants. His friendship with the President and with other prominent Texans in Washington, including the late Speaker Rayburn, undoubtedly has helped his career, especially when it comes to impressing people, but he has other assets that have contributed much.

Chief among these is a personable and enormously energetic wife, Lucy Virginia (known to everyone as "Scooter"), who is one of the capital's leading hostesses. Combined with this is another asset — sociability. Dale and Scooter Miller are among Washington's most indefatigable party-goers and party-givers; it seems as if they have been dancing incessantly for 25 years, and they appear on the local society pages almost as regularly as their good friend the President does on the front pages. Finally, Miller's reputation for hard work is a distinct asset. Members of Congress say that he prepares his lobbying presentations with great care, and he maintains close liaison with the executive agencies handling government programs that affect his clients.

Miller has represented the same four clients throughout his career — the Dallas Chamber of Commerce, the Texas Gulf Sulphur Company, the Intracoastal Canal Association of Louisiana and Texas, and the Port of Corpus Christi. He registers as a lobbyist for the first three but not for the Corpus Christi port, saying that his efforts for the latter involve no legislative work except appearances before the House and Senate Appropriations Committees. He is executive vice president of the canal association, composed chiefly of business firms and communities. Once a shallow ditch, the Louisiana-Texas intracoastal canal has been developed into a major waterway with more than $100,-000,000 in federal money, much of it obtained as a result of Miller's efforts, particularly his contacts with the Army's Corps of Engineers and the Coast Guard.

A tall, white-haired man, Miller was born in Corpus Christi in 1909. He received a bachelor of journalism degree from the University of Missouri in 1930 and a master's degree in journalism from the University of Texas two years later. For a time he wrote for the Texas Weekly, which he describes as "a magazine of editorial opinion" but which was subsidized by business interests. His writing was intensely conservative; he inveighed against the child labor, minimum wage and unemployment compensation programs of the New Deal.

In 1941 he came to Washington as lobbyist for the Dallas Chamber of Commerce. His father, Roy Miller, was already ensconced in Suite 371 at the Mayflower Hotel as Washington representative for the Texas Gulf Sulphur Company, making the Millers one of the few father-son teams in the lobbying business. When his father died in 1946, Miller took over his clients and his suite, which he still uses as his office and for frequent cocktail parties. His lobbying reports show an income of about $25,000 a year from the three clients for whom he registers. By lobbying standards, this is not munificent; presumably a generous expense account helps with Miller's entertainment costs.

Miller's father was instrumental in getting Lyndon Johnson his first Washington job in 1932, as secretary to Representative Richard Kleberg of Texas. The close friendship between the two families has developed into old-shoe easiness over the years. Publicly, Miller is at pains to play down his relationship with the President, contending that "a person acquires influence in Washington through integrity and effort — not through contacts." But his closeness to the President does not hurt; on the day before his State of the Union message in 1965, Johnson took 90 minutes from a busy schedule to meet with Miller and three Dallas businessmen to hear their plea for a new federal office building in Dallas. Miller served as chairman of the inaugural committee that year; his daughter, Mrs. Marta Ross, is an assistant to Mrs. Johnson's press secretary; and the Millers are frequent guests at White House dinners — none of which is lost on the lobbyist's Lone Star clients.

In "Presidential Power: The Politics of Leadership," a book that has had a wide impact on political thought, Richard E. Neustadt, a Truman aide and Kennedy adviser, coined the phrase "the Washington community" to describe "the men who share in governing this country." The Washington community, he said, consists of the top policy-making and career officials of the executive branch, the most influential members of Congress, leading politicians, military commanders, foreign diplomats, and lobbyists and veteran newspapermen — the more or less permanent cadre of men who dominate the machinery and attitudes of government.'

The subtle shadings between the lawyer and the lobbyist in Washington range from those who do no lobbying at all to those who do a great deal, with a large gray area in between. Nowhere is this better illustrated than in the small group of top-flight lawyers who form one of the inner power circles of the Washington community. These are the great political lawyers of Washington, men who have influence because they know the components of influence, who have power because they have been exercising it for a long time and know how to exercise it. As much as any one group, they typify what Alfred North Whitehead called "connexity" in men's affairs. Everything in government is interrelated. Each new event, each new policy, is connected in some way with events and policy of the past, and these men have been an intimate part of these interrelationships for years. They know everyone worth knowing; everyone worth knowing knows them. And they know how to get things done. They are the men to whom the great corporations turn when their vital interests clash with government.

Some of these lawyers are registered as lobbyists; many are not. But regardless of whether their work brings them within the purview of the Lobbying Act, they are the men who are called in when there are intricate and costly matters to be handled. Some are in government now; some have not held office for years but maintain an active interest from the sidelines, and others move easily in and out of government as their services are needed. Some of these men are nationally known, others only in the Washington community. The list includes Dean Acheson, Clark M. Clifford, George W. Ball, Fowler Hamilton, Thurman Arnold, Abe Fortas, Paul A. Porter, Thomas G. Corcoran, Edward H. Foley, James H. Rowe Jr., Thomas E. Dewey (although he does not live in Washington), Oscar L. Chapman, Charles S. Murphy, H. Graham Morison, Charles

Patrick Clark, Donald S. Dawson, Scott Lucas, Gerald D. Morgan, Bryce N. Harlow and Richard M. Nixon, whose New York law firm registered as lobbyist for the Talisman Sugar Corporation in 1965.

Acheson, the dominant figure in the Truman cabinet, undertook important foreign assignments for the Kennedy administration while continuing his private law practice, and he is one of President Johnson's principal unofficial advisors on foreign policy. Acheson, Fortas and Clifford form a triumvirate of confidants on whom Johnson relies heavily for counsel. Their influence is vast but largely unseen.

In 1962 Acheson appeared before the World Court on behalf of Cambodia in a dispute with Thailand. The Thai government charged bias on the part of the United States government in permitting him to take the case, and Representative Steven B. Derounian, New York Republican, asserted that Acheson was making a "personal profit" at the expense of one of this country's allies. Acheson won his case; by a nine-to-three vote the World Court ruled for Cambodia. His influential law firm, Covington and Burling, is registered under the Lobbying Act and as an agent for foreign interests. Covington and Burling filed lobbying reports in recent years on behalf of such clients as the International Business Machines Corporation, the Connecticut General Life Insurance Company, the Travelers Insurance Company, the National Association of Mutual Savings Banks and the Cuban-American Sugar Company. As an international lawyer, Acheson himself is registered under the Foreign Agents Act.

Under Secretary of State George W. Ball formerly was a member of the Washington law firm of Cleary, Gottlieb and Steen, which he helped establish. Before joining the State Department, Ball represented the French government, the European Common Market, the European Atomic Energy Community, the European Coal and Steel Community, the Conseil National du Patronat Francais (the French equivalent of the National Association of Manufacturers), and, in pre-Castro days, the Cuban sugar mill owners and cane growers association. Ball was registered as a lobbyist for the Woven Woolen Felt Industry between 1947 and 1949.

The Cleary, Gottlieb and Steen firm is registered under the foreign agents law and the Lobbying Act. It has lobbied for

E. I. du Pont de Nemours & Company, the Colonial Sugar Refining Company of Sydney, Australia and other Australian sugar interests, and the Savage Arms Company of Westfield, Massachusetts. Fowler Hamilton, who headed the foreign aid agency in the early part of the Kennedy administration, is a member of Cleary, Gottlieb and Steen. Hamilton registered as a lobbyist for the Caracas (Venezuela) Chamber of Commerce in 1950.

Another prominent Washington law firm is Arnold and Porter, formerly Arnold, Fortas and Porter. One partner in this firm is Thurman Arnold, an Assistant Attorney General in the Roosevelt administration. Another partner until recently was Abe Fortas, Under Secretary of the Interior from 1942 to 1946. In 1965 Johnson appointed him to the Supreme Court. Fortas has been one of Johnson's closest advisers for years; when presidential assistant Walter Jenkins was arrested on a morals charge during the 1964 campaign, Fortas was the first man to whom Johnson turned for help. Fortas and Clark Clifford visited the offices of the three Washington newspapers and urged them to suppress the story for "humanitarian" reasons. The editors agreed but the story got out anyway. Fortas and Clifford said they acted on their own initiative.

Another partner in Arnold and Porter is Paul Porter, former chairman of the Federal Communications Commission and head of the Office of Price Administration during World War II. Among the clients for whom the law firm has registered under the Lobbying Act are the National Retail Merchants Association, Investors Diversified Services, Inc., the American Tourist and Trade Association, the Council of Savings and Loan Financial Corporations, the Record Industry Association and organized baseball.

Chapman and Friedman, the law firm in which former Secretary of the Interior Oscar L. Chapman is a partner, has lobbied on behalf of the interests of the Texas Eastern Transmission Corporation of Houston (a large natural gas pipeline firm), a group of Mexican sugar producers seeking a quota from the United States, the American Taxicab Association, the Alaska Pipeline Company and Strohmeyer and Arpe Company.

The law firm of Morison, Murphy, Clapp and Abrams has registered as lobbyists for the Ford Motor Company, the Sperry & Hutchinson Company of New York and the American Reciprocal Insurance Association of Kansas City. H. Graham Morison, a member of this firm, was an Assistant Attorney General from 1948 to 1952. Charles S. Murphy, former Under Secretary of Agriculture and now a member of the Civil Aeronautics Board, was a member of the law firm from 1953 to 1961. From 1947 to 1950 Murphy was an administrative assistant to President Truman and from 1950 to 1953 he was Truman's special counsel, succeeding Clark Clifford.

Clark McAdams Clifford, who was Truman's special counsel from 1946 to 1950, is now senior partner in the law firm of Clifford and Miller. Tall, handsome, immensely personable, Clifford ranks as one of Washington's top lawyers and unofficial political sachems. Among his clients are some of the largest corporations in the United States — Standard Oil of California, the Phillips Petroleum Company, General Electric, Du Pont, the Hughes Tool Company, and several big mutual funds. Clifford also represents the Cocoa Manufacturers Association and other large cocoa interests. Another of his clients, on an unofficial, unpaid basis, was President Kennedy. When Drew Pearson charged that Kennedy's "Profiles in Courage" had been ghostwritten, Clifford was instrumental in getting a retraction from the American Broadcasting Company, apparently ghostwritten by Theodore Sorensen. In 1961 Clifford helped incorporate the "White House Historical Association."

Soon after he set up his Washington law practice, Clifford told an interviewer for Fortune magazine: "I have not and will not register as a lobbyist, for that is not the kind of work we do. We run a law office here, with a background of experience in the general practice of law, topped off by an intimate knowledge of how the government operates." This is still his position. Neither Clifford nor his firm registers under the Lobbying Act. In the words of one of Clifford's aides, the law firm advises corporations on "policy matters" involving the federal government, including how to plan their strategy on litigation before the courts and legislation in Congress.

Clifford and Miller, an associate has explained, advises its clients on what stand to take with respect to legislation affecting them and what tactics to use in supporting or opposing the legislation. The firm reports to its clients on the status of bills in which they are interested, but it does not appear before Congress on behalf of its clients and does not "communicate with Congress in any way," he added. If the legislative strategy worked out by the client in consultation with Clifford's firm calls for active lobbying, he emphasized, Clifford recommends someone else to do the lobbying.

In the case of the controversial du Pont-General Motors stock divestiture bill, Clifford, who is Washington counsel for du Pont, recommended John H. Sharon for the lobbying job. Sharon, who was then with Cleary, Gottlieb and Steen, registered as a lobbyist for du Pont as did the Cleary, Gottlieb and Steen firm. It was Sharon who suggested to Crawford H. Greenewalt, president of du Pont, that he come to Washington to lobby for the bill, as related in the first chapter of this book. Greenewalt bought the idea, and Sharon accompanied him on his visits to key members of Congress and administration officials. Later Sharon moved over to Clifford and Miller as a partner.

A rumor circulated among Washington lobbyists that the lobbying fee in the du Pont case was close to $1,000,000. It was widely referred to as "the million-dollar fee." Clifford's associates deny this. "It was a very reasonable fee — $1,000,000 is grossly exaggerated," said one of them. The lobbying fee went to Cleary, Gottlieb and Steen; Clifford and Miller received only its regular retainer as du Pont's Washington counsel, he added.

When John F. Kennedy was a Senator from Massachusetts, Clifford was his Washington attorney. The firm of Clifford and Miller served as a sort of unofficial counsel to Kennedy when he was President and to the White House staff and several members of the cabinet, including Attorney General Robert F. Kennedy. Johnson, too, calls Clifford to the White House frequently for advice, especially on intelligence matters.

The day after the 1960 election, President-elect Kennedy asked Clifford to coordinate the White House transition from the Eisenhower administration to the New Frontier. Clifford organized meetings and briefing sessions between officials of the incoming and outgoing administrations and was the liaison man between the President-elect and President Eisenhower.

In 1962 Clifford played a key behind-the-scenes role in the steel crisis. He accompanied then-Secretary of Labor Arthur J. Goldberg to New York for a crucial conference with Roger M.

Blough, board chairman of U.S. Steel. Administration sources said that Clifford was asked to take part in the meeting because he is respected by business, and as a neutral not officially connected with the White House he could bolster Goldberg's arguments. A year later, when the steel industry put into effect a selective price increase, Clifford was the first person called by Kennedy. The attorney attended a cabinet meeting at which the steel price boost was discussed and was given an assignment by the President which remains swathed in mystery. In the three years of the Kennedy administration, there were at least 12 other matters on which Clifford or members of his law firm assisted the White House.

In 1963 Clifford was appointed chairman of the President's Foreign Intelligence Advisory Board, succeeding Dr. James R. Killian of the Massachusetts Institute of Technology. Clifford, who had helped write the act that created the Central Intelligence Agency, was reported to have been the unanimous choice of the other members of the board to succeed Killian.

The attorney figured briefly in a Congressional investigation of the federal regulatory agencies in 1960. His name appeared on a list of representatives of natural gas companies who had private talks with Frederick Stueck, a member of the Federal Power Commission. Under questioning, Stueck acknowledged that he knew that Clifford was Washington counsel for Phillips Petroleum, one of the country's largest natural gas producers. The questioning brought out that Phillips Petroleum had many cases pending before the FPC at that time. Steuck declared, however, that he never discussed any details of these cases at the "eight or ten" luncheons he had with Clifford in 1959. He added that Clifford did not represent Phillips Petroleum on natural gas matters. Their conversations, the power commissioner said, were entirely social in nature. "We talked about what people who have known each other 35 years talk about," Stueck stated. He explained that his friendship with Clifford went back to the days when they were both law students at Washington University in St. Louis.

After the transition period between the Eisenhower and Kennedy administrations, President Kennedy spoke at a private dinner of the Alfalfa Club and expressed his appreciation for Clifford's services, calling him "a wonderful fellow." Then, in a jocular vein, Kennedy added that others wanted a reward for their efforts, but "you don't hear Clark clamoring. All he asked in return was that we advertise his law firm on the backs of the one-dollar bills."

Another leading Washington lawyer, a figure out of contemporary history who is still around to read what the historians are writing about him, is the ebullient, controversial Thomas Gardiner Corcoran — "Tommy the Cork" of New Deal days.

Thomas Corcoran was one of the most coruscating figures to come on the American political scene in this century. A phenomenal student at Harvard Law School, recipient of four degrees (including a doctorate in jurisprudence), law clerk to Justice Oliver Wendell Holmes (who called him the most brilliant of his clerks) — Corcoran blazed across the political firmament like a meteor. For five of the most hectic years of the New Deal, he was a close and powerful adviser to Franklin D. Roosevelt, F.D.R.'s chief legislative operator and a member of his "brain trust." With Benjamin V. Cohen and others, Corcoran helped write the Securities and Exchange Act, the Public Utility Holding Company Act, the Fair Labor Standards Act and other major New Deal legislation. He led the White House fight to "pack" the Supreme Court (although he had strong reservations about the court plan), and he played a prominent role in the largely unsuccessful effort to purge anti-F.D.R. Democrats in Congress.

"This generation has a rendezvous with destiny." Franklin Roosevelt made these words deathless — but Thomas Corcoran suggested them. Another of Corcoran's contributions to an F.D.R. speech was: "The immortal Dante tells us that Divine Justice weighs the sins of the cold-blooded and the sins of the warm-hearted in different scales." John F. Kennedy used this sentence repeatedly in the presidential campaign of 1960.

In the course of his career, Professor Louis W. Koenig has written, Corcoran has been "an adventurer who . . . sought to introduce banana-growing on the island fortress of Taiwan and to establish across the length and breadth of Brazil a chain of restaurants under the auspices of the Union News Company. In reality, he belongs not to the twentieth century, but to another age. He is a medieval character who operated in the era of the New Deal with the fervor, bravado and finesse of a top-notch grand duke of an Italian principality . . . Intrigue was his middle name . . . For the young and ambitious, Tom Corcoran offered a recipe of success, whose validity was amply demonstrated by his own public career. 'The way to get ahead,' he would say, 'is to fish in troubled waters.' " [5]

"Tommy the Cork" (the nickname was given him by F.D.R.) fished in many troubled waters and made many enemies, and in the end they had their revenge. When the post of Solicitor General became vacant in 1940, Corcoran sought it and let Roosevelt know that he wanted it. But F.D.R. knew that the Senate would never confirm Corcoran. The court packing plan, the purge and the bruised egos of Senators who had been on the receiving end of Corcoran's pressure tactics weighed too heavily in the scales. So Tommy the Cork, New Deal crusader, arch-foe of big business, passed from the picture. Thomas G. Corcoran, high-priced lawyer for big business interests, emerged almost overnight. Within a few months he was testifying before the Truman committee that he had received $100,000 in legal fees and had been forced to turn away clients "by the hundreds."

Again in 1960, a Congressional investigating subcommittee became curious about Corcoran's activities, this time in connection with alleged "ex parte" (off the record) contacts with members of the Federal Power Commission. In the federal regulatory agencies, an ex parte contact is one made outside the public hearing room and without the knowledge of the other parties to the case.

The House subcommittee had already traced a sordid pattern of pressure and influence in several of the big, important regulatory agencies, including Sherman Adams' intervention with the Federal Trade Commission and the Securities and Exchange Commission on behalf of his old friend, Bernard Goldfine of Boston; the "loans" (never repaid) from a Miami attorney to Richard A. Mack, a member of the Federal Communications Commission, and a long, sorry record of fraternization between members of the commissions and the industries they were supposed to regulate impartially. Instance after instance of freeloading, junketeering, expensive entertainment, "honorariums" and influence was uncovered. Bernard Schwartz, the thorny little lawyer who ran the first part of the investigation until the subcommittee fired him, wrote later that some of the regulatory

agencies were afflicted with "administrative arteriosclerosis." •
Riddled with an insidious and subtle form of corruption, they
had been taken over by industry and had long since forgotten
how to regulate in the public interest.

When the inquiry reached Corcoran, however, the subcommittee got out of its league. This was no plodding political hack
caught cozying up to industry, but a wily old pro who had forgotten more about the regulatory agencies and regulatory law
than the subcommittee members ever knew. Schwartz quoted
A. J. G. Priest, a veteran practitioner before federal commissions,
as saying that "many of us wince when we recall the instantane-
ous responses, 20 years ago, to 'this is Tommy Corcoran calling
from the White House.'" Corcoran ran rings around the subcommittee in some of the stormiest and funniest hearings ever
held on Capitol Hill. His jousts with Representative Derounian,
who had a penchant for taking on old Democratic buffalo, left
Derounian sputtering with ineffectual rage.

Derounian: "Just answer the question, Mr. Corcoran. I don't
want you to be a long-playing record, because you have been
doing that for two days now. Your contacts with members of
the Senate has (sic) gotten you into their habit of filibuster and
we have to get through with this hearing."

Corcoran: "Thank you, Mr. Derounian, if you think I am that
long-winded that I have talked for two days. I have only been
here for a half session."

Derounian: "Yesterday you talked all morning and you didn't
answer one of the eight questions that I was concerned with.
I think I am justified in that comment . . ."

Corcoran: "May I finish, Mr. Derounian. I know I am not
like your friend Tom Dewey, I don't come down here in the
same kind of a case as your friend Tom Dewey came down, who
is also a friend of mine, with a long, long time sheet justification
as to how he charged more than I did in the case. No, I didn't
do that."

Derounian (shouting): "First of all, Tom Dewey is not my
friend. He couldn't care less about what happens to me, and
I couldn't care less about what happens to him. He can take
care of himself as, apparently, you proved you can."

Corcoran: "I know what you want me to do."

Derounian: "Let's get the record straight about my friendship."

Corcoran: "All right."

Derounian: "And stop winking at the chairman [Representative Oren Harris of Arkansas] with your left eye. Maybe he is your friend too. That is all right but let's keep this thing strictly business."

Corcoran: "All right, Mr. Derounian."

The Chairman: "The committee will be in order."

Derounian: "I have noted here, Mr. Corcoran —"

Corcoran: "I am not going to use any right eye on you, it is just that I have been having a little trouble."

Derounian: "It is all right, use your other eye. I will look you straight back. We are trying to get to the facts here, let's not have a filibuster."

Corcoran: "Have I, I assume I have answered the question." [7]

In between the fun and games, the subcommittee managed to elicit a few facts about Corcoran's activities on behalf of his client, Midwestern Gas Transmission Company of Houston, Texas, which was seeking permission from the Federal Power Commission to build a $50,000,000 pipeline serving four Middle Western states.

Corcoran admitted that he had off-the-record talks with FPC Chairman Jerome K. Kuykendall and two other members of the commission, Arthur Kline and William R. Connole, while the case was pending, but he said the conversations were "in full conformity" with FPC laws and regulations and did not affect the commission's decision. He admitted that he mentioned the 7 percent rate of return being sought by the company in a telephone conversation with Chairman Kuykendall, but asserted he brought this up purely as a procedural matter, not as a discussion of the issues in the case.

When Midwestern Gas's application to build the pipeline came before the commission, the FPC staff recommended that the company be allowed a 6¼ percent annual rate of return on its investment. This was the rate the FPC had granted Midwestern on a companion pipeline a year before. The company had accepted 6¼ percent in the earlier case, but it said it wanted 7 percent on the new pipeline. Midwestern contended that unless it was given the higher rate, it would not be able to obtain financing to build the new facility and consumers in the Middle West would be deprived of needed natural gas. The rate of return would determine the company's profit.

On October 23, 1959, the commission heard oral arguments — a public proceeding — on the application. On October 31, it issued its decision in the case. Between those two dates, Corcoran called on Kuykendall, Kline and Connole in their offices and also telephoned Kuykendall. The FPC members said their decision in the Midwestern case was not influenced by these visits, although Kuykendall testified that "I would say the phone call to me, where he [Corcoran] reiterated to me about the 7 percent, was improper."

Kuykendall told the subcommittee that when the commission began its deliberations, it was split, with two members in favor of giving Midwestern only $6\frac{1}{4}$ percent, and two, including himself, in favor of approving the application to build the pipeline but postponing a decision on what rate of return to allow the company. Nevertheless, he acknowledged that the commission first instructed its opinion writers to draft an order upholding the staff and giving Midwestern $6\frac{1}{4}$ percent. The chairman called this "one of the most regrettable innocent things I ever did," since news of this preliminary order leaked out and gave rise to the impression that the FPC had initially decided to grant only a $6\frac{1}{4}$ percent rate, before Corcoran made his visits. Not so, said Kuykendall. He explained that there was nothing final about the first draft. No decision had been reached at that time, and the preliminary order was intended only to serve as a basis for discussion, he told the subcommittee. "We draft and redraft these orders as we go along," he added.

When the final order came out on October 31, it left the rate of return open, to be determined later. The order stated on page 10 that the FPC could not predict what rate of return Midwestern would need to obtain its financing. "We shall, therefore, require Midwestern to file with the commission, prior to commencing construction, the firm proposals for financing as finally consummated, and we shall at that time fix a rate of return," the order said. On page 14, however, were these words: "Obviously, the company (Midwestern) will be able to sell the gas at the rates it is required herein to file reflecting a $6\frac{1}{4}$ percent rate of return."

Then on November 6, the commission put out another order

making several corrections and amendments in the October 31 order. The wording on page 14 was changed to read: "Obviously, in the light of the company's market requirements hereinafter discussed, it will be able to sell the gas at the rates it is required herein to file." The reference to a 6¼ percent rate was deleted.

Almost a year later, after Midwestern had filed cost of service data with the FPC, the commission gave the company a 6½ percent rate of return on the pipeline. FPC engineers estimate that the difference of one-fourth of 1 percent is costing consumers an extra $217,000 a year.

In the end the Democratic majority on the subcommittee absolved Corcoran of any impropriety. The Democrats said they were "not seeking to condemn or exculpate either the commission or Mr. Corcoran," but they added that "from the record, it would appear that Mr. Corcoran was actually encouraged by the commission to have ex parte contacts with it in order to expedite the granting of the [pipeline] certificate," and "in any event, it would appear that Mr. Corcoran's communications were in conformity with commission practice and were sanctioned by the Administrative Procedure Act." [8]

The Republican members of the subcommittee, in their dissenting report, saw things in a different light. "Perhaps the most shocking political whitewash to come out of a Congressional committee in many years," they declared, "is that which is accorded Thomas G. Corcoran. The [subcommittee] majority and its staff have sought to exonerate one of Washington's best-known influence peddlers."

The G.O.P. Congressmen described Corcoran's activities as "obviously improper." They said that "the type of conduct engaged in by Corcoran has been revealed and condemned many times, most recently in the Landis report." This referred to a 1960 report to President-elect Kennedy by James M. Landis, former dean of the Harvard Law School and a leading authority on the federal regulatory agencies. The Republicans cited this language from the Landis report:

"Much attention has recently been centered on efforts, unfortunately too frequently successful, to sway the judgment of the members of regulatory agencies by so-called ex parte approaches

or arguments, usually personalized, made off the record in proceedings that should be decided on the record . . . Many of them
emanate from lawyers striving to press their clients' cause; indeed, one of the worst phases of this situation is the existence
of groups of lawyers, concentrated in Washington itself, who
implicitly hold out to clients that they have means of access
to various regulatory agencies off the record that are more important than those that can be made on the record. These lawyers
have generally previously held positions of more or less importance in the government."

With these mixed reviews from Congress, Tommy the Cork
went his way, back to his lucrative law practice with the firm
of Corcoran, Foley, Youngman and Rowe. One partner, Edward
H. Foley, was Under Secretary of the Treasury in the Truman
administration and chairman of President Kennedy's inaugural
committee in 1961; another, James H. Rowe Jr., was an administrative assistant to President Franklin Roosevelt and later an
Assistant Attorney General.

In 1962 Corcoran received a fee of $31,875 from Midwestern
Gas Transmission and $70,283 from its parent firm, Tennessee
Gas Transmission Company, according to reports filed by the
two companies with the Federal Power Commission. He was
listed as Midwestern's general counsel, but Tennessee Gas's report did not indicate what he did for the parent firm. The FPC
staff tried to find out. The company politely refused to say.
Midwestern's 1964 report again listed a fee of $31,875 to Cor-
coran as its general attorney. Tennessee Gas's report in that year
listed no payment to Tommy the Cork.

Corcoran himself may have shed some indirect illumination
on what made him worth $100,000 a year to the two big firms.
At one point in the House investigation, he held forth briefly
on the subject of Thomas Corcoran in a conversation with a subcommittee staff member. Said Tommy the Cork: "I am a very
intelligent and resourceful Irishman."

8

METHODS

"Public sentiment is everything. With public sentiment, nothing can fail; without it, nothing can succeed. Consequently, he who molds public sentiment goes deeper than he who enacts statutes or pronounces decisions. He makes statutes and decisions possible or impossible to be executed." — *Abraham Lincoln.*

". . . the public is a monster, like the idol we saw in Owyhee, with the head of a jackass, the body of a baboon, and the tail of a scorpion." — *Herman Melville, "White-Jacket."*

In a recent study of Washington folkways, Merriman Smith, veteran White House reporter for United Press International, has this to say about the methods of a "typical" Washington lobbyist:

"He arises when he feels like it, usually mid-morning, in a spacious, comfortable but definitely unflashy home in the northwest residential section of town. Over breakfast, he reads four or five major morning newspapers. If interested, he skims through the Congressional Record for the day before. These are the golden hours of his day. He may earn his keep more from intelligent reading than from any other single activity. Years of experience have taught him to read between the lines and to search for indicative but seemingly small details . . .

"Once 'read' for the day, he may make it to town for luncheon with one or two key men in government at the Carlton or the Mayflower. Mostly, they talk about golf or fishing. Possibly in parting, he may ask casually, 'You fellows heard anything new on depreciation allowances?' . . . This man is more effective for his employer than a dozen more energetic fellows patrolling the halls of the Senate and House office buildings . . . By being highly selective in his friendships, he manages to keep in touch with virtually any government move that might help or hinder his

company. Our man's effectiveness would be destroyed if he had
to play the lobbyist's conventional role in attempting to push or
halt specific bills before Congress." [1]

This description of the lobbyist at work makes him sound like
a pretty casual fellow. A word here, a hint there and he collects
his fee. There is some truth to it, in the sense that the experienced lobbyist is a man with very sensitive antennae. And
Smith correctly emphasizes the role of the lobbyist as a commu-
nicator. He is expected to keep abreast of governmental activities that may affect his client and to report these developments
as quickly as possible. If legislation is in the wind that may hurt
his client, he wants to know about it early so that it can be
nipped in the bud. If this is not possible, an early warning will
at least give time to mount a counterattack.

So the lobbyist keeps a very close eye on the committees
handling legislation that touches his client's interests. He culti-
vates the members of these committees and their staffs. He is
an avid reader of the trade journals in his client's field. These
publications concentrate on specialized areas, and when it comes
to developments in these fields their Washington reporters frequently are ahead of the correspondents working for newspapers
and general-interest magazines. The lobbyist thus has extra
eyes and ears on which to rely.

The communicative function often is used as an excuse for
not registering under the Lobbying Act. Some Washington representatives of corporations and trade associations do not register
as lobbyists because, they insist, their only function is to inform
their home offices on the status and prospects of legislation.
A typical case is the Washington "rep" employed by a retail
group with its main headquarters in New York. In describing
his duties, he says that he spends almost all his time on Capitol
Hill getting information from various Congressional committees.
Asked whether he is registered as a lobbyist, he replies with
a smile that he is not. Why not? "Because I don't make any
attempt to influence legislation. I just gather information."

Lobbying, by the same token, is not quite as offhand or casual
as Merriman Smith suggests. Most lobbyists work fairly hard
and some work very hard. Their activities are not confined to
palsy-walsy lunches with friends who have risen to key positions
in government. They do get up to Capitol Hill frequently. They

do try to push or block specific bills; that also is part of what they are paid for. Moreover, the working lobbyist is also involved in legislative drudgery — particularly hearings, the long, sweaty sessions at which laws are hammered out amid interminable talk. The picture of our man at work over martinis at lunch is incomplete.

Lobbying methods fall into three main categories: direct contact with members of Congress and Congressional staffs; indirect or grassroots campaigns to stimulate pressure on Congressmen from the public, and cross-lobbying. This last term refers to a common practice in which one special interest group gives its indorsement and assistance to another group on an issue in which the first organization may not be primarily interested, in return for a similar favor later. It can be summed up in the famous political maxim attributed to Simon Cameron, Lincoln's Secretary of War: "You scratch my back and I'll scratch yours."

Direct contact is the method most often associated with lobbying. Despite an ever-increasing emphasis on grassroots campaigns, the direct contact remains a prime technique. In his survey of 100 Washington lobbyists, Milbrath found that 65 listed the direct contact as the method they prefer and generally use. On a scale of 0 to 10, personal presentation of arguments to members of Congress was given a rating of 10 by 58 of the lobbyists. Only 19 lobbyists rated it below eight on the scale.[2]

Approximately the same findings resulted from a questionnaire sent out by John F. Kennedy when he was chairman of a Senate government operations subcommittee. The questionnaire went to a representative group of registered lobbyists. Direct contact with members of Congress ranked first among the methods listed, with 43 responses. Testimony before Congressional committees was second, with 37. Printed matter — bulletins, newsletters, press releases and the like — was third, with 23. Contact with members of organizations, suggesting that they get in touch with their Congressmen, was fourth, with 16. The last two, however, can be considered grassroots lobbying; together they gave this method a total of 39 responses.[3]

In the Milbrath survey of 100 lobbyists, personal presentation of arguments to members of Congress received a mean score of 8.43. Presentation of research results to Congressmen, which most lobbyists consider an integral part of the first method, had a mean score of 7.40. Testifying at Congressional hearings rated 6.55. All three of these methods involve personal, direct contact by the lobbyist with members of Congress. When these three techniques are compared with indirect contact through intermediaries, the Milbrath survey shows some interesting results. Contact with the Congressman by a constituent (arranged by the lobbyist) rated 5.90 and contact by a close friend of the Congressman rated 3.76. Public relations campaigns received a mean score of 5.55. Letter and telegram campaigns were rated 4.55, and publicizing voting records of Congressmen rated 2.05.

In other words, the two principal techniques of indirect, grassroots lobbying — public relations campaigns and letter and telegram campaigns — are ranked by the lobbyists themselves as lower on the effectiveness scale than personal, direct dealings. Contacts by constituents, which partake of both direct and grassroots lobbying, rank right in between direct and indirect lobbying. While 58 lobbyists gave personal presentation of arguments a top effectiveness rating of ten, only two lobbyists rated it zero in effectiveness. On the other hand, only 17 lobbyists gave public relations campaigns a top score of ten, while 21 rated this method of grassroots lobbying at zero. Seven lobbyists rated letter and telegram campaigns at ten while 20 put this kind of indirect pressure at zero in effectiveness.

Milbrath's observations about public relations campaigns offer some clues as to why lobbyists do not rate this method as high as the direct contact. The public relations campaign, he pointed out, is expensive, and its effects are so diffuse and delayed that they are extraordinarily hard to measure. The lobbyist, in other words, may not get all the credit he thinks he deserves.

However, Milbrath notes that some lobbyists feel that public relations campaigns are of use "even though they were not sure their message was getting through to the public, not to mention getting from the public back to the decision makers. They reasoned that the decision makers are quite likely to conclude that the campaign is very persuasive and [is] convincing many people how they should vote. Therefore, the decision maker may possibly alter his behavior in the desired way in anticipation of the reaction from his constituents, without receiving direct communication from many of them." Putting it another way, the massive public relations campaign, handsomely presented, oiled, perfumed and motivationally researched, intimidates the Congressman or bureaucrat before he knows whether anyone in the hinterlands is paying any attention to it. He reads the full-page ads and the facile brochures, is impressed by them and assumes that the voters will be similarly beguiled.

Although the lobbyists rate the direct contact most effective, 75 percent of those interviewed by Milbrath reported that they spend less than 10 percent of their time calling on members of Congress and no more than another 10 percent calling on staff assistants. The explanation is that these personal presentations require careful advance preparation, mainly research. Three-fourths of the lobbyists interviewed reported that they spend more than 40 percent of their time in their offices. The importance of research is emphasized again and again by most lobbyists. "The important thing is the research work done in your office," said lobbyist Scott Lucas. "Off and on, I may spend three or four weeks on research for a 10 or 15-minute appointment with a Senator. I could have a lot of time with that Senator because I'm a former Senator, but I don't want to take up that good man's time. So I brief myself thoroughly before I go up — that's where the work comes."

As much as any lobbyist in Washington, Charles Patrick Clark exemplifies the direct contact tactician. He refers to his operation as "counter propaganda with a personal approach." He runs a one-man show with no law partners. He does some personal grassroots propagandizing but no mass mailing. He concentrates on Congress.

At the beginning, Clark worked against substantial odds. His old boss, Truman, was against aid to Spain, as were the State Department and influential liberals in and out of government. Not only did Clark prevail, but for more than a decade Spain was one of the few nations in the world for which U.S. money was specifically earmarked in the annual foreign aid bill, meaning that the State Department and the foreign aid agency had no leeway. The money had to go to Spain. This favored treatment was strongly protested by Secretary of State John Foster Dulles and his successors.

How did Clark do it? Confronted with solid opposition from the executive branch, he centered his efforts on Congress.

Sam Ward once explained his operations as merely a matter of "stating on all occasions, where it was proper to do so, that I was in favor of the measure." Clark's words are reminiscent of Sam Ward. He says that he simply "presented the facts about Spain at every opportunity to members of Congress, the press, labor leaders, university groups and the like."

It is not enough, of course, to say that Clark has been indefatigable in wooing Congress and let it go at that. The essence of the direct contact, effectively used, is that the contact is with the right members, the key men. What is important is not that Clark used this method but that he used it with skill and discrimination.

It is instructive to examine the list of Congressmen on whom Clark concentrated his lobbying efforts. For the most part, they are members of key committees, men of seniority and influence. Many of them belong to the inside, little-known power structure that runs the House and Senate. Among them are Representatives Eugene J. Keogh of New York and Michael J. Kirwan of Ohio, both Democrats. Clark also enjoyed the friendship of the late Representative William J. Green Jr. of Pennsylvania, the Democratic boss of Philadelphia and a chief of the Pennsylvania delegation in the House.

Keogh is a member of the powerful House Ways and Means Committee, best known as the committee that writes tax legislation. What is less well known is that it is one of the most influential *political* groups in Congress. The Democratic members of Ways and Means constitute the Democratic "committee on committees" — they determine the committee assignments of all Democratic Representatives.

Then there is garrulous, shrewd old Michael Joseph Kirwan of Youngstown, Ohio. Although by no means a great figure on the national scene, he is nevertheless one of the most powerful men in Congress. Two mighty wellsprings furnish his power. He is chairman of the House Democratic campaign committee, which allocates campaign funds to party candidates for the House. And, equally important, Kirwan is chairman of the House Appropriations subcommittee on public works — one of the chief custodians of the pork barrel.

These are two of the men, in other words, to whom the other Democratic members of the House must come — for the committee assignment they want, for a federal project in their district, for money with which to get re-elected, for the lifeblood of their political existence.

When Clark spoke at Marquette University a few years ago, he obtained letters from several members of Congress dealing with their views on Spain, to which he referred in his speech. Among those from whom he received letters were Senators A. Willis Robertson of Virginia, Milton R. Young of North Dakota and Margaret Chase Smith of Maine, all members of the Senate Appropriations Committee, which handles the foreign aid appropriation. Robertson headed his letter: "Dear Charles." Young, second-ranking Republican member of Appropriations, addressed his: "Dear Charlie." Mrs. Smith started off with "Dear Mr. Clark." Others from whom Clark obtained letters were Senate Republican Leader Everett M. Dirksen ("Dear Charles"); the late Senator Styles Bridges of New Hampshire, who at that time was ranking G.O.P. member of the Appropriations Committee ("Dear Charles"); Representative Emanuel Celler of New York, chairman of the House Judiciary Committee ("Dear Charlie" and signed "Mannie"); Representative Hale Boggs of Louisiana, assistant Democratic leader of the House ("Dear Charlie"); Senator Stuart Symington of Missouri, an influential member of the Senate Armed Services Committee ("Dear Charlie"); Chairman L. Mendel Rivers of the House Armed Services Committee ("Dear Charlie"), and Representative A. Sydney Herlong Jr. of Florida, a member of Ways and Means ("Dear Charlie").

The direct contact as a method of influencing the course of government is not confined to Congress. Pressures on the executive branch are equally intense and just as likely to affect the public interest. One recent example of this concerned the efforts of a drug firm, the William S. Merrell Company of Cincinnati, in connection with a tranquilizer whose chief ingredient was a drug known as thalidomide.

To market the pill, Merrell needed the approval of the Food and Drug Administration. The company filed an application for FDA clearance on September 12, 1960 — and the stage was set for a remarkable story of individual steadfastness under pressure.

The application was referred to Dr. Frances Oldham Kelsey, a Canadian-born physician and pharmacologist employed by the FDA as a medical officer. From the first, she was skeptical about the drug and about the evidence submitted by the company as to its safety — evidence that she regarded as "incomplete in many respects." She was troubled, for instance, by the fact that thalidomide did not make experimental animals sleepy. Rather than proving that the drug would be safe for humans, she reasoned, this might indicate that the animal research did not show anything one way or the other about the drug's effect on humans.

Dr. Kelsey's refusal to certify the drug as safe subjected her to insinuations that she was a bureaucratic nitpicker, that she was unreasonable and that she was stupid. In a 14-month period between September 12, 1960 and November 30, 1961, representatives of the Merrell company made almost 50 contacts with Dr. Kelsey and other FDA officials to urge approval of the application. Most of these visits and telephone calls were by Dr. F. Joseph Murray of Merrell's scientific relations division. At one point Dr. Murray informed Dr. Ralph Smith, then Dr. Kelsey's superior officer, that "his firm thought some pressure should be exerted. Accordingly, their vice president intended to see Mr. Larrick [Commissioner George P. Larrick of the FDA] if nothing were going to be done. They wanted a 'yes' or 'no' decision . . ."

Thirty-nine of the contacts — all urging approval of the application — took place *after* the FDA had notified Merrell that some Europeans who had taken thalidomide had developed peripheral neuritis, an inflammation of the nerves in the feet and hands. The company contended that the incidence of this condition was small, one case among 300,000 users. (Later Dr. Kelsey found that the incidence among adults who took thalidomide regularly was one in 250.)

In a letter to the company, Dr. Kelsey expressed concern that "evidence of neurological toxicity [the nerve inflammation] apparently was known to the applicant [Merrell] without being forthrightly disclosed in the application," according to FDA records. Dr. Murray responded with a call to Dr. Smith in which he said he considered this letter somewhat libelous. There were indications that Murray himself was having some trouble with his home office. In one conversation with Smith, he spoke of "being under pressure to 'get it through' because of the need for preparation for marketing." At another point, Murray "expressed hope for early action in view of his management's dissatisfaction with his own efforts in 'pushing the application.'"

On November 30, 1961, Dr. Murray called Dr. Kelsey and informed her that the drug was being withdrawn from the market in West Germany because of reports that it caused gruesome deformities in babies. Three months later, on March 8, 1962, Merrell withdrew its application to sell the drug in the United States.

Many questions remain unanswered in this connection. One of the most important is whether the interests of the American people are adequately safeguarded by an ill-defined relationship between government and private interests in which the protection of the public may depend on happenstance. Americans are fond of saying that they have a government of laws and not of men, but suppose there had been no Dr. Kelsey?

The thalidomide case might have remained an obscure bureaucratic incident, unknown to the general public, had it not been for a front-page story in the Washington Post of July 15, 1962. Reporter Morton Mintz's account of Dr. Kelsey's role, in addition to making the woman doctor a household name, set in motion a train of events that led Congress to place stiff controls on the American drug industry.

Only three days before the story appeared, however, the Senate Judiciary Committee had completed the gutting of a strong drug bill introduced by Senator Estes Kefauver of Tennessee. Lobbyists for the drug industry played an important role in the emasculation of the bill.

In December 1959, the Senate antitrust and monopoly subcommittee headed by Kefauver began an investigation of drug prices. The hearings went on for two and a half years and produced a mountain of evidence showing that the public interest was being adversely affected. The subcommittee's majority report declared that the drug industry was under the "monopolistic control" of a few large firms, that some drug manufacturers took advantage of loopholes in the law to put unsafe and ineffective drugs on the market and that in many cases drug prices and profits were "unreasonably high."

The production cost of prednisone, an arthritis drug, was revealed to be $8.99 per thousand tablets, the retail cost as much as $170 per thousand, a markup of almost 1,900 percent over factory cost. Reserpine, a sedative, had a factory cost of 63 cents per thousand and retailed for as high as $39.50 per thousand, a markup of 6,270 percent. Tetracycline cost $1.67 per 100 tablets in the factory and retailed for as much as $26.01 per 100, a markup of 1,500 percent.

The drug industry's profits as a percentage of net worth averaged 21.9 percent, almost twice the average profit of all manufacturing companies, according to the First National City Bank of New York. In defending their high prices, the drug companies pointed to the large sums they spent on research, but when the Senate subcommittee pinned them down, the 22 largest drug firms admitted that they spent only 6.3 cents out of every sales dollar on research — and 24.8 cents on high-powered promotion and advertising.[4]

From the start, the Kefauver investigation encountered resistance from the subcommittee's ranking minority member, Senate Republican Leader Dirksen. Time after time, Dirksen objected to subcommittee meetings while the Senate was in session. On one occasion his tactics forced Kefauver to hold a hearing at 1 o'clock in the morning. At another point the mellifluous Dirksen declared: "I deem it unobjective and unfair . . . to bring before the subcommittee witnesses whom the subcommittee knows to be critical of the drug profession and the medical profession."

There were interesting sidelights in the fight over the Kefauver drug bill. A leading United States drug company is E. R. Squibb & Sons, a wholly-owned subsidiary of the Olin Mathieson Chemical Corporation. According to the subcommittee, Olin Mathieson's profits from its drug operations alone were 6.8 percent of sales in one year. Without its drug subsidiary the company's profits were .3 percent of sales. Squibb, in other words, is highly important in Olin Mathieson's profit picture. One of the directors of Olin Mathieson is Spencer T. Olin of Alton, Illinois, former finance chairman of the Republican National Committee. In 1956 Olin contributed a total of $34,600 to the G.O.P and other officers and directors of Olin Mathieson brought this up to $100,000. In 1962 Olin contributed $2,000 to the Republican

National Committee and in the first quarter of 1963 he added another $1,000.

Kefauver finally got his drug bill through the subcommittee, but a funny thing happened to it on the way to the full Judiciary Committee. Senator James O. Eastland, the Mississippi Dixiecrat who heads the full committee, called a little meeting. Among those present were Lloyd N. Cutler, counsel for the Pharmaceutical Manufacturers Association, and Marshall Hornblower, one of his associates. Kefauver was not invited to the meeting. He was not told about it.

The meeting was held on June 8, 1962 in the Judiciary Committee office and lasted for 10 hours. Others present were Thomas B. Collins, a Judiciary Committee staff member, representing Eastland; Peter N. Chumbris, minority counsel of the subcommittee, representing Dirksen; Ronald D. Raitt, another minority counsel of the subcommittee, representing Senator Roman L. Hruska, Nebraska Republican, and Jerome N. Sonosky and Theodore Ellenbogen of the Department of Health, Education and Welfare. Republican and southern Democratic members of the Judiciary Committee were represented, the drug industry was represented — but not the Senator who conducted two and a half years of painstaking inquiry into the drug companies and wrote the drug bill. Eastland said later that to have invited Kefauver would have been "a futile act."

The Kefauver bill was rewritten at the meeting. Out came the Tennesseean's proposal to do away with the time restriction on the Food and Drug Administration in acting on new drug applications. It was only by bending this time limit, sending the Merrell application back for more data, that Dr. Kelsey was able to keep thalidomide off the market. In like fashion, the rest of Kefauver's proposals were watered down or eliminated entirely, leaving, in his words, "a mere shadow" of the original bill.

Sonosky told this writer in an interview that the 13 amendments drafted at the June 8 meeting in effect constituted "a whole new bill." He contended that the administration won some concessions, but he acknowledged that on points where no compromise could be reached, the drug industry prevailed. "We knew they had the votes in the Judiciary Committee," he explained. On balance, he said, "they [the drug industry] got much more than we got." When Dirksen presented the 13 new provisions to the full committee, he read from summaries prepared by the drug industry. The committee adopted the amendments on a series of 9 to 2 and 9 to 3 votes.

While the committee work was going on, the drug companies mounted an outside grassroots lobbying campaign against the Kefauver findings. The Pharmaceutical Manufacturers Association hired Hill and Knowlton of New York and Washington, one of the country's largest public relations organizations, to prepare its basic public relations reply to Kefauver. The fee paid to the firm was $5,000 a month and Bert Goss, its president, personally directed the work. Millions of pamphlets and brochures were distributed. Drug company officials and salesmen made hundreds of speeches across the country. Hill and Knowlton provided the "detail men" with instructions on what to say in their talks to women's groups and clubs. These 15,000 salesmen give the drug industry a built-in grassroots lobbying force.

Eli Lilly & Company hired Arthur Newmyer Associates of Washington, a high-priced public relations firm, to handle its grassroots campaign against the Kefauver bill. Newmyer's clients are select, usually one leading company in an industry. Among his other clients: Standard Oil Company of New Jersey, the Ford Motor Company and General Foods. Another Washington public relations firm headed by Paul Duncan handled the grassroots campaign for Merck & Company.

The drug industry surrounded itself with top legal talent in its fight against the Kefauver bill. The Pharmaceutical Manufacturers Association hired Edward H. Foley of Thomas Corcoran's law firm to argue against the bill. William Douglas McAdams Inc. of New York, one of the largest drug advertising companies, retained Cleary, Gottlieb and Steen during the Kefauver hearings, and later Clark Clifford's law firm. Clifford is McAdams' nephew. L. W. Frohlich of New York, another large drug advertising firm, retained Arnold, Fortas and Porter. Other Washington law firms in the drug picture included Covington and Burling, and Morison, Murphy, Clapp and Abrams.

The long, bitter fight over drug legislation illustrated both the direct contact and indirect grassroots methods of pressure. It also illustrated something else: although compromise and the interplay of interests are vital parts of the democratic system, the

public welfare is not served when the compromise is not really
a compromise but a top-heavy victory for one side, and when
the interplay is not really an interplay but a run-away. There
is nothing wrong with compromises. They are indispensable in
the legislative process. But all major interests should be represented in a compromise. The conservative elements of Congress,
in this instance and in many others, prevented a legitimate
bargain.

When the balance was re-established later, it was only by
chance, in the person of Dr. Kelsey. The decision of the Judiciary Committee was reversed and some of the original Kefauver
proposals were restored. An effective drug law was enacted. But
this did not result from the ordinary give and take of the democratic process. It was occasioned by deformed West German
babies, the kind of circumstance on which we should not have
to rely for good laws.

If the danger of direct contact lobbying is that the balance of
interests may be upset by private, exclusive arrangements, the
danger of indirect grassroots lobbying is distortion of the facts.

Most Washington lobbyists emphasize that there are sound,
practical reasons why the information they furnish to members
of Congress should be accurate. They try to put the best possible
face on the facts, but they seldom omit directly relevant data
and, except for the fly-by-night operators, they almost never try
outright fabrication. If a Congressman makes a speech based
on information provided by a lobbyist and the opposing side
is able to catch him in a misstatement of fact or a glaring omis-
sion, the relationship between the Congressman and the lobbyist
is likely to come to an end. Virtually every lobbyist speaks in
this vein: "I've got a living to make in this town. I can't afford
to mislead a Congressman to gain an advantage on one particular
issue. I will be around long after that issue is gone, and so will
the Congressman."

This practical consideration does not apply with equal force
to the grassroots campaign. Distortion often seems to be the
hallmark of this kind of lobbying. A recent example was the
successful campaign by savings and loan associations to kill President Kennedy's proposal to withhold federal income taxes on
interest and dividends.

When Kennedy submitted this plan in 1961, he was proposing only an extension of an existing law. Income taxes on salaries and wages have been subject to withholding since 1942. Moreover, Kennedy was not proposing a new tax. Stock dividends and interest on savings accounts have been taxable right along. He simply recommended that a major tax loophole be closed by extending the withholding feature to interest and dividends. "This is not a new tax," the House Ways and Means Committee stated. "It is a method of collecting taxes already imposed under existing law."

The impact of this loophole on the public was painfully obvious. The honest taxpayer who reported and paid taxes on his interest and/or dividends carried his own tax burden and the burden of the evaders as well. The proposal would have affected only those who were not paying taxes that, by law, they should have paid. "That is tax evasion," Kennedy said, "which must be made up by other taxpayers who pay their taxes." The figures showed the burden on the honest taxpayer. The tax loss to the Treasury from unreported dividend and interest income in 1959 was put at $880,000,000; in 1960, $1,040,000,000 and in 1963, as a result of the defeat of the withholding plan, $1,150,-000,000. Later the Internal Revenue Service installed computers that catch unreported dividend and interest income, but until this was done the honest taxpayer was being penalized.

Savings and loan institutions across the country mounted one of the most intensive grassroots lobbying campaigns in history against the withholding proposal. The campaign leaned heavily on misleading implications, innuendo and scare tactics. This is an old tactic not made honorable by repetition. The big black type in the advertisements screams out and the eye slides over the small print that keeps the message just inside the bounds of truth.

The campaign against the withholding proposal was led by the United States Savings and Loan League. Founded in 1892, the League represents about 5,000 of the country's 6,000 savings and loan associations. Its member associations have about 95 percent of the savings and loan assets in the nation and some 30,000,000 depositors. Long considered one of the most powerful lobbying organizations in Washington, the League was once indicted for alleged violation of the Lobbying Act. The case was dismissed when the organization complied with the law.

Former President Truman referred to the League as part of the real estate lobby which fought public housing, slum clearance and rent control during his administration, even though the first two programs were co-authored by "Mr. Republican," Senator Robert A. Taft. (The late Representative Adolph J. Sabath of Chicago, a greatly respected legislator, called the real estate lobby, led by the the National Association of Real Estate Boards, "one of the rottenest" lobbies "that ever infested Washington.") The Savings and Loan League maintains its interest in housing matters to this day; it played an important role in the defeat of the cabinet-level Department of Urban Affairs during the Kennedy administration. Heading the League's Washington office (its national headquarters are in Chicago) are Stephen G. Slipher and Glenwood S. (Glen) Troop, considered two of the ablest lobbyists in town.

There were interesting cross-currents in the League's fight against the tax withholding plan. In the House the big savings and loan group registered only nominal opposition. This was part of a deal with the House Democratic leadership under which the League would go easy on the withholding proposal in return for a break on the section of the tax bill dealing with the taxes on savings and loan associations. For years these associations had been paying virtually no federal income taxes at all. They were permitted to put their annual income into a tax-free bad debt reserve up to an amount equal to 12 percent of their assets. Between 1952 and 1961 all the savings and loan associations and mutual savings banks in the United States paid a total of less than $70,000,000 in federal income taxes while retaining $5,500,-000,000 in the same period in the form of additions to reserves, undivided profits and surplus.

"We knew this was too good to last," one savings and loan executive admitted candidly. The Ways and Means Committee finally settled on a formula that would raise taxes on the associations to approximately $200,000,000 a year in the first year. The Treasury favored a higher figure. The League judged the Ways and Means formula to be the best deal obtainable and downplayed its opposition to the withholding plan in the House in order to retain the committee figure on the savings and loan taxes.

When the tax bill reached the Senate, however, the gloves came off. On March 26, 1962, top officials of the League met in a private dining room at the Palmer House in Chicago to map a campaign against the withholding plan in the Senate. M. L. Dye, then president of the League, chaired the meeting. About 25 men were present, including 10 former League presidents.

According to some of the participants, three basic decisions were taken at the meeting. First, a letter would go out to the 5,000 savings and loan associations affiliated with the League, urging them to communicate with their Senators in opposition to the withholding proposal. Second, the associations would urge individual depositors and borrowers to do likewise. Third, the League would try to discourage local associations from using advertising to fight the withholding proposal. This last should be noted in the light of later developments.

The letter went out on March 30 from Norman Strunk, executive vice president of the League. It was a signal for action. "The time has come," it said, "for every savings and loan executive, officer and director to write a letter to both his United States Senators covering either or both the savings and loan tax law and the proposed withholding on interest and dividends. The time also has come for associations to address letters to their savers, borrowers, and builder and realtor friends. You will recall that earlier this year we asked every association to get ready for such a mailing to savers and others by addressing envelopes, etc. This is the time when these envelopes should be used."

The result was an avalanche, a flood, a torrent of letters to members of the Senate. So many stacks of letters piled up that Senatorial staffs had to drop everything else to cope with the deluge. The Senate postoffice said there had been nothing to compare with it since Truman fired General Douglas MacArthur, or possibly the Army-McCarthy hearings.

Senator Paul H. Douglas, Illinois Democrat who was one of the chief sponsors of the withholding plan, got 75,000 letters, almost all of them opposed. Senator John Sherman Cooper, Kentucky Republican, got about 60,000 similar letters. Senator Clifford P. Case, New Jersey Republican, received 5,000 letters *in one day*, 80 percent of them opposed. Senator Joseph S. Clark, Pennsylvania Democrat, got 26,000 letters of protest, and only

20 in favor, in one month. Senator Russell B. Long, Louisiana Democrat, received more than 10,000 letters, and Senator George A. Smathers, Florida Democrat, got 50,000 letters, the overwhelming majority opposed to the withholding plan. Senator Eugene J. McCarthy, Minnesota Democrat, received 12,000 letters, all but a handful opposed.

The heaviest barrages were directed at members of the Senate Finance Committee, which was considering the tax bill. Douglas, Long, Smathers and McCarthy are members of the Finance Committee.

A great many of the letter writers were flatly mistaken in two key respects. They thought the tax bill called for a new tax and that it would be a tax on their *savings*. Actually, it merely related to the basic withholding rate applicable to the *interest* on their savings, not the principal —a vast difference. A high proportion of the letters came from elderly persons whose plaintive, sometimes pathetic messages made it clear that they had been led to believe their savings were going to be taxed. "They were scared," a Treasury official observed.

Despite the strenuous efforts of Senator Douglas and a few others to set the facts straight, the League's campaign was a smashing success. Starting with only 35 Republican Senators in its camp, the League at the end had battered down the administration forces in the Senate to a ragged 20 votes. On July 11 the Finance Committee knocked the withholding plan out of the tax bill on a vote of 10 to 5. Senators Robert S. Kerr, Clinton P. Anderson, Albert Gore, Vance Hartke and Douglas, all Democrats, voted for withholding. Senators Long, Smathers and McCarthy, the latter ordinarily an administration stalwart, were among those who voted against it. When the tax bill reached the Senate floor its supporters lacked the votes to restore the withholding plan, and a House effort to revive it in conference failed.

Senate Majority Leader Mike Mansfield, who saw his majority pounded to pieces by the barrage of mail, paid tribute to the League's grassroots lobbying campaign. "Under the pressure from home," he said, "Senators made commitments. We couldn't change them when the bill came to the floor."

When, at Mansfield's urging, President Kennedy finally made a public statement on the withholding issue, it was a strong one.

At a press conference on May 9, he bluntly accused the savings
and loan associations of "misinforming . . . millions of people."
But he did not follow this up. Had he done so, even at that late
date, the outcome just might have been different. The Savings
and Loan League was acutely nervous about an open confron-
tation with the President.

The day after Kennedy's press conference, Strunk sent a confidential memorandum to officials of the national League and
executives of state savings and loan leagues.

"Basically, we are not anxious to get into a public 'cat and
dog fight' with the President," the memorandum said. "We feel
that in any public discussion in the press or otherwise, the White
House has all the advantages in terms of communication with
the American public. We do not want to fan this flame."

"We hope this publicity generated by the President yesterday
will not be picked up and repeated and repeated," Strunk said
at another point. "Our own handling of this is deliberately
designed not to fan any fire . . . We have reason to believe and
hope that this will not be a repetition of the steel incident, where
there was a planned follow-up of the President's attack," the
memo stated.

The League was biting its nails. Strunk sent out another memo
to executives of local savings and loan associations, calling their
attention to a press release issued by the national League after
the President's news conference. "It is temperate, deliberately
so," he said. And Dye, the president of the League, wrote Kennedy a long letter in which he acknowledged that "there has
been some misinformation and misunderstanding about the withholding proposal" but contended that this was "primarily due
to the extreme complexity of the proposal."

But the League need not have worried. After his one statement, Kennedy remained silent.

The charge that the public was misinformed about the withholding proposal stemmed from a sample letter sent out by the
League and from newspaper advertisements placed by some individual savings and loan associations. The sample letter went
out with Strunk's March 30 alert to the League's members, who
in turn used it widely as a model for their letters to individual
depositors.

Addressed "Dear Saver," the sample letter at first correctly identified the proposal as a withholding plan on the interest on savings. But the concluding paragraph, which exhorted depositors to write their Senators, spoke of "this proposed withholding tax against your savings and investments." This gave the misleading impression that it was a tax on the principal. The letter contained several other major inaccuracies and omissions, including a statement that only a "few" people did not report all their interest and dividends on their income tax returns. Actually, as Senator Douglas pointed out, an estimated 12,000,000 people, more than 70 percent of them in the $10,000-a-year bracket or above, failed to pay federal taxes on this income. More than a third of all the interest paid by banks and savings and loan institutions was not being reported on income tax forms when Kennedy made his proposal.

Nor did the savings and loan associations mention that approval of the withholding plan would have cost them a tidy additional income derived from money that belonged, by law, to the Treasury. Since most depositors do not withdraw their interest as it is credited to their accounts, the associations can and do retain this money and invest it, leaving it up to the depositor whether he reports the interest on his income tax return. If the withholding plan had passed, the associations would have been required to forward 20 percent of the interest to the Treasury, just as employers forward a percentage of wages and salaries. Treasury officials believe that this undoubtedly was a factor in the bitter S. and L. opposition to withholding.

In many instances the newspaper ads taken by savings and loan institutions were calculated to give the impression that the withholding plan was a tax on savings. One ad, in Oak Park, Illinois, alerted suburban savers to "a threatening new 20 percent tax." Repeatedly, the ads displayed the words "20 percent tax" in big bold type and the words "on interest and dividends" in smaller print. An ad in Norfolk, Virginia, declared: "Twenty percent of your savings would be deducted at the source and forwarded directly to the federal government whether or not you owe the tax."

An ad in the Cleveland Plain Dealer declared: "Do you want your earnings from savings and investments taxed . . . in advance? You can do something about it if you act now . . . Remember, this insidious bill is not yet passed but hearings to decide the outcome are being held in Washington. If you feel that this withholding tax *against your savings* is unfair, now is the time to protest — not after the bill is passed. Write the President, your Congressman and Senators today." (Italics supplied.)

The widows and orphans appeal, an ancient wheeze, was trotted out. In Lima, Ohio, a full-page ad stated: "Even little children must file complicated tax forms to obtain refunds. Can you imagine the red tape involved in getting a fifty-cent refund for a two-year-old child?" A heartrending picture, had it been true. In vain did Senator Douglas point out that children under 18 would have been exempt from the withholding requirement.

After the dust had cleared, the Savings and Loan League said it had tried to discourage the use of advertisements by local associations. It is true that the League's Washington professionals killed a proposal that the League itself conduct an ad campaign. "The trouble with an ad campaign is that you can't control it," one of them said. "There is bound to be misleading information in the ads, and that can hurt you." To some extent, the local associations may have run away from the Washington staff, as sometimes happens when the grassroots decides that it, too, knows how to lobby. But there is little evidence that the League made any formal nationwide move to stop the ads.

In this connection, another League communication should be noted. On March 30, the same day that the letter went out to League members, Strunk sent a memorandum to executives of state savings and loan leagues. The memorandum, marked "Confidential — not for publication or quotation in any form," stated at one point: "With respect to the fight against withholding . . . we feel that now is the time for the big push. *There is no reason for holding back on anything.*" (Italics added.)

How effective is grassroots lobbying? Some members of Congress discount it as having little influence on how they vote. The big stacks of mail that come in, they say, are easily recognizable as resulting from organized campaigns directed by special interest groups. The letters and telegrams often use identical language and the same canned arguments. To hear some legislators tell it, the letters are stacked in a closet or corner, and that's that.

But is it? Although the Congressman may downplay the effectiveness of organized pressure tactics (no politician likes to admit that he responds to pressure), the fact is that these lobbying efforts frequently are successful in delaying a bill for several sessions or forcing the adoption of weakening amendments. Sometimes, although less often, these campaigns can kill a bill outright, as in the case of the savings and loan industry's fight against the interest and dividend withholding proposal. An instance in which grassroots pressure delayed a major bill for several years and compelled a watering down of the final version was the recent campaign by the National Rifle Association and other groups against some major aspects of proposed legislation to regulate and control the interstate sale of various types of guns.

In August 1963, after a lengthy study by the Senate subcommittee on juvenile delinquency, Senator Thomas J. Dodd introduced a bill to establish a measure of control over the merchandizing of firearms. The subcommittee's hearings had produced an abundance of evidence that such a law was needed.

In Los Angeles, the Senate unit learned, a mentally-ill youngster read a magazine advertisement for mail-order guns, ordered and received a revolver and used it to kill his 14-year-old brother. "My brother was an inferior person," he explained. In Pittsburgh a 16-year-old youth shot a playmate with a mail-order gun obtained from an out-of-state firm. When a court directed that the boy be sent to a detention home, he committed suicide with his father's rifle. In Baltimore a 15-year-old boy slaughtered his family with a revolver purchased through the mail. In Fairfax, Virginia, a 16-year-old accidentally shot and killed his 14-year-old companion with a .38 caliber revolver purchased from a Los Angeles mail-order house. When the gun dealer was told about it, he said: "I didn't break the law, did I? If they've got the money, I sell them the gun. I'm not responsible for what they do with it."

The evidence amassed was not confined to teenagers. Convicted criminals can and do order firearms through the mail with impunity, often in violation of state and local gun control laws that do not apply to interstate commerce. The Chicago police department reported that 4,069 guns were shipped into that city in a three-year period by just two mail-order gun firms and that 25 percent of these weapons went to persons with criminal records. Mail-order guns were purchased by convicted felons in Los Angeles who used them to commit armed robberies. In Pittsburgh convicted criminals purchased guns through the mail in violation of the Pennsylvania firearms act. In the District of Columbia 25 percent of those who bought mail-order guns had criminal records ranging from assault with a deadly weapon to homicide.

In 1963, the Federal Bureau of Investigation reported, there were 8,500 homicides in the United States. About 56 percent of them were committed with firearms. Of this number, 70 percent were committed with revolvers and automatic pistols, 20 percent with shotguns and 10 percent with rifles. Criminals with guns commit about 40,000 armed robberies every year and more than 25,000 aggravated assaults. Upwards of 120,000 persons are maimed by firearms annually. Treasury Department officials recently uncovered in Illinois an arms cache that included 100 submachine guns, five tripod-mounted machine guns, a flame-thrower, several 25-pound aerial bombs, mortars and live ammunition for all these weapons. An agent of the Senate subcommittee joined the Minutemen, an organization that seeks to recruit a guerrilla army to prevent the Communists from taking over the United States. He was instructed to purchase weapons, and with no questions asked he bought an 81 mm. Russian mortar, a 50 mm. Finnish mortar, a 2.36 mm. bazooka, a rifle with a grenade launcher and grenades, and several bazooka rockets and 81 mm. shells. A judge in Chicago reports that he collects a bushel basketful of guns every ten days from teen-agers brought before his court. A student at the University of Mississippi bought a "souvenir" mail-order submachine gun that could easily be made operable with a few simple adjustments.

It is estimated that Americans spend about two billion dollars a year on firearms. Some states have laws regulating the purchase of weapons, but these laws are of no effect against mail-order guns sold and delivered in interstate commerce. "States with gun control laws now stand helplessly by while those laws are flouted daily by the unchecked sale of guns by mail," President Johnson pointed out in his 1966 crime message to Congress.

Except for some gangster-era statutes aimed at sawed-off shotguns and the like, the interstate traffic in firearms is virtually
unregulated.

It was against a long and grisly background of uncontrolled
violence that Senator Dodd introduced his bill. Four months
after he submitted it, Lee Harvey Oswald, using a mail-order
rifle, shot and killed the President of the United States as he
rode through the streets of Dallas, Texas. Oswald bought his
rifle for $12.78 from a Chicago sporting goods store. In ordering
it, he used a fictitious name, "A. Hidell." He had no permit for
the rifle. No one checked his record of mental instability. The
rifle was ordered and delivered through the mail. Oswald picked
it up at a post office box in Dallas, with no questions asked.

Despite the national trauma produced by the brutal slaying
of John F. Kennedy, two and a half years elapsed before the
Dodd bill came to a vote in the juvenile delinquency subcommittee and began to work its way through the legislative mill.
And the bill had been weakened in significant respects that left
the way open for potential Oswalds to obtain high-powered rifles
through the mail. A massive grassroots pressure campaign by
the National Rifle Association and other sportsmen and wildlife
organizations was primarily responsible for a delay that must
rank as unconscionable in a civilized society, and for diluting
the bill as it affected mail-order sales of rifles and shotguns.
As so frequently happens in this kind of lobbying, the campaign
against major aspects of the Dodd bill was marked by serious
charges of misleading information and misstatement of fact.

The version approved by the subcommittee in March 1966
prohibited the interstate sale and delivery of handguns except
between licensed gun dealers, manufacturers and importers. No
longer could a private individual, regardless of age, order a revolver or automatic pistol by mail from a dealer in another state
and have it shipped directly to him by mail or common carrier.
Under the bill, a person 21 years old or older could buy a handgun over the counter from a dealer in his own state if he supplied
credible identification.

For rifles and shotguns, the bill was less restrictive. It permitted over-the-counter sales of long guns to persons 18 or older,
again with credible identification, and it also permitted mail-
order purchases of these weapons from out-of-state dealers, as

long as the rifle or shotgun was suitable for lawful sporting purposes and was not a military surplus weapon. The mail-order
traffic in rifles and shotguns was not closed down — a concession
wrung by the grassroots pressure of the National Rifle Association. The right to buy hunting and sporting rifles and shotguns
by mail was preserved, for responsible citizens and potential Lee
Harvey Oswalds alike.

The Dodd bill did contain some safeguards in this area. The
purchaser of a long gun by mail was required under the legislation to submit with his order a notarized affidavit giving his
correct name and address, stating that he was 18 or older, that
he had not been convicted of a crime punishable by a year's
imprisonment or more and was not under indictment for such
a crime, that he was not a fugitive from justice and that he had
complied with state and local firearms laws, meaning that he had
obtained a local permit if one was required. The purchaser was
further required to furnish the name of the chief law enforcement
officer in his community, and the dealer was required to forward
a copy of the affidavit to this official. This would give local
chiefs of police advance notice of who in their community was
buying mail-order rifles and shotguns. The police chief could
not block the sale — even if he knew the purchaser to be a dangerous schizoid, for instance. Seven days after the police chief
received the affidavit by registered mail, the dealer would be
free to ship the weapon to the purchaser.

Dodd, it has been noted, introduced his bill before Kennedy
was assassinated. After the assassination, he amended it, at the
request of the Johnson administration, to prohibit all mail-order
sales of rifles and shotguns, except between licensed gun dealers,
manufacturers and importers. The amendment, in other words,
applied the same restrictions to long guns as to revolvers and
automatics. It was this provision that drew the heaviest fire
from the National Rifle Association, the National Shooting Sports
Foundation and other firearms and wildlife groups. Under intense pressure, the amendment disappeared from the version
finally approved by the subcommittee.

The National Rifle Association was founded as a non-profit
corporation in 1871 by a group of National Guard officers. Its
purpose was "the improvement of its members in marksmanship,

and to promote the introduction of the system of aiming drill and rifle practice as part of the military drill of the National Guard." Later the organization's objectives were expanded to include other salutary goals, among them: "to promote social welfare and public safety, law and order and the national defense; to educate and train citizens of good repute in the safe and efficient handling of small arms [and] generally to encourage the lawful ownership and use of small arms by citizens of good repute." It is wondrous that the association found the Dodd bill so objectionable; their stated objectives were so similar.

The NRA is housed in a handsome building on Scott Circle in Washington. It has an annual budget of more than $4,000,000, net assets of more than $8,000,000 and immense prestige in its field. More significantly from a legislative standpoint, the association has nearly 750,000 individual members and 12,500 affiliated organizations that bring its total strength to well over 1,000,000 persons. It thus possesses the vital weapon of grass-roots lobbying — a big "constituency," a large membership that can be aroused to real or fancied dangers. Moreover, there are some 14,600,000 registered hunters in the United States and an estimated 22,000,000 persons take part in target, trap and skeet, and pistol-shooting sports every year. Orchestrated into a mighty pressure force, these millions of hunters and sportsmen command attention on Capitol Hill. The NRA does not lack the means of organizing them.

Like most large special interest associations, the NRA utilizes several techniques of communicating with its members and the nation as a whole. One is the *National Rifleman,* official publication of the NRA. A total of 8,601,748 copies of this monthly magazine were printed in 1964, and sale of advertising space in its pages brought the NRA 25 percent of its revenue that year. A regular feature of the magazine is a section entitled "What the Lawmakers Are Doing," which keeps members up to date on firearms legislation at the federal, state and local levels. In 1964 the magazine devoted a total of 57 columns to reports on pending firearms bills, and the association's annual report boasted that "no other organization carries on such a continuous and successful effort to inform its members about proposed anti-gun laws which would restrict the ownership and use of shotgun, handgun and rifle alike."

When necessary, the National Rifle Association puts out special bulletins and memoranda on legislation. Twenty-six legislative bulletins were mailed out to 141,000 NRA members and clubs in 11 states in 1964. Thus informed about proposed gun control legislation in their states, "NRA members reacted promptly, firmly and in force," the annual report stated. "As a result, no severe legislation was enacted," it added.

Moreover, the association uses direct mail and telegrams to inform its members about urgent legislative matters. Thus, on April 0, 1065, a letter went out to all NRA members — about 700,000 of them at that time — from Franklin L. Orth, executive vice president of the organization. The letter alerted NRA members to the version of the Dodd bill under consideration at that time, which included the administration-backed ban on mail-order sale of rifles and shotguns. This ban, Orth asserted, would place "harsh and unreasonable restrictions upon law-abiding citizens who wish to order sporting firearms . . . by mail, especially those citizens who do not have convenient access to licensed dealers for over-the-counter sales."

The NRA centered its sharpest criticism on the amendment containing the proposed ban. "This bill," Orth's letter declared, "conceivably could lead to administrative decisions imposing such a burden on the sale, possession and use of firearms for legitimate purposes as to totally discourage, and thus to eliminate, the private ownership of all guns." The NRA was gazing into its crystal ball and seeing therein all manner of evil shapes, an old trick in grassroots lobbying.

"We strongly urge you, as a sportsman and law-abiding citizen," the letter concluded, "immediately to write to your Senators and Congressmen respectfully to voice your views as to S. 1592 [the Dodd bill] and to insist that public hearings are held on this bill. We also urge you and your friends to write the President and express your opinions and concern. Write now, or it may be too late!"

This last paragraph deserves comment. The NRA was urging its members to write their Senators and Representatives about a specific piece of pending legislation and "to voice your views" on it, although the letter did not specifically ask NRA members to urge their Congressmen to oppose the bill.

The generally accepted interpretation of the Supreme Court's decision in U.S. v. Harriss is that it exempts organizations conducting indirect grassroots pressure campaigns from registering under the Lobbying Act. But the court stated at one point that lobbying "through an artificially stimulated letter campaign" should be subject to the registration and financial disclosure requirements of the law. Does this include general appeals to "voice your views" and "express your opinions and concern"? Or does it mean that the Lobbying Act applies only to instances in which citizens are specifically urged to ask their Congressmen to vote for or against a bill? No one really knows. The lawyers differ. No government official or agency, as will be seen in the next chapter, is authorized to make such determinations. It is a vast murky area.

At any rate, the National Rifle Association is not registered under the Lobbying Act. Officers of the organization say that registration as a lobbying group would violate the NRA's charter. When Orth testified before the Senate subcommittee concerned about firearms, he said he did not think of the NRA as a lobbying group. "I think," he explained, "that the great patriotic organizations of America, non-profit organizations, such as the American Legion, the Veterans of Foreign Wars, the National Rifle Association of America, and others, should have, on public issues concerning their membership, an opportunity to discuss these things with the members of the Congress and with others who are interested, for the benefit of the people as a whole. It has nothing to do with monetary or personal profit. It is for the purpose only of the good of the United States."

The American Legion apparently does not agree entirely with the National Rifle Association. It registers under the Lobbying Act. Neither does Senator Dodd agree. "It seems to me," he told Orth, "that your organization is doing what I would call lobbying against this measure. I think your comparative statement of income and expenses shows that this must be so. In reading over the Lobbying Act, it seems to me that this kind of activity gets pretty close to it, if it is not actually engaged in lobbying under the Act."

When Dodd referred to the NRA's comparative statement of income and expenses, he had in mind the fact that the association's expenditures for legislative and public affairs rose from $76,563 in 1962 to $157,388 in 1964 and expenditures for its editorial division went from $1,315,167 to $1,617,303 in the same period. By multiplying five cents postage times the 700,000 letters sent out by the NRA on April 9, 1965, Senate sources calculated that this mailing cost alone amounted to $35,000. Since the organization is not registered under the lobbying law, none of these expenses were reported to Congress and the public, although some of the items were listed in the NRA's annual report to its members.

The executive committee of the association officially indorsed the first version of the Dodd bill, and Orth testified in support of this version. Nevertheless, when Dodd introduced the measure, thousands of letters poured in from riflemen and hunters across the country. The opposition, Dodd told Orth, was so strong "that I could not get a vote on the bill in the Commerce Committee. So I was in the position of having your support and that of your directors, but your members just flooded the members of the committee with letters in opposition. I don't hold you responsible for that. But it certainly worked that way."

Replied Orth: "In an organization of 700,000 individuals . . . there are many who do not agree with the policy necessarily of the governors of that organization . . . We have in America some 20,000,000 sportsmen, and there are many gun magazines, a great many of them who came out flatly against S. 1975 [the earlier version]. As a matter of fact, there were a great many of these magazines who said the National Rifle Association was selling the sportsman short. And I received a great many telegrams, letters and so forth for my action in this respect."

While it is clear that the NRA opposed a ban on mail-order sale of rifles and shotguns, as proposed in a later version of the Dodd bill, nailing down the association's position in the subcommittee's hearings is difficult. "While controls on the interstate shipment of firearms are definitely needed, the complete prohibition of such commerce to all but the licensed few is not the answer," Orth said at one point. And at another point: "In principle, I must object to any law which would prohibit the delivery of firearms in interstate or foreign commerce to all persons except licensed dealers, importers or manufacturers." But Orth said he agreed with Dodd "absolutely" that some legislation was needed, and he added, "I will do all that I can to assist you and your committee in obtaining it." The NRA, he vowed, "will support legislation which can effectively reduce the criminal use of firearms, but the NRA stands squarely on the premise that the ownership of firearms must not be denied American citizens of good repute so long as they use them for lawful purposes." Later, the NRA announced that it was backing a three-part legislative package as an alternative to the the the Dodd bill. The association proposed (1) to make it a federal crime to use a firearm transported in interstate commerce in the commission of a major crime, (2) to make it a federal offense for a licensed gun dealer "knowingly" to ship a firearm in interstate commerce in violation of any state statute, and (3) to amend existing federal law to provide control over so-called destructive devices such as bazookas, grenades, bombs and mines. The second proposal came closest to the Dodd bill. The proposed ban on interstate shipment of firearms would apply to mail-order sales of rifles and shotguns as well as handguns, but Frank Daniel, secretary of the NRA, acknowledged that most state laws cover only weapons that can be concealed, meaning revolvers and automatics. Nor did the NRA propose any machinery to insure that dealers would know when an order for a gun violated state law.

It is clear that the NRA considers grassroots pressure an effective legislative weapon, regardless of what the Congressmen say. In an article in *The Nation,* Robert G. Sherrill quoted Daniel as saying: "We sent letters to our 730,000 members and told them to let their opinions be known. Well, we really got results. There was probably no other response like it to anything happening in Congress. Changed a lot of opinions on Capitol Hill, too. After that, Dodd couldn't even get a quorum of his subcommittee." [5] Sherill also quoted NRA officials as claiming that the association can hit Congress with a half million letters on 72 hours' notice. This may be an exaggeration but probably not by much. The letters and telegrams from hunters and sportsmen inundated Capitol Hill at crucial points in the consideration of the gun control bill. On March 16, 1966, the juvenile delinquency subcommittee held a closed meeting to work on the bill. Although the meeting was not announced to the press, the day before it was held 350 telegrams and several thousand letters poured in, referring to the meeting and urging Senators to vote against the measure.

The NRA is endlessly alert to legislation that it considers hostile to the rights of riflemen. "Through available reporting machinery," its 1964 annual report said, "legislation proposed at the federal and state levels usually can be discovered in time to inform our members when effective action is deemed necessary. Local legislation, however, may be enacted much more swiftly than state or national laws . . . [NRA] members in a local community must be alert and must act quickly and decisively, in a well-organized manner, to defeat such threats. Some communities have met the situation by means of a 'watchdog' committee consisting of local NRA members and club representatives who are capable of quickly detecting restrictive measures and as quickly generating concerted, well-timed action."

When the Senate subcommittee voted on the Dodd bill on March 22, 1966, it was approved by a vote of six to three, but without the ban on mail-order sales of rifles and shotguns. The first Congressional action on the gun control measure had come two years and four months after the assassination of John F. Kennedy, and despite President Johnson's strong indorsement of the bill, a long and perilous road still lay ahead in Congress. Voting against the measure in subcommittee were two prominent Democratic liberals from states where hunting is an important source of tourist revenue — Senators Philip A. Hart of Michigan and Quentin N. Burdick of North Dakota. The third vote against the bill was cast by Republican Senator Roman L. Hruska of Nebraska.

The campaign against the gun bill, Senator Dodd charged, was marked by repeated misstatements of fact and misleading information that caused unfounded opposition to the bill in Congress and the nation. Dodd fought back with a series of speeches in which he replied to the alleged distortions, but the campaign continued. Finally, his patience exhausted, he lashed out directly at the National Rifle Association in some of the strongest language ever used by a Senator against a powerful special interest group. In a statement to the Senate on March 10, 1966, he charged that the NRA and other organizations had "deliberately deceived the public with respect to the provisions of this bill." Opponents of the bill, he said, "have been deplorably two-faced in their statements and actions . . . The officers of the National Rifle Association have indicated their support of some of the provisions we have proposed, yet newsletters going out under their organization's letterhead have misrepresented the bill and urged all gun enthusiasts to oppose it . . . Apparently the majority of the leadership of the National Rifle Association will have to be dragged, kicking and screaming, into the twentieth century."

"In a similar vein," Dodd continued, "bulletins distributed by other organizations with a special interest in firearms, such as the National Shooting Sports Foundation, have helped to mount an unbelievable propaganda campaign against [the bill]. Together, these opponents of S. 1592 have been guilty of dishonesty against the American people, and I for one would charge them with intentionally perpetrating harm against this country."

Among the misstatements spread by some opponents of the bill, Dodd charged, were these: It would be the first step toward eventually prohibiting all private ownership of firearms in the United States; it would establish federal regulation of firearms; it would forbid hunters to transport their rifles and shotguns across state lines for legitimate sporting purposes; it would give the Secretary of the Treasury or some other federal official arbitrary powers to regulate the handling and ownership of guns by the public; it would drive reputable gun dealers out of business, and it would violate the Second Amendment to the Constitution. These and other assertions, Dodd said, added up to "a campaign of falsehoods and deceptions."

The charges of misrepresentation were aired at several points in the subcommittee's hearings on the gun control bill, notably in the questioning of Thomas J. Siatos, publisher and editorial director of *Guns & Ammo* magazine. Dodd considered Siatos "about the most violent critic of this legislation." An article in the July 1965 issue of the periodical, the Senator said, contained 28 paragraphs referring to the gun control measure, "and 27 of them are not anywhere near truthful. They distort the provisions of this bill through conjecture or actual misstatement of fact." The first paragraph of the article read as follows: "On March 28, Senator Dodd of Connecticut introduced firearms bills numbered S. 1591 and S. 1592, and if you as a collector, hunter, target shooter, gun dealer, gunsmith or small manufacturer wish to lose your rights to own guns, to go hunting, target shooting, deal in firearms, read no further. This bill will confiscate your guns, make it impossible for you to hunt or stay in business." [8]

At a subcommittee hearing, Dodd questioned Siatos about the article.

Dodd: "You have read this bill, have you?"

Siatos: "Yes, sir; I have, Senator.

Dodd: "You point out to me where confiscation is mentioned in this bill.

Siatos: "It is not mentioned in the bill specifically, Senator, but we sincerely feel that such a bill as S. 1592 will ultimately become, there will be additions made to it because we also sincerely feel that it will not accomplish the purpose that it states.

Dodd: "Is that the best explanation you can give for writing a paragraph like that about this bill?

Siatos: "Yes, sir. We sincerely feel that it will not accomplish its purpose.

Dodd: "You sincerely feel it will cause confiscation of the guns of hunters, people who want to target shoot, to own guns, to deal in firearms. Do you really believe that?

Siatos: "S. 1592, as you indicate, Senator, does not mention the word 'confiscation,' but as I have indicated previously, we do feel that it could conceivably lead to much more stringent type of legislation which may ultimately end up in confiscation of firearms."

At another point, Dodd quoted the 19th paragraph of the *Guns & Ammo* article as saying that: "The bill would prohibit a hunter or target shooter going from one state to another taking his gun with him."

Siatos: "Yes, there seems to be some confusion —

Dodd: "The bill specifically says that a man can transport — any man transporting his rifle or shotgun for lawful purposes may do so.

Siatos: "But, I am not an attorney on this point, Senator, and possibly you can help me out, but that is providing he adhered to the laws and ordinances of the state in which he was traveling.

Dodd: "He has to do that now, doesn't he?

Siatos: "Up to a point.

Dodd: "Up to what point? You are not suggesting that he violate the laws of the state, are you?

Siatos: "No, I am not, Senator. But this simply would be another bill which would add to the confusion that already exists.

Dodd: "You know that it is one thing to say, but to write an article of this kind and just nakedly say, 'prohibit a hunter or target shooter going from one state to another and taking his gun with him.' This morning you say, well, it is possible it could happen. But to your readers, and you have the largest circulation, that kind of a statement is certainly misleading, because you state categorically that this bill would prohibit the hunter or target shooter from carrying his gun from one state to another. Do you really think that is a fair thing to do about this bill?

Siatos: "Well, we, again I must reiterate my sincere opinion that it would ultimately lead to the statements outlined in this particular article, Senator.

Dodd: "Even though the bill says otherwise?

Siatos: "Even though the bill was conceived in utmost sincerity on your part.

Dodd: "Don't give me that sincerity bunk. I just want to know why you wrote an article like this?

Siatos: "Because we do feel that it [the bill] would lead to this manner of confusion.

Dodd: "Well, I can't think of any greater confusion that has been contributed to the discussion of this bill than your article. You baldly state what I am sure you know is not true. You say you have read the bill. And for you to write an article that it would prohibit a hunter or target shooter from taking his gun from one state to another is about as willful a misrepresentation of this bill as I have read or heard of. And thousands of people have read it. The mail is pouring into the Congressmen and Senators, into the White House, and some of it is almost word for word from your article."

The Connecticut Senator then quoted another paragraph as saying: "Do not be fooled by any of the double talk. What it all comes down to is that without obtaining special licenses, permits, probably from the federal government and every state, you will not be allowed to travel out of your state with a firearm under any circumstances unless you are fully licensed, and even then that is questionable."

Dodd: "Do you really believe that, having read the bill?

Siatos: "The bill does not state that, Senator. But it is again conceivable to us, because of the broad regulatory powers given to the Treasury Department, that this could be the ultimate —

Dodd: "I don't think you ever have read it, or else your imagination has run wild. When referring to the standards set forth to obtain licenses under Section Three, you say in paragraph 27, and I quote it: 'In other words, if for any reason they do not like your looks, your politics, your religion or anything else, you may not be allowed to have a license in the first place.' Do you believe that?

Siatos: "Do I specifically — does this article specifically say that?

Dodd: "In paragraph 27. I am reading from it. Do you believe the Secretary of the Treasury is going to enforce this law on the basis of not liking a citizen's looks or his politics or his religion? Have you ever known a Secretary to do that?

Siatos: "Senator, all I can say is this is what we call editorializing.

Dodd: "Is that what you call it?

Siatos: "Yes, sir.

Dodd: "That is pretty good. Some people call it lying, and I am one of them. You know better than that. I think you maliciously misrepresented this bill. You are one. There have been several others. No wonder that the Congressmen and Senators are being swamped with mail by people who have become excited and confused when you write this kind of falsehood about the bill.

Siatos: "Senator, I honestly don't think that we intended it as a malicious falsehood. We sincerely feel —

Dodd: "If you didn't, I don't know what you intended. But I come back to the fact that you are a man of considerable background in this field. You are a graduate, I believe, of the University of California, you are a ballistics expert, you have written books and articles and manuals on guns, you are not an innocent by a long shot. You just show me anywhere in this bill where there is any reference to a man's religion and his politics.

Siatos: "As I indicated a moment ago, Senator, this is just editorializing.

Dodd: "It is a pretty name."

In a statement submitted to the subcommittee, Siatos gave seven reasons for opposing the gun control bill: (1) It would not, he claimed, disarm criminals who wanted to obtain firearms;

(2) it would "in effect, make it difficult if not impossible for many American citizens to own and use firearms — a right that dates back to Constitutional law . . . and in custom to our earliest colonial history"; (3) "the multiplicity of dealer fees, registration requirements, occupational fees, gun transportation restrictions and new burdens of paperwork inherent in S. 1592 will, if carried to their logical enforcement conclusion, in many cases force legitimate dealers of sporting guns out of business and open the door for future restrictive amendments . . . which could virtually eliminate gun ownership and use by law-abiding hunters, sports shooters and gun hobbyists"; (4) it would "create a potentially huge new federal policing and bureaucratic organization"; (5) "it specifically implies a federal distrust of U.S. citizens who have given no cause to be distrusted"; (6) "the total effect of the bill is, by implication, to tar all firearms generically with a black brush"; and (7) the bill "represents an infringement upon the American citizen's right to possess and bear arms guaranteed by the Second Amendment."

Again and again, Senator Dodd and other backers of the bill denied this litany of charges against the gun control legislation. With respect to the Second Amendment, for instance, which protects "the right of the people to keep and bear arms," they pointed out that the Supreme Court has held that the requirements of this amendment are met by the maintenance of a militia, which these days means the National Guard. In U.S. v. Miller, they noted, the court ruled that the Second Amendment does not prohibit enactment of federal legislation respecting firearms. Repeatedly, Dodd pointed out that his bill would prohibit only felons and fugitives from transporting rifles across state lines, not legitimate hunters. But still the letters bombarded Congress as hunters and sportsmen read the gun lobby's appeals and grew fearful that their rights would be infringed by the bill.

When Orth, the executive vice president of the NRA, appeared before the subcommittee, Dodd referred to the letter sent out April 9, 1965, to NRA members. "I have read it and reread it many times," he told Orth, "and I must say it is not an accurate presentation of the provisions of the bill." The following colloquy ensued:

Dodd: "Paragraph five of that letter says, and I quote from it, 'anyone engaged in the manufacture of ammunition would be required to have a $1,000 manufacturer's license.' Now, this is simply not true. The facts are, first, that shotgun ammunition is excluded from the coverage altogether. Secondly, the license fee for manufacturers of ammunition other than for destructive devices is $500. How did you happen to make that mistake?

Orth: "Well, Mr. Chairman, the NRA policy on the content of S. 1592, which is reflected verbatim in my letter of April 9, 1965, was prepared by a committee of the NRA board of directors. Serving on that committee were two presiding court judges and four prominent practicing attorneys. They studied S. 1592 conscientiously and earnestly, and in light of what the bill says, and what interpretations could be placed upon it, and found the broad administrative powers delegated to the Secretary of the Treasury . . . Mr. Chairman, if this committee of ours is guilty of an error as you charge, I would say that — very definitely — that it is not with any intent to mislead . . . whether the amount is $1,000 or $500 is rather immaterial. We think in all honesty, either a fee of $500 or $1,000 would have the same severe regulatory effects.

Dodd: "I don't want to make a big thing of it. The fact is it is not $1,000.

Orth: "That is correct. I admit that that is true.

Dodd: "And it is not the only untrue statement in that newsletter. The next sentence, after the one I read, says: 'Apparently this would apply to a club engaged in reloading for its members.' Now, again, there is no such language in the bill . . . But yet your letter to your membership makes it appear that this is so. How could that mistake have been made?

Orth: "Well, Mr. Chairman, the committee deliberately used the qualifying term 'apparently,' which is designed to convey the idea that in their opinion and understanding of the ammunition license provision this requirement would also apply to a club engaged in reloading for its members as a convenience.

Dodd: "I know they said 'apparently.' But you see the harm that was done. Members of Congress were deluded, particularly on this score, and it has caused a great deal of confusion about the bill. My colleagues have been calling me, and speaking to me about it, saying, 'is this in the bill?' And I pointed out to them there was no such language . . .

Orth: "Well, Mr. Chairman, I think it can be so misconstrued by looking at it. Very honestly — the language is such that it is susceptible to that construction, in my opinion."

Then Dodd took up another portion of the NRA letter: "If you transported your rifle or shotgun to another state for a lawful purpose, such as hunting, you would have to comply with such burdensome restrictions and red tape as might be required by the regulations." This "patently untrue" sentence, the Senator declared, caused more unfounded opposition to the gun bill than any other statement.

Dodd: "There are no restrictions in the bill pertaining to a **person, other than a criminal or a fugitive,** traveling in interstate or foreign commerce who transports his rifle or shotgun for a lawful purpose such as hunting. And this, I think, has caused the greatest difficulties for us. Decent sportsmen, good citizens, as a result of your letter, have understood that if this bill is passed they would not be allowed to take their shotguns from Connecticut to, say, Colorado, and hunt. Now, this is just not so.

Orth: "Well, within the overall authority granted to the Secretary of the Treasury, the language is so broad that he could make such determination, if he chose.

Dodd: "Oh, no. You point that out to me, will you? Show me what language you construe that by? In any event, I suppose the important thing is that maybe you and I can agree this is just not so, it is not in the bill, it never was intended to be. This has been my greatest task — explaining to my friends and my colleagues that there is no such language, no such intent.

Orth: "Well, Mr. Chairman, I can say this. There has been no attempt to give the impression that these things are so when they were not so. This letter was drafted by a committee as soon as they got the bill. There is no attempt at deliberate misrepresentation of the nature and scope of the bill in order to win suport for our approach.

Dodd: "I am not charging malice. But you see the dreadful effect that this mistake has had — I want to be charitable with you fellows and say it was a mistake."

Orth repeated that there had been no intent to mislead in the NRA letter, but he acknowledged that "sometimes in the heat of battle there are regrettable excesses which are not deliberate, or are born in misunderstanding." He thus pinpointed one of

the most serious problems arising from unregulated grassroots
lobbying.

At length the Senator and the NRA official, differing over interpretation, differing over approach, agreed to disagree.

Orth: "I guess we just don't like S. 1592.

Dodd: "I guess you just don't want this bill passed."

Virtually every major legislative issue that comes before Congress involves cross lobbying, also known as intergroup lobbying or, sometimes, logrolling. Since every organized pressure
group is anxious to convince Congress that its stand on a particular issue is in the public interest, it seeks to enlist the support of other organizations whose membership will add numerical
weight to the argument. Essentially, cross lobbying is based on
the theory that the public interest is composed of the sum
of the private interests. The more special interests that can be
swung behind a proposal, the reasoning goes, the closer it will
approximate the overall public interest, or seem to.

Just as labor has its natural allies, there are informal alliances
between the big business and professional organizations. When
the interest and dividend withholding plan came before the Senate Finance Committee, the U.S. Savings and Loan League
found a friend in the National Association of Manufacturers.
The "N.A.M. News" trotted out the boldface type and declared:
"It is imperative . . . that opponents of the legislation express
their views immediately to members of the Finance Committee
and to other members of the Senate." It added that "an avalanche of communications could determine the outcome." Just
what the Savings and Loan League had in mind.

When the United States Chamber of Commerce discussed
health care for the elderly through Social Security, the Chamber's wording caused no consternation in the offices of the American Medical Association. While the Medicare battle was on,
a Chamber bulletin devoted six paragraphs to arguments for the
Social Security approach and 35 paragraphs to arguments against
it. The bulletin concluded: "The health care situation of some
aged today does not warrant the adoption of a huge permanent
Social Security program. Medical care is available. The Kerr-
Mills bill should be given a chance. Voluntary health insurance
is growing." [7]

No organization places more reliance on cross lobbying than the American Medical Association, which sought to surround itself with as many kindred souls as possible in its fight against Medicare. This desire for friends dates back to the halcyon days of 1949 when the public relations firm of Whitaker and Baxter reported to the A.M.A. that it had lined up 1,829 organizations to oppose President Truman's health insurance program.

But inexorable social and economic forces — the growing proportion of elderly persons in the population, the unconscionably high cost of hospital care — worked to thin the lines of A.M.A. allies in the Medicare battle. The Chamber of Commerce and the National Association of Manufacturers stayed in camp, but the American Hospital Association, with more expertise in the field of hospital costs, "edged perceptibly closer to a working relationship with the government," even before Congress passed the Medicare bill, Michael J. O'Neill pointed out.[8] Despite intense pressure from the A.M.A., the hospital association, at a special meeting in 1962, conceded the need for further government aid to meet the health problems of the elderly. This was significant. While the A.M.A. solicited the support of every conceivable type of organization, it made a special effort to keep other health groups on its side in the Medicare fight.

The A.M.A.'s bitterest pill, in all likelihood, was the stand taken by the American Nurses' Association, which supported the original Forand bill and later the King-Anderson program that was enacted. For the nurses, however, their "venture in independent thinking has been costly," O'Neill reported. Miss Mathilda Scheuer, president of the nurses' association, charged that the A.M.A. used "rather unethical pressures" in its effort to persuade nurses to repudiate their national organization — to the point where some nurses expressed the fear "that if they continue to support the King-Anderson bill, they may lose their jobs [in] the hospitals."

Similar views were expressed by Miss Julia C. Thompson, Washinton representative of the nurses' association, in a statement in which she said: "There have been a variety of approaches, some through the district medical societies, some through individual physicians, some through the state medical society. Sometimes they [the doctors] have come to the state nurses' annual meetings with resolutions, asking the nurses' asso-

ciations to adopt them. They have asked to appear on the program without prior request. They have gone to board meetings
of state nurses' associations asking to present their views . . .
[although] the board meeting of an association is considered
a closed meeting . . . There have been instances where nurses
have been advised not to join the American Nurses' Association
because of the stand that we have taken on this legislation."

The nurses' group added that in areas where the A.M.A. pressure was heaviest there was a serious decline in membership in
the nurses' association.

When the Y.W.C.A. announced its support of the King-
Anderson bill, the A.M.A. broke into a rash. In an indignant
letter, Dr. F. J. L. (Bing) Blasingame, the A.M.A.'s executive
vice president, wrote to Miss Edith M. Lerrigo, general secretary
of the Young Women's Christian Association of the United
States, as follows: "The American Medical Association has been
shocked by the report that the resident national board of the
Y.W.C.A. has taken a stand favoring, in effect, socialized medicine . . . You can imagine our distress and the concern which
many Americans must feel when they learn that the resident
national board took a stand on a highly controversial political
matter, involving a very technical subject that has widespread
ramifications."

As one of their contributions to public enlightenment on this
very technical subject, A.M.A. spokesmen went around the country questioning the financial stability of the Social Security fund
on which 20,000,000 elderly persons, disabled workers and children rely. In a speech in 1963 before the Economic Club of
Detroit, for instance, Dr. Edward R. Annis, president of the
A.M.A., declared: "It's no secret to you that Social Security
is already in difficulty . . . There is nothing in the Social Security fund but I.O.U.'s . . . The future is bleak indeed. It's going
to have enough trouble standing on its own feet . . . And, if on
top of this we add any other scheme of financing, it's merely
going to add to the already overburdened Social Security
system."

As a result of these and other foreboding words from organized
medicine, the Social Security Administration received a large
number of pathetic letters from old folks fearful that their world
was about to come crashing down. Under Secretary of Health,

222 THE LOBBYISTS

Education and Welfare Ivan A. Nestingen and other government officials denounced the A.M.A. statements on Social Security as completely false and accused the medical group of "misleading, misinforming and deceiving the public on the basic issues."

The A.M.A.'s leaders were no more impressed by these categorical denials than they were by the fact that the Social Security funds have more than 22 billion dollars and are expected to face the bleak future in 1970 with assets of almost 33 billion dollars

One of Washington's oldest established, permanent floating lobbying alliances is that between the big business groups and the American Farm Bureau Federation, the country's largest and most conservative farming organization. For a business group, the U.S. Chamber pays a remarkable amount of attention to agricultural matters. And the Farm Bureau Federation frequently lays aside its hoe and delves into non-agricultural fiscal policy. When it does, the phraseology would gladden a businessmen's heart.

To work out the broad outlines of Chamber-N.A.M.-Farm Bureau-A.M.A. legislative strategy, a summit meeting is held each year at the plush Greenbrier Hotel in the West Virginia mountains. The Greenbrier Conference, as it is called, brings together the top officials of these four organizations and other sympathetic groups for three days of legislative discussions. The meeting is highly secret. Reporters are barred.

The conference grew out of informal meetings in 1950 between officials of the Farm Bureau Federation and the N.A.M. The original purpose was to coordinate a campaign of opposition to controls during the Korean war. After two meetings in Philadelphia in 1951, the group moved to the Greenbrier. The meetings have been held annually ever since.

Between 75 and 100 persons attended the 1963 conference, held on the weekend of January 18-20. Among those present were Philip M. Talbott, past president of the U.S. Chamber, and other Chamber officials; John C. Davidson, a vice president of the N.A.M., and Lambert H. Miller, N.A.M. general counsel; Charles B. Shuman, president of the Farm Bureau Federation and chairman of the conference committee; Dr. George M. Fister, then president of the A.M.A.; M. Monroe Kimbrel, president of the American Bankers Association; Harold D. Hodgkinson, president of the American Retail Federation; H. C. Lumb, a vice president of Republic Steel Corp. and a director of the N.A.M.; Dr. Austin Smith, president of the Pharmaceutical Manufacturers Association; Arthur P. Wilcox, president of the National Association of Real Estate Boards; Robert H. Craft, past president of the Investment Bankers Association; former Under Secretary of the Interior Clarence Davis, a guest of the U.S. Chamber; Joseph W. Hathcock of Standard Oil of New Jersey, and John Exter, senior vice president of the First National City Bank of New York.

At five plenary sessions and more informally at cocktail receptions in the Greenbrier's West Virginia Room and dinner in the Crystal Dining Room, the conference participants discussed such topics as the federal budget, tax reduction, "pressures and activities for consumer protection," "labor union power," and unemployment.

MONEY

"Before you can begin to think about politics at all, you have to abandon the notion that there is a war between good men and bad men . . . If politics is merely a guerrilla warfare between the bribed and the unbribed, then statecraft is not a human service but a moral testing ground." — *Walter Lippmann, A Preface to Politics.*

"You just put good, green folding money in their lily-white hands and be goddamn sure they know why you put it there." — *The regional counsel for a large oil company, quoted by Robert Engler.*[1]

In lobbying, money is not like an iceberg. Not even the tip shows. Just a very small sliver. Using a broad definition of lobbying, the Buchanan committee concluded that the business of influencing government is a billion-dollar-a-year industry. Yet in 1964 the amount reported to Congress as having been spent on lobbying was only $4,223,277.

A few of the activities which the Buchanan group defined as lobbying may belong more properly in the area of general propaganda, since they do not refer to specific legislative issues. Even without these, however, the committee's conclusion is still true today: only a small amount, a very small amount, of the money expended to enact or defeat legislation is disclosed to Congress and the public.

As the result of an imprecise law, a confusing Supreme Court decision and a total lack of enforcement, every person engaged in legislative activity is free to decide whether to register under the Lobbying Act, and if registered, how much money to report as having been spent on lobbying. Some do not register at all, and there is no one to gainsay them. Among those who do register, there are wide variations in the amount of money reported for lobbying. Many individual registrants report only trifling, strictly nominal sums. Others list a percentage of their income and expenses as attributable to lobbying. A few hardy souls report their entire income or close to it.

Among organizations that maintain a Washington office, there are all sorts of variations. Some do not register and report at all. A number of organizations report only a small percentage of the cost of operating their Washington office — salaries, rent, telephone, office supplies, printing and the like — as lobbying expenditures. These relatively small outlays make up the bulk of the four to five million-dollar total publicly recorded each year as spent on lobbying.

When it comes to the money expended on indirect, grassroots lobbying, the intent of the lobbying law to compel disclosure breaks down entirely. In this area the gap between appearance and reality is so enormous as to make mockery of Congress's desire — if it was Congress's desire. Of the hundreds of millions of dollars poured out every year to pass, defeat or amend legislation by arousing the voters to bring pressure on their Congressmen, only a few faint greenbacks find their way into the lobbying reports.

The basic lobbying law was enacted by Congress in 1946 as part of the LaFollette-Monroney Legislative Reorganization Act signed by President Truman on August 2 of that year. Formally known as the Regulation of Lobbying Act, or Title III of the Legislative Reorganization Act, it is a comparatively short law covering three and a half pages. It requires, in essence, that any person "who shall engage himself for pay or for any consideration for the purpose of attempting to influence the passage or defeat of any legislation by the Congress of the United States shall, before doing anything in furtherance of such object, register with the Clerk of the House of Representatives and the Secretary of the Senate."[2]

Registration as a lobbyist is required of any person who seeks to influence legislation, but only if he is being paid for this work or receiving some consideration of value. (There is a further big exemption, the "principal purpose" clause, which will be discussed later.) The term "person" includes individuals, partnerships, committees, associations, corporations and any other organization or group of persons.

Those who do no more than appear before a committee of

Congress to testify in support of or in opposition to legislation
are not subject to the registration requirement. Nor does it apply
to the extensive lobbying activities of public officials or to newspapers and magazines publishing editorial material or advertisements designed to influence legislation. There is no similar specific exemption for radio and television stations — in this respect,
as in many others, the lobbying law is not up to date.

The registration statement requires the lobbyist to state under
oath "his name and business address, the name and address of
the person by whom he is employed, and in whose interest he
appears or works, the duration of such employment, how much
he is paid and is to receive, by whom he is paid or is to be paid,
how much he is to be paid for expenses, and what expenses are
to be included." Thereafter, as long as his legislative activities
continue, the lobbyist (or lobbying organization) is required
to file a "detailed report" every three months, stating under oath
how much money he received and expended for lobbying in that
quarter, to whom he paid money and for what purpose, the proposed legislation he is supporting or opposing and the names
of any newspapers or magazines in which he "caused to be published any articles or editorials." In these quarterly reports, the
lobbyist is supposed to list the amount and source of all income
of $500 or more, and all expenditures of $10 or more. He must
report the name and address of each person to whom he paid $10
or more, the amount paid, the date of the payment and the
purpose.

However — and this is a big however — Section 307 of the
Lobbying Act states that the statute "shall apply to any person . . . who . . . directly or indirectly, solicits, collects, or receives
money or any other thing of value to be used *principally to aid,*
or *the principal purpose* of which person is to aid, in the accom-
plishment of any of the following purposes: (a) The passage or
defeat of any legislation by the Congress of the United States.
(b) To influence, directly or indirectly, the passage or defeat
of any legislation by the Congress of the United States." (Emphasis added.) The Lobbying Act, in other words, does not
apply unless the "principal purpose" of an individual or organization is lobbying.

The phrase "principal purpose" has been a merry-go-round
of confusion over the years. It is the biggest loophole in the

lobbying law. How do you define "principal purpose"? What measurement do you use? Invoking this clause, many Washington attorneys and representatives of corporations and trade associations assert that their principal purpose is not lobbying. They describe their main function as reporting to their employer on the status of legislation and/or governmental affairs generally. They analyze legislation. They say they deal with the executive branch of government (where the lobbying law does not apply) as much as the legislative branch, or more.

Many, in short, who are very much concerned with legislative matters do not register as lobbyists. Others register but report only a very small part of their salary — or none at all — as having been paid for the principal purpose of lobbying. Their expenses are treated in the same modest way — the cost of a few taxi fares to and from Capitol Hill, perhaps a lunch or two.

Early in the game, the "principal purpose" phrase was seized upon by some large organizations as exempting them from registering and reporting under the lobbying law. The National Association of Manufacturers, in particular, resisted the Lobbying Act from the start. After analyzing the law, the N.A.M. concluded that it was not covered, on the ground that it was a multipurpose organization, that influencing legislation was not its principal purpose, that its lobbying activities were minimal and that none of its income was received for this specific purpose.

In 1947, after the Lobbying Act had been in effect for a little more than a year, the Justice Department made its only attempt at administering and policing the law. The Attorney General at that time, Tom C. Clark (now an Associate Justice of the Supreme Court), set up a special lobbying unit in the department. The unit was headed by Special Assistant Attorney General Irving R. Kaufman and had a staff of ten lawyers and six assistants. Copies of all lobbying registrations and reports were sent to this group, which checked them for accuracy, completeness and compliance with the law. The unit looked into alleged violations of the lobbying law and saw to it that those who were required to register did so.

A year later Kaufman was appointed a federal appellate judge and the work of the special unit was transferred to the department's criminal division. For a time the lobbying group preserved a degree of identity within the criminal division, but

in 1953 it was broken up. From then on the Justice Department
ceased to administer the Lobbying Act.

In the brief period that he directed the unit, Kaufman admin-
istered the lobbying law energetically. His eye soon fell on the
N.A.M. Officers of the big business organization were called in
and asked to furnish information on the N.A.M.'s legislative operation. Subsequently Kaufman informed the N.A.M. that in the
opinion of the Justice Department it had not complied fully with
the lobbying law and requested that it do so by submitting a
more complete account of its receipts and expenditures.

The N.A.M. complied, under protest, and then filed suit for
a declaratory judgment in the United States district court for the
District of Columbia. A three-judge panel of the district court
upheld the N.A.M. and ruled that the financial disclosure requirements of the Lobbying Act, including Section 307, were unconstitutional. The court held that the disclosure provisions were
"manifestly too indefinite and vague to constitute an ascertain-
able standard of guilt" and therefore violated the due process
clause of the Fifth Amendment.[3] In the opinion of the judges
the Lobbying Act had failed to state precisely what would constitute an offense under the Act. But when the ruling reached
the Supreme Court, on an appeal by the Justice Department, the
high court overruled the district court on a technical point and
directed the lower court to dismiss the N.A.M.'s complaint. The
Lobbying Act remained in effect.

Nevertheless, the N.A.M. ceased reporting any expenditures,
as an organization, under the lobbying law. It has not done so
since 1950. Some other large organizations — among them the
American Bankers Association, Americans for Constitutional Action and the American Public Power Association — likewise do
not register or report as organizations, although some of their
individual employees register as lobbyists. The United States
Chamber of Commerce and the American Medical Association file
reports but under protest. A good many organizations, pro-
fessing complete confusion as to whether the Lobbying Act
applies to them, register and report at least some expenditures
on the assumption that "when in doubt, file."

Again in 1954, the Lobbying Act reached the Supreme Court
in the test case of U.S. v. Harriss. This time the court handed
down a full decision on the lobbying law but just what the deci-

sion meant has been a matter of considerable uncertainty ever since. In effect, the court rewrote the Lobbying Act, but its version was almost as murky as Congress's originial product.

The defendants in the case were Robert M. Harriss, a New York cotton broker; Ralph W. Moore, a Washington commodity trader; James E. McDonald, agriculture commissioner of Texas; Tom Linder, agriculture commissioner of Georgia, and the National Farm Committee, a Texas corporation. They were charged with attempting to influence the passage of agriculture legislation without registering or reporting under the Lobbying Act. In order to test the lobbying law, Harriss had refused to register when he raised money to lobby for farm price supports. The Justice Department indictments charged that Harriss made payments to Moore, who was secretary of the National Farm Committee, for the purpose of pressuring Congress on legislation, and that Moore made similar payments to McDonald and Linder, all without registering as lobbyists.

A federal district court dismissed the charges against Harriss and the others on the ground that the Lobbying Act was unconstitutional. As in the initial ruling on the N.A.M., the court held that the law was too vague and indefinite to meet the constitutional requirement that no person shall be fined or imprisoned without due process of law. The issue was whether the lobbying law specified what would constitute an offense in terms that a person of ordinary intelligence could understand, and the district court held that it did not. The court ruled further that the registration and financial reporting requirements of the Act violated the First Amendment's guarantees of freedom of speech and assembly, and that some of its penalty provisions violated the First Amendment's guarantee of the right to petition Congress. The Justice Department appealed this ruling to the Supreme Court.

The Supreme Court, in a 5 to 3 decision on June 7, 1954, held that the lobbying law was constitutional and that Congress could compel the disclosure of lobbying activities. To hold otherwise, Chief Justice Earl Warren wrote in the majority opinion, "would be to deny Congress in large measure the power of self-protection." [4] But the court went on to change the Lobbying Act in major respects. The majority opinion held that, in order to be subject to the Act, a person must solicit, collect or receive contributions (salary, dues, etc.); that "one of the main purposes" of such person or such contributions must be to influence the passage or defeat of legislation, and that the intended method of influencing legislation must be through *direct* communication with members of Congress. All three tests had to apply before an individual or organization was required to register and report. If the individual or group came under one, another might not apply. In many cases, this is exactly what has happened.

The Supreme Court opinion in U.S. v. Harriss did a lot of things, not all of them consistent:

1. It removed a major lobbying technique — indirect or grass-roots lobbying — from the scrutiny of the Lobbying Act. Henceforth, the vast sums spent on grassroots campaigns to bring pressure did not have to be disclosed.

2. It limited the disclosure requirement to the sums spent on direct communication with Congress. Or did it? At one point the court declared that "the legislative history of the [Lobbying] Act makes clear that, at the very least, Congress sought disclosure of such direct pressures, exerted by the lobbyists themselves or through their hirelings *or through an artificially stimulated letter campaign.*" (Emphasis supplied.) So it seemed that one form of indirect lobbying was to be covered, to an undefined extent, by the Lobbying Act. The Supreme Court defined letter campaigns as a form of direct lobbying. Some lobbyists agree with this definition; some do not. Some lobbying organizations report the cost of printing and mailing out material aimed at arousing their members to write letters to their Congressmen; some do not. The test apparently is whether the material specifically urges the recipient to write his Senator or Representative on a piece of legislation, or whether it is general in tone.

3. It replaced the "principal purpose" test with a "substantial" or "one of the main purposes" test. "The legislative history of the Act," said the court, "indicates that the term 'principal' was adopted merely to exclude . . . those contributions and persons having only an 'incidental' purpose of influencing legislation. Conversely, the 'principal purpose' requirement does not exclude a contribution which *in substantial part* is to be used to influence legislation through direct communication with Congress or a person whose activities *in substantial part* are directed to influencing

legislation through direct communication with Congress." (Emphasis added.) "Substantial purpose" may be a little easier to measure, although it still leaves a lot of room for argument. Even so, all three tests must still apply before registration and financial reporting are required.

Warren said that the court was construing the Act narrowly in order to avoid doubts as to its constitutionality, and that as construed the Act did not violate the First Amendment's guarantees of free speech and petition or the Fifth Amendment's requirement of definiteness (due process). The principal respect in which the court narrowed the lobbying law was to limit registration and reporting to those who engage in direct contact lobbying.

The provisions of the Lobbying Act, Warren declared in the majority opinion, should be construed as referring only to "lobbying in its commonly accepted sense," i.e., direct contact with members of Congress. With this limitation, he then went on to state what has become the most widely accepted justification for enactment of a law dealing with lobbying: "Present-day legislative complexities are such," the Chief Justice wrote, "that individual members of Congress cannot be expected to explore the myriad pressures to which they are regularly subjected. Yet full realization of the American ideal of government by elected representatives depends to no small extent on their ability to properly evaluate such pressures. Otherwise the voice of the people may all too easily be drowned out by the voice of special interest groups seeking favored treatment while masquerading as proponents of the public weal. This is the evil which the Lobbying Act was designed to help prevent.

"Toward that end, Congress has not sought to prohibit these pressures. It has merely provided for a modicum of information from those who, for hire, attempt to influence legislation or who collect or spend funds for that purpose. It wants only to know who is being hired, who is putting up the money, and how much. It acted in the same spirit and for a similar purpose in passing the Federal Corrupt Practices Act — to maintain the integrity of a basic governmental process . . . Under these circumstances, we believe that Congress, at least within the bounds of the [Lobbying] Act as we have construed it, is not constitutionally forbidden to require the disclosure of lobbying activities. To do so would be to deny Congress in large measure the power of self-protection."

Warren was right, of course, when he warned that the voice of the people all too easily can be drowned out by the thunder of special interest groups posing as proponents of the public weal. But his argument in other respects is open to question.

Is it true that individual members of Congress cannot be expected to know the sources of the myriad pressures to which they are regularly subjected? As far as direct contact lobbying is concerned, it is a rare instance indeed in which the Congressman does not know the identity of the man who comes to see him in his office, as well as the identity of the lobbyist's employer. The Congressman is not naive. He knows who is trying to persuade him, and usually why. The court's majority opinion upheld the Lobbying Act's requirement that this type of pressure must be disclosed to the Congressman, which is fine but probably not really necessary.

It may be somewhat more difficult for members of Congress to be as fully aware of the sources of indirect, grassroots pressure. The letters and telegrams that pour in from constituents often influence the legislator's vote. In some instances, however, he may not know or fully comprehend that they were prompted by an organized pressure campaign. It is precisely this kind of lobbying pressure that the Supreme Court decision in U.S. v. Harriss appeared to have removed in large measure from the requirements of the Lobbying Act. The majority opinion said that members of Congress must be able to evaluate such pressures, to put them in perspective, and then took away the chief means of doing so.

Even so, most Congressmen and their staffs usually are able to spot an organized grassroots pressure campaign. The letters and telegrams tend to use similar wording; sometimes they are even mimeographed. In this instance, too, the legislator knows that he is being pressured and who is doing it, although he may lack information about some of the details and usually does not know how much money is being spent to put on the heat. It is the public, more than the Congressman, that is in the dark about the organized pressure campaigns that operate against the public interest. Congress would benefit if the financial disclosure re-

quirement for indirect lobbying were restored to the Lobbying
Act, and the public would benefit even more.

Despite the Supreme Court's effort to retain the constitutionality of the lobbying law by interpreting it narrowly, the
decision in U.S. v. Harriss left the law in bad shape. While the
court succeeded to some extent in defining who and what were
covered by the Lobbying Act, it removed the real lobbying
money from public scrutiny. Justice Robert H. Jackson, in his
dissent from the Harriss decision, noted that Congress had
enacted a statute to cover "the raising and spending of funds
for the purpose of influencing Congressional action *directly or
indirectly.*" (Emphasis added.) "But," said Jackson, "the majority opinion entirely deletes 'indirectly' and narrows 'directly'
to mean 'direct communication with members of Congress.' "
These two interpretations, he declared, "leave the [Lobbying]
Act touching only a part of the practices Congress deemed sinister." A very small part, he might have added.

However, Justice Jackson contended that the constitutionality
of the lobbying law, as written, could not be defended. "I think,"
he said, "we should point out the defects and limitations which
condemn this act so clearly that the court cannot sustain it as
written, and leave its rewriting to Congress. After all, it is Congress that should know from experience both the good in the
right of petition and the evils of professional lobbying."

Similar concern about the constitutionality of the law was
expressed by Justices William O. Douglas and Hugo L. Black,
the other dissenters. (Justice Clark, having been Attorney General, took no part in the decision.) Douglas argued that the
question was whether the lobbying law "either forbids or requires the doing of an act in terms so vague that men of common
intelligence must necessarily guess at its meaning and differ as
to its application." In his opinion the lobbying law was vague
in this respect and therefore "fails to meet the standards required
by due process of law." The language of the law, Douglas said,
"is so broad that one who writes a letter or makes a speech or
publishes an article or distributes literature or does many of the
other things with which appellees [Harriss and the others] are
charged has no fair notice when he is close to the prohibited line."

Authorities on lobbying, including the staff of Congressional

Quarterly, have concluded that the original wording of the Act, together with the Supreme Court decision, left many loopholes.

First is the matter of collecting and receiving money. The Supreme Court's decision held that the lobbying law applies only to individuals and groups that solicit, collect or receive money for a substantial purpose of influencing legislation through direct contact with members of Congress. Under the court's interpretation, individuals or groups that spend their own funds for this purpose, rather than receiving or collecting money from others, do not have to register and report under the Lobbying Act.

The second loophole is the "principal purpose" clause in the original lobbying law, which has been discussed previously.

Another loophole is the court's decision that the lobbying law applies only to direct contact with Congress. Although the court said that direct contact included "artificially stimulated" letter-writing campaigns, many groups do not report the cost of this type of grassroots lobbying, even when their advertisements and other exhortations urge the writing of letters to Congressmen on specific legislation.

Still another ambiguity arises because the lobbying law and the Supreme Court decision are not clear as to what kinds of contacts with Congress are covered by the registration and financial disclosure requirements. This is related to the third loophole. The Lobbying Act itself specifically exempts testimony before Congressional committees from the provisions of the Act, and in a 1950 case involving ex-Representative Roger C. Slaughter of Missouri, a federal court held that this extends to those who help prepare such testimony. Beyond that, however, there are vast areas of uncertainty. Some individuals and organizations, public relations firms among them, assert that the material they present to Congress is strictly informational and therefore not subject to the lobbying law. Others say that their legislative function is confined to reporting to their employers on the status of legislation and that they, too, are not required to register as lobbyists because they do not try to influence legislation.

Another loophole in the lobbying law is that it leaves it up to the individual lobbyist and pressure group to determine what portion of their expenditures they report as lobbying spending. As Congressional Quarterly points out, some organizations have gained reputations as big lobbying spenders simply because they interpret the law more strictly and list a larger percentage of their Washington expenditures in their lobbying reports. To some extent this accounts for the American Medical Association's consistent ranking at or near the top of the annual list of big lobbying spenders. The A.M.A. simply ascribes a larger percentage of its Washington operation to lobbying than do many other organizations.

Another weakness in the Lobbying Act is the fact that it applies only to efforts to influence Congress and not to lobbying in the executive branch and the federal regulatory agencies.

Still another loophole in the Act is the lack of any agency to enforce it. The lobbying law does not designate anyone to investigate the truthfulness of the spending reports and to take action against those who should file and do not or those who file inaccurate or incomplete reports. There have been proposals in recent years that the Comptroller General be designated to enforce the lobbying law, but Congress has taken no action on these recommendations. Since the Act carries criminal penalties for violations, the Justice Department has power to prosecute violators, but Congress gave the department no instructions to investigate the lobbying reports for truthfulness and completeness. There is a prosecutor, in other words, but no policeman.

The Harriss case, incidentally, was remanded to the federal district court for further proceedings. The charge against Harriss subsequently was dismissed on the ground that he had not received or solicited money for the purpose of lobbying but was, in fact, the person who had furnished the money. The charge against Linder was dismissed on the ground that he was a public official who had been acting in his official capacity. The indictment against Moore was dismissed because a key witness had died. The National Farm Committee pleaded nolo contendere and was acquitted.

Except for the few who report their entire income, the individual lobbyist usually decides how much of his salary to report by determining how much of his time is devoted to the principal purpose of direct lobbying. He then reports that percentage of his income as lobbying income. The same formula generally is used for reporting expenses. The expenses are seldom itemized as to amount, recipient, date and purpose, although this is required by law if the outlay is $10 or more.

A lobbyist who had been a regulatory agency official in the Eisenhower administration filed a report stating that he had worked for enactment of an amendment to an international trade law. He listed $24 in expenses for the quarter, and no salary. A sugar lobbyist filed a report stating that he had been interested in three bills. He listed $198 in expenses for the quarter, and no salary. A lobbyist for one of the nation's leading manufacturers listed $120 in salary and expenses of $5 for travel, food, lodging and entertainment.

The reasons cited by these three men — and many others — are essentially the same. They say their salaries are not paid for the principal purpose of lobbying and therefore, under the law, do not have to be reported. "None of my salary is ever allocated to any specific activity," one of the lobbyists insisted. Said another: "My association would pay my salary if I never went near Congress, and therefore I refrain from reporting any of my salary as received for lobbying." The third was equally frank: "If I go to see Congressman X, all that is involved is the cost of a taxi fare, say $1.50, and 30 minutes of my time. You have to see a lot of Congressmen to run that up." This is the prevailing pattern in the never-never land of lobbying money.

The sugar lobbyist spoke of his Congressional work as an incidental part of his job, occupying "not more than 5 to 10 percent of my time." He said his principal function is to serve as a sort of "central listening post in Washington," reporting to his employer on all governmental activities affecting the sugar industry. This involves regular contacts with the State Department, the Agriculture Department, the Commerce Department, the foreign aid agency and the Alliance for Progress as well as Congress. These contacts with the executive branch do not come under the lobbying law.

Terry Rice, until recently chief lobbyist for the United States Chamber of Commerce, states in his lobbying reports that he was advised by legal counsel that there was some "uncertainty" about whether he was required to register and report under the Lobbying Act, in the light of U.S. v. Harriss. Rice asserted that if it should later be held that he was covered by the law, the portion of his salary which could be considered remuneration for lobbying would not exceed $1,250 a quarter, or $5,000 a year, which he reported. His listed expenses were small — $25 in one three-month period, for example.

Similarly, Ted Compton, chief lobbyist for the N.A.M., stated that the part of his salary that "by any possibility could be called remuneration for lobbying" amounted to $2,000, or $8,000 a year. His reported expenses for that quarter were $592. In the next quarter he again listed $2,000, and expenses of $501. For one three-month period he did not report any salary or expenses at all, explaining that Congress was not in session. Compton files his lobbying reports in the form of letters to the Clerk of the House, saying that he has been advised by counsel to report in that manner. The financial reporting space on the regular lobbying form is left blank. In his letters, the N.A.M. lobbyist, who is a vice president of the organization, declares: "My principal responsibility in connection with legislation is to analyze and report on important legislative programs affecting industry."

Andrew Biemiller, chief lobbyist for the AFL-CIO, reported $18,700 in salary in a recent year, and $1,769 in lobbying expenses. One of his assistants, John H. Beidler, reported $13,939 in salary and $758 in expenses. Sidney Zagri, legislative counsel for the Teamsters Union, reported $25,652 in salary.

On the other hand, a lobbyist for one of the nation's best-known professional organizations reported total salary of $194 and total expenses of 50 cents in a recent quarter. In the next three months, his salary went up — to $387. But his expenses tapered off. He reported nothing in this category. The six lobbyists for this organization reported a total of $6,157 in salaries, or a little over $1,000 each, in one quarter. That would make their annual salaries, on the face of it, about $4,000 each. Their combined expenses in one three-month period were reported as $526. During this period their organization was engaged in a massive lobbying effort against a major bill.

It is instructive to compare the lobbying data filed by a lady who represents a peace group with those filed by five lobbyists for one of America's largest corporations, with annual net profits of well over a billion dollars. The lady lobbyist reported total receipts of more than $64,000 and lobbying expenses of over $20,000. In the same year the corporate lobbyists reported total salary of $6,107 and $730 in expenses — for all five of them. At that time, they were engaged in a successful lobbying campaign to put through an important bill of great advantage to their company. The five lobbyists attached statements to their reports asserting that influencing the passage or defeat of legislation was not their principal purpose or that of their company. They said they presented the views of their employer on legislation to members of Congress "as the occasion arises," but they added that their "legislative activities" comprised only "a minor part" of their duties. They further stated that the filing of lobbying reports was not to be construed as an admission that the lobbying law applied to them or their company.

Senator William Proxmire, Wisconsin Democrat, made a study of oil and gas lobbyists and reported: "Of the 41 lobbyists who did file reports, 36 violated the law by failing to give their specific legislative interests, 21 failed to comply with the law by stating whether they had received contributions of more than $500, 20 illegally refused to list the parties they had paid money to, and 17 did not state the nature of their employers' businesses as the law requires."

The lobbying law leaves it entirely up to the individual to determine how much income and expenses he reports. The lobbyist alone decides how much, if any, of his salary and expenditures are for the "principal purpose" or "main purpose" of lobbying. And he decides what these terms mean in the first place.

There is no enforcement. The Lobbying Act is a law without an enforcement provision, except for the general prosecution powers of the Justice Department. Although specific penalties for violations are provided, the Act is entirely silent on who shall administer it and who shall enforce it. No one checks the hundreds of lobbying registrations and reports that come in each year. They are filed with the Clerk of the House and the Secretary of the Senate, neither of whom has the statutory authority or the staff to scrutinize the information for accuracy, completeness or compliance with the law. The Clerk and the Secretary merely act as repositories for the reports. Four times a year the reports are published in the Congressional Record in small print.

And that's it. The lobbying reports, once filed, vanish into a limbo of indifference. They are stored away in a dusty, obscure office of the House file clerk on the fifth floor of the old House

office building. They can be viewed by Congressmen, reporters
or citizens who know how to track down the out-of-the-way
office, but few are interested. After a report is two years old,
the permission of the House clerk is required to inspect it, and
this is seldom given.

Since 1953 the Justice Department has taken the position
that it does not have the responsibility for administering the
Lobbying Act. When Representative John H. Dent, Pennsylvania Democrat, asked Attorney General Robert F. Kennedy
about this in 1961, Kennedy replied: "The Department of Justice does not administer the so-called Lobbying Act, and has
no authority to investigate 'lobbying' as such. This department's
only function with respect to 'lobbying' is to investigate and
prosecute those who, being required to register and file reports
under the provisions of the so-called Lobbying Act, fail to do so."

Judson Bowles, the Justice Department attorney who receives
complaints of non-compliance with the lobbying law, says he gets
five or six complaints a year. Some come from organizations
which have registered and feel they are at a disadvantage because
another organization has not; others are from members of Congress. Some of the complaints involve small groups which did
not register because of unfamiliarity with the law. These usually
turn out to be cases in which registration is not required, or
else the organization registers after being informed of the
complaint.

Bowles' office has only five lawyers and many other duties.
If he receives an outside complaint of non-compliance with the
Lobbying Act and if the complaint appears to to warrant investigation, he refers it to the Federal Bureau of Investigation.
But the Justice Department does not initiate such inquiries on
its own, since it is not the administering agency. It no longer
receives copies of the lobbying registrations and reports. Between
1946 and 1965 a total of 7,151 individuals and organizations
registered as lobbyists. But only four prosecutions have ever
been brought for violation of the Lobbying Act, the last one
in 1956. In only one case, involving the Superior Oil Company,
were the defendants found guilty — and they pleaded guilty.

The amount of money spent by large organizations which
maintain permanent lobbying operations in Washington is sub-

ject, in most cases, to the same modesty that afflicts most individual lobbyists. Since 1950 there has been a general downward trend in the amount of lobbying spending reported to Congress. As compiled by Congressional Quarterly, the totals since 1947 have been as follows:

1947	$ 5,191,856		1956	$ 3,957,120
1948	6,763,480		1957	3,818,177
1949	7,969,710		1958	4,132,719
1950	10,303,204		1959	4,281,468
1951	8,771,096		1960	3,854,374
1952	4,823,981		1961	3,986,095
1953	4,445,841		1962	4,211,304
1954	4,286,158		1963	4,223,605
1955	4,365,843		1964	4,223,277

Taken at their face value, these figures would indicate that the total amount spent annually to influence Congress dropped by $6,500,000 between 1950 and 1960. In the same period the cost of living rose by 20 percent.

The 1954 decision in U.S. v. Harriss is generally credited with starting the downward trend, by removing the disclosure requirement for money spent on indirect lobbying. However, the Congressional Quarterly figures show that the trend began before 1954. The big break came between 1951 and 1952. Some possible reasons suggest themselves: the American Medical Association's successful lobbying effort against President Truman's health care plan was pretty well over, and most of the big lobbying groups probably decided that the district court decision in the earlier N.A.M. case meant that they could reduce the amount of lobbying spending they reported. Moreover, the Justice Department's lobbying unit virtually ceased to function about this time.

There is no doubt that the Harriss decision helped accelerate the downward trend. In 1953 the National Association of Electric Companies reported lobbying spending of $547,789; in 1954 it reported $110,537. In 1953 the Association of American Railroads reported $235,728; $185,380 in 1954 and $104,806 in 1955. The Supreme Court decision came on June 7, 1954, giving the big lobbying organizations two more quarters in that year in which to revise their financial reports downward.

Congressional Quarterly's figures for lobbying spending re-

ported to Congress from 1947 through 1964 add up to a total
of $93,609,326. Using the Buchanan committee's billion-a-year
rule of thumb, the actual total would be in the neighborhood
of 18 billion dollars.

From 1948 through 1962 the top reported lobbying spender
was the American Medical Association, with total expenditures
of $4,075,804 in that period. The National Association of Elec-
tric Companies was next, with $2,948,842, followed by:

Committee for Constitutional Government	$2,484,403
AFL-CIO	2,119,671
American Farm Bureau Federation	2,041,702
Association of American Railroads	1,947,396
National Co-Operative Milk Producers Federation	1,443,641
United Federation of Postal Clerks	1,427,578
American Legion	1,339,861
National Association of Real Estate Boards	1,297,679
Southern States Industrial Council	1,216,760
United States Savings and Loan League	962,420
United World Federalists	952,635
National Housing Conference	893,141
National Small Business Association	815,432
International Association of Machinists, District Lodge 44	758,627
National Farmers Union	751,298
United States Chamber of Commerce	715,947
National Committee for Insurance Taxation	701,238
Townsend Plan, Inc.	699,666

Congressional Quarterly's tabulations show that the business
community continues to outspend other special interest groups
and general welfare lobbyists. In every year since 1949 the
amounts spent on lobbying by business groups have exceeded
the outlays of labor unions, citizens' groups, and agriculture,
military and veterans and professional organizations, usually
by wide margins. In 1964 the reported lobbying totals were:
business, $1,361,428; citizens' groups, $1,065,197; employee and
labor organizations, $945,071; farm groups, $365,472; professional groups, $331,616, and military and veterans organizations,
$154,493.

The ten top reported lobbying spenders in 1964 were:

Coordinating Committee for Fundamental American Freedoms	$319,825
AFL-CIO	153,542
United Federation of Postal Clerks	131,913

Council for a Livable World (a group of scientists interested primarily in disarmament) 123,982
American Legion 123,914
American Farm Bureau Federation 123,645
International Association of Machinists, District Lodge 44............ 123,569
United States Savings and Loan League 98,233
National Housing Conference 88,224
National Farmers Union 80,946

The top reported spender, the Coordinating Committee for Fundamental American Freedoms, conducted an intensive lobbying campaign against the Civil Rights Act of 1964. The committee was financed by such groups as the Mississippi State Sovereignty Commission, and after the civil rights bill was enacted, the committee ceased its lobbying activities. Its reported spending of $319,825 was the largest amount listed by any single organization between 1953 and 1964. In 1963 the coordinating committee was among the top lobbying spenders with $127,827.

Even before the Harriss decision, when the cost of grassroots lobbying still had to be reported, the lobbying figures submitted to Congress often were subject to dispute. In the four years from 1949 through 1952 the American Medical Association reported total lobbying expenditures of $3,310,994. But Whitaker and Baxter, the public relations firm that ran the A.M.A.'s gigantic lobbying campaign against Truman's health insurance plan, reported to the A.M.A. board of trustees that the campaign cost $4,678,157 from the beginning of 1949 to the middle of 1952.[5]

What the A.M.A. spent in its *Gotterdammerung* grassroots effort against the Kennedy-Johnson version of the health care plan is its own business, thanks to the Harriss decision. The National Council of Senior Citizens, which backed the Medicare plan, estimated that the A.M.A. spent more than $7,000,000 in 1962 to convince the American people that the doctor-patient relationship would be destroyed and the national will enervated if the Social Security system were extended to include health care for the elderly. The senior citizens council arrived at its estimate this way:

The American Medical Political Action Committee, political fund-raising arm of the A.M.A., claimed that one-fourth to one-third of the A.M.A.'s 188,000 doctor members had joined AMPAC. Memberships in AMPAC range from $5 (for students) to $99. The senior citizens council estimated that one-fourth of the A.M.A.'s members contributed an average total of $50 to AMPAC or its state or county equivalents, for a figure of $2,500,000, which it called a conservative estimate. Further, Dr. Edward R. Annis, then president of the A.M.A., reportedly told a meeting of the Public Relations Society of America in Boston that the A.M.A.'s public relations budget to defeat the Medicare bill was $1,300,000 in 1962 and would be considerably higher in 1963. In addition, thousands of doctors mailed out A.M.A. literature to their patients along with their bills. It has been estimated that a mailing of this size would have cost the A.M.A. about $1,000,000.

The National Council of Senior Citizens pointed out that the 2,000 state and county medical societies were offered prepared advertisements from A.M.A. headquarters in Chicago. These were placed in thousands of community newspapers from coast to coast at the expense of the state and local societies at an estimated cost of $2,000,000. A limited appeal by the council to elderly persons to send in examples of these ads produced more than 250 responses. Adding in the cost of letter-writing campaigns by physicians' wives and medical students brought the estimated 1962 total to more than $7,000,000. Other estimates ranged as high as $12,000,000.

In 1962 the A.M.A. reported to Congress that it spent a total of $83,076 on lobbying. This sum represented part of the cost of operating the A.M.A.'s Washington office, including 10 percent of the office overhead and part of the salaries of its six registered lobbyists, all but one of whom are based in Washington, together with their travel expenses. In the fourth quarter of 1962, for instance, the overhead for the A.M.A.'s Washington office was $8,107, of which $810 was reported as lobbying expenditures. Telegraph and telephone costs in that three-month period were $4,518, of which $451 was reported as lobbying expenses. In the first quarter of 1962 the A.M.A. listed as lobbying expenditures $24,000 for printing and distribution of various types of material.

Partly because it reports some of its Washington overhead as attributable to lobbying, the A.M.A. has the distinction of having submitted the three highest individual lobbying figures of all time — $1,522,683 in 1949 and $1,326,078 in 1950, when it was campaigning against the Truman health plan, and $951,570 in the first quarter of 1965, when its effort to defeat the new Medicare bill was reaching a climax.

As part of the 1965 campaign, according to the A.M.A. News, advertisements were placed in Readers Digest, TV Guide, Time, Newsweek, U.S. News and World Report, Broadcasting, Editor and Publisher, Life, the Saturday Evening Post, the Saturday Review and Nation's Agriculture. On June 9, 1965, the A.M.A. ran advertisements in about 100 major daily newspapers opposing the Johnson administration's Medicare bill and urging the public to "let your Senators, your Congressman and the President know your views on this vital issue." On June 17, the A.M.A. presented a nationwide television broadcast on the American Broadcasting Company network, entitled "Health Care at the Crossroads." It was all in vain. The Medicare bill was approved by both houses of Congress and signed into law by President Johnson on July 30, 1965, ending a 30-year struggle.

Perhaps sensing that night was falling, the A.M.A. spent heavily in 1964 and 1965. The amount it reported spending in 1964 was not especially high — $45,515 — but the actual outlay was huge. In October of that year the medical group conducted a press, radio and television campaign against the Medicare bill but did not report the cost of this under the lobbying law because the public was not directly urged to communicate with Congress on the issue. The October campaign included a series of spot announcements on the ABC television network aimed at reaching 142 major population areas. There were also spot broadcasts on radio and advertisements in no less than 8,000 daily and weekly newspapers, at an estimated cost of $1,000,000. Expensive magazine ads were another feature; one in Life magazine on October 16, 1964 stated: "The supporters of the proposed Medicare tax would have you believe that passage of this controversial bill is urgent . . . that persons over 65 are deprived of needed medical care because they can't pay for it. Nothing could be further from the truth." The campaign was handled by the Madison Avenue advertising firm of Fuller, Smith and Ross, among whose other clients have been Barry Goldwater and Robert A. Taft Sr.

The backers of the Medicare plan were equally active. The National Council of Senior Citizens persuaded radio and tele-

vision stations on several occasions to give it free time in which
to reply to the A.M.A.'s anti-Medicare broadcasts. On October 25,
1964, the council got a free half-hour of television time from
the Columbia Broadcasting System to present a program, "Rx
for a Nightmare," and on June 18, 1965, a free half-hour from
ABC television for a show, "Medicare, the American Way."
ABC not only gave the council the free half hour but absorbed
most of the production costs.

The senior citizens council had a budget of about $150,000 in
each of the three years 1963 through 1965. About two-thirds of
this came from dues and contributions from affiliated organizations; the remaining third was supplied by the Democratic Party
and the AFL-CIO. Although the AFL-CIO and the council were
the leading non-governmental lobbyists for the Medicare bill,
the council did not register as a lobbying group. Its deputy
director, William R. Hutton, explained that the group construed
its function as being primarily to conduct informational and educational work among elderly persons and the general public,
rather than putting pressure on Congress directly.

This was another example of the use of "informational and
educational" work as a euphemism for grassroots lobbying, the
cost of which does not have to be disclosed to Congress or the
public. The council's indirect lobbying undoubtedly played a
major role in whipping up sentiment for the Medicare program.
In 1962 the council helped organize 35 mass rallies in support
of the bill around the nation, topped off by a rally at Madison
Square Garden with President Kennedy as the main speaker.
The group also organized petitions and letter-writing campaigns
directed at Congress and arranged for visits to Washington by
delegations of elderly persons backing the Medicare bill.

Many other large organizations follow the A.M.A.'s practice
of reporting a percentage of their office costs and salaries as
attributable to lobbying. The United States Savings and Loan
League, for example, allocates varying percentages of the salaries
of some of its officers and employees to lobbying. In a recent
year, Norman Strunk, executive vice president of the League,
was listed as having received a salary of $65,000, of which the
League reported $6,500 (10 percent) as applicable to legislative
activity, i.e., lobbying. Stephen G. Slipher, an assistant vice

president and one of the League's chief Washington lobbyists, received $45,000, of which $11,250 (25 percent) was reported by the League as lobbying costs. Glen Troop, another League lobbyist, received $26,000, of which 25 percent was reported as lobbying expenditures in the first quarter and 50 percent in each of the next three quarters, for a total of $11,373.

Altogether, the League lists 18 or 20 employees in its Chicago and Washington offices whose work is to some extent connected with lobbying and reports portions of their salaries ranging from 2 to 50 percent. One-third of the League's printing costs is allocated to lobbying. Part of the overhead of the Washington office — usually 15 to 18 percent — is reported as lobbying expenditures. The percentage reported is the same as the average percentage of salaries allocated to lobbying in a given quarter. The Savings and Loan League reported total lobbying spending of $113,014 in 1962 — the year in which the savings and loan industry staged a massive grassroots lobbying campaign against President Kennedy's interest and dividend withholding plan.

The largest part of the AFL-CIO's lobbying expenditures goes for the salaries of a five- or six-man lobbying staff headed by Andrew Biemiller. In a recent quarter the salaries of these men accounted for $23,903 out of a total of $39,625. The AFL-CIO also reports part of the cost of printing the weekly AFL-CIO News and the monthly magazine, the American Federationist, saying that the amount reported represents that part of the material in these two publications that might be regarded as falling under the Lobbying Act. Part of the cost of radio broadcasts sponsored by the AFL-CIO is reported on the same basis. The AFL-CIO reported total lobbying spending of $153,542 in 1964.

Similarly, salaries account for a large part of the lobbying expenditures reported by the United Federation of Postal Clerks. In a recent quarter salaries were $10,962 out of a total of $18,118. Public relations and advertising costs were reported as $2,698; office overhead, $501; telephones and telegraph, $108; travel, food, lodging and entertainment, $111, and other expenses, $3,739. The postal clerks reported a total of $131,913 in lobbying spending in 1964.

The reporting picture is not consistent. Many lobbying groups do not list any of their office overhead as lobbying spending.

According to James W. Riddell, a partner in the Washington

law firm of Dawson, Griffin, Pickens and Riddell, "perhaps 20 percent of our fees and retainers — not more than that — are received for lobbying." He added that "we don't interpret the Lobbying Act as requiring us to determine 20 percent of our overhead — rent, stenographers' salaries, office supplies and the like — and report that as lobbying expense." Among the companies and organizations for which the Dawson firm has registered as lobbyist are the Hilton Hotels Corporation, the C.I.T. Financial Corporation of New York, the Equitable Life Insurance Company, the Air Transport Association of America, the Transportation Corporation of America, Variable Annuity Life Insurance Company and the Indian Sugar Mills Association. One of the partners in this law firm is Donald S. Dawson, a presidential aide in the Truman administration.

The United States Chamber of Commerce files reports under the Lobbying Act but attaches a disclaimer stating that "legal counsel has advised that in the light of the . . . decision in U.S. v. Harriss . . . it does not appear that the functions and purposes of the Chamber . . .are of such character as to require reporting under the Regulation of Lobbying Act." The Chamber states it is a multi-purpose organization, that its "principal purpose" is not lobbying, that all of its membership dues and other receipts go for the full purposes of the Chamber and that none are earmarked for specific purposes, legislative or otherwise.

If it should be held that, "under any reasonable construction" of the Lobbying Act, any Chamber expenditures were subject to the Act, they would not be in excess of the amounts shown in its report, the Chamber states. Accordingly, it reported a total of $4,973,526 in dues and contributions in 1961. Expenditures that might be construed as subject to the lobbying law were reported as $43,773 in that year. In the first three quarters of 1962, the Chamber reported $4,001,175 in dues and contributions, and lobbying expenditures of $45,019. The Chamber's total operating budget in 1962, however, was $11,500,000. Of this amount, some $7,500,000 was for field costs, including the printing of Nation's Business. The remainder, about $4,000,000, was budgeted for the Washington office (national headquarters). About 75 percent of the time of the Washington office, according to Terry Rice, is spent on research on governmental matters, and this research goes into the material sent out to Chamber members "in the hope that they will exert their influence on legislation." In other words, about $3,000,000 a year goes into grassroots lobbying.

Although the Chamber considers only a fraction of its budget as possibly subject to the lobbying law, it does report that fraction. Not so the National Association of Manufacturers, which does not report, as an organization, at all. Yet the N.A.M.'s expenditures for "public information activities" totaled $2,199,-966 in 1961. This included $172,039 for speakers and programs for industry and for women's and clerical groups; $152,906 for radio and television programs; $132,401 for the N.A.M.'s "education department" and distribution of printed material in schools (in 1963 the N.A.M. provided high schools with a debate kit on the subject of health care for the elderly, including such topics as "The Federal Role in Medical Care: Compulsion and Conformity"); $116,454 for the N.A.M.'s industrial press service and service for company publications; $113,766 for printed materials and films for public distribution; $109,377 for "executive planning and programming"; $80,051 for a public affairs program; $77,754 for press relations — and $1,245,218 for N.A.M. divisional and regional offices. This last item was described as "implementation of public relations, public affairs and economic education activities on local and regional levels." Most of these are euphemisms for grassroots lobbying.

Other N.A.M. expenditures in 1961 had at least a partial relation to lobbying. Among these were the Washington office, budgeted at $318,155; the law department, $144, 570; the N.A.M. News and other publications, $125,058; the employee relations department, $102,976, and the operations of the N.A.M.'s committees, $416,330. These committees deal with such matters as taxation, government economy, national defense, conservation, money, banking and credit, patents, industrial relations and nuclear energy, among others. The cost of the above activities added up to $3,307,055, out of a total N.A.M. budget of $5,773,664 in 1961. None of this was reported as lobbying expenses.

Most lobbyists, as we have seen, assert that the amounts they report as having been spent on direct contacts with Congress accurately reflect their outlays, in the light of the "principal purpose" clause. But these amounts are a drop in the bucket compared with what does not, under the Harriss decision, have to be reported at all: the hundreds of millions of dollars spent on grassroots lobbying campaigns aimed at passing or defeating specific legislation. The massive grassroots effort by the oil and gas industry to secure approval of the Harris-Fulbright natural gas bill is a case in point.

On June 7, 1954, the Supreme Court handed down its decision in the case of Phillips Petroleum Company v. Wisconsin. The court held that producers of natural gas were subject to regulation by the Federal Power Commission under the Natural Gas Act. In so doing, the court touched off a bitter fight. Fearing that the decision ultimately might lead to federal regulation of the closely related oil industry, the nation's oil and gas men sought to have the court's decision overturned. A bill to do this was introduced by Representative Oren Harris, chairman of the House Interstate Commerce Committee, and Senator J. William Fulbright, both Arkansas Democrats.

The oil industry has often demonstrated its muscle in Congress, notably in the successful effort to block the renomination of Leland Olds to the Federal Power Commission because he had stood for the consumer, and the attack on Federal Trade Commissioner Stephen Spingarn, "whose character, mental stability and loyalty were publicly questioned because of his role in the release of a report on the international oil cartel in 1952." [•] And, of course, there is the industry's long and successful defense of the 27½ percent oil depletion allowance, one of the biggest special interest loopholes in the tax laws.

The lobbying campaign to put through the Harris-Fulbright bill was just a romp for the oil industry. Then, irony of ironies, the activities of an oil man, Howard B. Keck, threw away the whole show. Keck, president of the Superior Oil Company, tried, through intermediaries, to give a $2,500 campaign contribution to Senator Francis Case, South Dakota Republican. Case implied that this was an attempt to influence his vote on the Harris-Fulbright bill. A Republican President normally sympathetic to the oil industry vetoed the bill as a result, and there never has been a successful effort to resurrect it. As Kaiser Wilhelm remarked: "Someone's always spitting in the soup."

Six months after the Phillips decision was handed down, the oil and gas industry organized the Natural Gas and Oil Resources

Committee (NGO). Chairman of the committee was Leonard F. McCollum, president of Continental Oil Company. Vice chairman was Paul Kayser, president of El Paso Natural Gas Company. The committee's executive director was Baird H. Markham, formerly with the American Petroleum Institute. The API is the oil industry's chief (although far from only) lobbying outlet in Washington.

The NGO's avowed purpose was to carry out a nationwide public information and education program about the oil and gas industry. But when a special committee headed by Senator John L. McClellan questioned NGO officials, it developed that there was a legislative purpose as well, the legislation being the Harris-Fulbright bill. This exchange was illustrative:

George M. Fay, chief counsel of the McClellan committee: "Would you say that it was correct or incorrect to conclude that one of the ultimate aims [of NGO] was to influence legislation which would exempt gas producers from regulation or control?"

McCollum: "You said one of the ultimate aims. Now, I can answer your question this way: in the record is a statement of purpose, which . . . stated that . . . this committee . . . was a long-range information and education committee . . . Certainly if the public were informed on a subject as we understood it . . . one thing ultimately could be legislation of some form or the other . . . To answer your question, yes; it is conceivable that one of the results would be legislation." [7]

To finance its operations, NGO received contributions totaling $1,950,000 from more than 1,000 contributors. About 80 percent of this amount, $1,646,500 to be exact, came from 26 large oil and natural gas companies. Those which contributed $100,000 or more were: Humble Oil and Refining Company (a subsidiary of Standard Oil of New Jersey), $175,000; the Texas Company, $153,000; Shell Oil, $138,000; Standard Oil of California, $119,000; Socony Mobil, $114,000; Standard Oil and Gas Company, $112,500; Gulf Oil, $111,000, and Standard Oil of Indiana, $100,000.

The NGO did not register under the Lobbying Act and did not report any of this money, on the grounds that it was engaged solely in conducting an information and education program, without any direct legislative contact work. The Supreme Court decision in the Phillips case came on the same day as its ruling in U.S. v. Harriss. The NGO was set up on the following October 24. Handy timing for the oil industry.

The $1,950,000 donated to NGO does not tell the whole story. To carry out its extensive program of speeches, contacts with newspaper editors, radio broadcasts and the like, NGO borrowed the services of some 3,000 officials and employees of oil companies, on a part-time basis. The salaries of these men were paid by their regular employers while they worked for NGO. It is not possible to determine the value of these donated services with accuracy. But the NGO campaign went on for about 18 months, and if we assume that an average of $5,000 is a reasonable estimate for each man's services to NGO in that time, then NGO got another $15,000,000. The total now is close to $17,000,000.

It does not end there. McCollum testified that his own company undertook a campaign independently of NGO. Through its field men, jobbers, agents and credit customers, it distributed anti-regulation pamphlets to 586,750 people. There was no estimate of the cost of this, but McCollum also testified that Continental Oil regularly spent $500,000 a year to educate the public on the oil and gas business. The regular education program of 1955 probably can be assumed to have paid some attention to the dangers of regulation. Say $500,000 altogether, for both the special and regular programs in late 1954, 1955 and early 1956. New total: $17,500,000.

There's more. Another oil and gas industry committee, the General Gas Committee (GGC), was set up on October 4, 1954, with the avowed sole purpose of securing legislation to exempt the production of natural gas from federal control. The GGC was headed by Maston Nixon, president of Southern Minerals Corporation. This committee received $118,625 in contributions, including many of the same oil companies that contributed to NGO, and spent the same amount. At this point in the narrative, something unusual occurred. The GGC registered under the Lobbying Act and reported its expenditures. New total: about $17,600,000.

Still more. In addition to loaning personnel to NGO, several of the major oil companies, on their own, distributed material dealing with the gas regulation controversy to their employees, dealers, stockholders and credit-card holders. Socony Mobil, for instance, loaned 95 employees to NGO at various times and distributed approximately 1,000,000 pieces of printed material to its 170,000 stockholders, 45,000 employees and hundreds of thousands of credit-card holders and other customers. Shell Oil loaned a number of employees to NGO on a full-time basis, others part-time, and distributed material to its employees, dealers, stockholders and to 250,000 credit-card holders. Standard Oil of Indiana educated its employees through discussion groups, pamphlets, letters and house organs, and sent printed material to stockholders, dealers and 350,000 credit-card holders.

It is equally difficult to pinpoint the cost of these and similar efforts; none of the amounts spent were reported under the Lobbying Act. But adding in the company activities, a very conservative estimate of the amount spent to lobby for the Harris-Fulbright bill would be $20,000,000 to $25,000,000. Of which, $118,625 was disclosed to Congress and the public.

To plan its grassroots lobbying campaign, NGO retained the public relations firm of Hill and Knowlton. One of the first moves in the campaign, at the suggestion of Hill and Knowlton, was to call in Opinion Research Corporation, which made a survey of leaders of public opinion — editors, teachers, clergymen, professional men, businessmen and farm leaders — to get their views on the gas industry. For a fee of $10,000, Opinion Research interviewed 561 persons and submitted a comprehensive report on its findings. Under the broad outlines prepared by Hill and Knowlton, NGO then divided the country into 15 regional districts, with a chairman for each region. A chairman also was designated for each state, and there were more chairmen at the county and local levels. The oil and gas companies furnished the chairmen.

All media of mass communication — newspaper and magazine advertisements, radio and television programs, films, speeches and printed material — were used. The NGO prepared elaborate kits which were distributed to its personnel around the country. Among other things, the kits contained material for newspaper editors, press releases, speeches tailored for various types of audiences, and scripts for radio and television broadcasts.

By September 1955, NGO estimated that it had distributed 5,000,000 pieces of printed material. The oil and gas men on loan to the committee gave thousands of speeches and talked with thousands of daily and weekly newspaper editors and members of civic groups such as chambers of commerce. The NGO representatives, by September 1, had made about 500 radio broadcasts, and a film entitled "You, the People" had been widely shown. Between October 1955 and March 1956, NGO spent $798,-305 for newspaper and magazine advertising; $499,182 for printing; $234,733 for administrative expenses; $87,033 for national publicity, and $85,160 for Hill and Knowlton's fee, none of which was reported to Congress and the public under the lobbying law.

The campaign against gas regulation had some offbeat aspects. The McClellan committee brought out that Standard Oil of Indiana originated and paid for a barrage of phony telegrams sent to Senator Edward J. Thye, Minnesota Republican. Nine hundred telegrams urging support of the Harris-Fulbright bill poured into Thye's office in January 1956. It was not discovered until some seven months later that many of the telegrams were sent without the knowledge or permission of the purported senders. Standard Oil acknowledged paying for the wires but denied knowing that many of them were spurious. Minnesota officials of the company admitted, however, that they were responsible for the phony telegrams.

The McClellan investigation elicited another interesting little fact about the money spent on the natural gas campaign. Under prodding by Senator Clinton P. Anderson, New Mexico Democrat, most of the oil and gas companies admitted that they were charging off their contributions to NGO as ordinary business expenses for income tax purposes. This meant that the Treasury — the American taxpayer — would put up 52 cents of every dollar contributed to NGO. Humble Oil, Socony Mobil, Standard Oil of California, Shell, Gulf and Standard Oil of Indiana were among the companies that already had or intended to charge off their NGO contribution as a business expense. The McClellan committee took a dim view of this, noting that the Treasury would lose the taxes on almost $2,000,000 if all contributors to NGO claimed the deduction and got away with it. McClellan informed the Treasury. The Treasury instructed the Internal Revenue Service to disallow the deductions, and then some of the oil companies changed their minds and said they didn't plan to claim them after all.

But the other big costs of the grassroots lobbying campaign —

salaries of company personnel loaned to NGO, material mailed out to employees, stockholders and so on — presumably were treated as ordinary business expenses and claimed as income tax deductions. On this occasion, as on so many others, the American taxpayer paid half the cost of being propagandized. It brought to mind George Orwell's words about the British middle class: They had been bought — and with their own money.

REMEDIES

"The best lack all conviction, while the worst are full of passionate intensity." — *W. B. Yeats, The Second Coming.*

"I do not believe in democracy. I think it stinks." — *Herbert U. Nelson, former executive vice president of the National Association of Real Estate Boards.*

On those occasions when Congress has one of its spasmodic twinges of concern about lobbying, the remedies that are proposed invariably reflect Washington's preoccupation with effect rather than cause. Various suggestions are put forth to supervise lobbying more closely by tightening the existing law, to add an enforcement provision or to prohibit this or that type of lobbying arrangement, particularly contingent-fee lobbying.

In the midst of the furor over natural gas lobbying, Senator John F. Kennedy pointed out that "the effective supervision and surveillance of the lobbyist remains as a continuing challenge to the people and the Congress." That is still true. The chief defect of the lobbying law, he declared, was its failure to designate an agency or official to administer and enforce the law. "Until this is done," he said, "there is little hope that the [Lobbying] Act will accomplish its intended purposes." [1]

Political scientists, politicians and the lobbyists themselves generally agree that the Lobbying Act of 1946 is an inadequate, loosely written, confusing and unenforced law and that the confusion has been compounded by the Supreme Court decision in U.S. v. Harriss. Professor Belle Zeller of Brooklyn College, an authority on lobbying, describes the wording of the law as "vague and ambiguous." The Act, she states, has "serious defects," the most serious being the ambiguity of the words "principal purpose." [2]

Many other experts on government, among them Dr. George B.

255

Galloway of the Library of Congress, call attention to the grave shortcomings of the Lobbying Act as originally written. And, as noted earlier, Dean Robert F. Drinan of the Boston College Law School has expressed the view that court decisions have left the lobbying law "a judicial shambles."

The lobbyists, too, hold a low opinion of the law that is supposed to publicize their identities and expenditures, and thereby, in some intangible way, keep their operations honest and aboveboard. "Out of date," "unrealistic," "meaningless" and "unenforceable" are some of the adjectives they use to describe the law. A member of one of Washington's leading law firms, who has registered as a lobbyist, sums up the prevailing sentiment: "The law is not enforced — there is no provision for enforcement. It badly needs to be tightened up. As it is now, it is a mockery."

The Lobbying Act needs to be overhauled; there is little dispute about that. Some constructive and thoughtful proposals have been advanced in recent years to strengthen one of the weakest laws on the books. But valuable as they have been, all these proposals have a fundamental flaw. They deal with lobbying as an effect, lobbying after it happens. They recommend ways to correct old wrongs and, hopefully, to prevent new ones, to intensify supervision, to enforce. They treat the effects, not the causes of lobbying abuses.

After its two-year study of lobbying, the House committee headed by Representative Frank Buchanan of Pennsylvania proposed a series of amendments to the Lobbying Act. The first was a suggestion that the law itself be renamed. The committee said that although it did not feel there was any stigma attached to the word lobbyist, "a great many persons have felt uncomfortable in complying" with a law known as the Regulation of Lobbying Act. The committee proposed renaming the law "An Act to require the reporting of certain information on efforts to influence legislation" or, for short, "the Legislative Interests Reports Act."

To cut the amount of detailed reporting, the committee recommended that reports be required only on lobbying expenditures of $50 or more, rather than $10, and that persons or organizations receiving or spending less than $1,000 a year to influence legislation not be required to report at all. The committee further recommended that contingent-fee lobbying be prohibited, that radio and television stations be exempted from the lobbying law as newspapers are, that the Justice Department be required and empowered to enforce the Lobbying Act, and that Congress consider setting up a permanent Joint Committee on the Legislative Process to examine the ties between lobbying and campaign contributions. On this last point, the committee commented in typically restrained fashion: "We believe that the business of influencing elections often bears a close relation to the business of influencing legislation." Since the Buchanan investigation took place when the Lobbying Act still covered indirect, grassroots pressure, the committee made no recommendations in this area. Nor did it suggest any change in the "principal purpose" clause.

After the Supreme Court's decision in the Harriss case, John Kennedy developed an interest in the problem. A junior Senator at that time, he introduced a new lobbying law. His recommendations were greeted with the thundering silence which the Senate customarily accords to reform proposals. Nevertheless, Kennedy persevered. As chairman of a Senate government operations subcommittee, he sent a questionnaire to more than 200 registered lobbyists, and he reported that the responses indicated general agreement that "substantial revision" of the lobbying law was needed.

The new statute proposed by Kennedy was a mixed bag. It had both strong and weak features. Its chief strength was that it tried to do something about the "principal purpose" confusion. The measure set up a new classification — "legislative agent" — and defined this as any person who, for pay, "engages himself to influence legislation . . . and who . . . devotes *any portion of his time* to efforts to influence legislation." (Emphasis added.) This was simple and direct. A person who devoted any part of his time to lobbying would be required to register and to report "the total amount received by him as compensation" for lobbying and "the total amount received by him for expenses," together with the name and address of his employer, his legislative interests and every lobbying expenditure of $50 or more. To exempt the ordinary citizen petitioning his government, the "for pay" provision was included.

The Kennedy proposal was obviously not foolproof. In all

probability, many professional lobbyists would still have reported only part of their salaries and expenses. But the new plan would have made it difficult not to report any or to list only a nominal amount. The phrase, "any portion of his time" would prevent that and end the "principal purpose" evasion.

Kennedy's measure drew a distinction between legislative agents who lobby personally and organizations that receive or spend money to influence legislation but do not do the actual lobbying themselves. The bill, in other words, recognized the common lobbying arrangement in which a corporation, trade association or labor union hires lobbyists or maintains a regular lobbying staff. The existing law does not make this distinction, leaving it up to the employing organization to decide whether it, like its individual lobbyists, should register and report. Under the Kennedy bill, these organizations would be required to register and report the total amount of money they received and spent "to influence legislation" if the amount exceeded $250 a quarter, as well as the name and address of each person contributing $100 or more. The wording was simply "to influence legislation," not "for the principal purpose of influencing legislation." This might still have permitted large special interest groups to report only a small amount of their actual lobbying outlays, but it would have prevented them from refusing to report at all on the ground that lobbying was not their principal purpose.

The Kennedy bill had some other good points. It outlawed contingent-fee lobbying, exempted radio and television stations, and required the Attorney General to report annually to Congress on the actions he had taken to insure compliance with the lobbying law. Kennedy made it clear that this meant the Justice Department was to be charged specifically with enforcing the Lobbying Act. Kennedy called his bill "the Federal Lobbying Registration Act." By removing the word "regulation" from the title, he dealt with the misconception that the present Lobbying Act regulates lobbying. It does not. It places no restrictions on lobbying. It sets up no rules governing the conduct of lobbyists. It merely requires registration and minimal disclosure.

The Kennedy bill, however, had one resounding defect. It defined the term "to influence legislation" as relating only to direct contacts with members of Congress. The huge sums spent to stimulate indirect, grassroots pressure — the real lobbying money — would have continued to be exempt from the disclosure requirement. Kennedy explained that he did this to remove objections to the law on constitutional grounds.

When the natural gas scandal came along, Kennedy's efforts were shunted aside. He had hoped to make a full-scale investigation of lobbying, but the Senate elders assigned this task first to the venerable Walter F. George of Georgia, who looked into the $2,500 campaign offer to Senator Case, and then to Senator John L. McClellan of Arkansas, whose committee investigated the broader ramifications — lobbying in conjunction with political activities and campaign contributions.

The McClellan committee came up with a proposed "Legislative Activities Disclosure Act" which represented a long step toward an effective lobbying law. The committee adopted Kennedy's "legislative agent" idea; its bill would have required financial reports from persons and organizations receiving or spending more than $300 a quarter to influence legislation by employing lobbyists; it made it a felony to knowingly send false communications to Congress (harking back to the phony telegrams in the natural gas fight); it designated the Comptroller General as the official responsible for administering and enforcing the Act, and it made other worthwhile recommendations.

But most important, the McClellan committee's bill provided for disclosure of grassroots lobbying costs under certain circumstances. It would have required financial reports from persons and organizations who conduct big campaigns to whip up public sentiment for or against a specific legislative issue in Congress. The committee made a persuasive case for this proposal.

"If a member of Congress," it said, "receives several hundred authentic letters or wires *opposing* a particular bill, he knows that those writing were sufficiently interested to communicate with him, and this indicates opinion on the part of the people he is trying to represent. But what of those who *favored* the bill? If the interest of the opponents has been aroused by the expenditure of large sums of money for newspaper, radio and television advertisements which impliedly seek 'a letter to your Congressman' [and] if no similar appeals have been made on the other side of the legislative issue, and if he knows of the expenditures

for the [opposing] advertising, the Congressman can better evaluate the true feeling of his constituency. Similarly, it is helpful
to Congress to know of the existence of widespread public relations campaigns which are calculated to produce direct communications but do not specifically call for such communications."

This kind of pressure, the committee said, "can and should be
subject to some disclosure provisions." It noted that the majority opinion in U.S. v. Harriss had said it would be constitutional to require disclosure of the cost of "artificially stimulated"
letter-writing drives. On the other hand, the committee con-
concluded that a lobbying statute could not cover the kind of
general campaign which Justice Felix Frankfurter, in an earlier
case, had described as "efforts . . . to influence public opinion . . .
however remote the radiations of influence which they may exert
upon the ultimate legislative process."

The law proposed by the McClellan group covered grassroots
lobbying campaigns if they related to specific pending legislation.
The bill would have required a financial report to Congress by
"any person [or organization] who has made expenditures ex-
ceeding $50,000 in the aggregate within the preceding 12 months
in presenting a program addressed to the public, a substantial
portion of which is intended, designed or calculated to influence
legislation."

There are three principles that justify requiring disclosure of
the cost of indirect lobbying if it relates to pending legislation.
They are that public business should be transacted publicly,
that Congress must be adequately informed in order to legislate
wisely and that it has a right to protect itself against misleading
information.

The McClellan committee came to grips with a hard problem,
a conundrum that has plagued all efforts to legislate in the field
of lobbying: how to see to it that Congress and the public are
informed about the money spent on massive grassroots pressure
campaigns — and the identity of the sponsors — without violating the constitutional right of free speech. It may be argued
that the committee did not go far enough, but it at least made
a try at clearing up one of the toughest problems of lobbying
regulation. The significance of the committee's recommendation
was simply that until and unless grassroots lobbying costs are

included, the present lobbying law is — and any future statute would be — meaningless.

The guiding principle, Dr. Galloway says, must be "full disclosure by all persons and groups whose purpose and substantial effort is to influence legislation. This principle applies not only to attempts to influence legislation through direct communication with Congress, but also to indirect 'lobbying at the grassroots.' " How to do this is a big problem, as he acknowledges. "In the Harriss case, the Supreme Court, feeling that it was faced with the choice of striking out or striking down, construed the Lobbying Act narrowly as applying only to attempts to influence legislation 'through direct communication with Congress.' The court implied that if the lobbying law were more broadly construed — to cover attempts to influence legislation through indirect educational activities — it would violate the freedom guaranteed by the First Amendment — freedom to speak, publish and petition the government . . . Thus, the principle of full disclosure comes into apparent conflict with the rights guaranteed by the First Amendment." [3]

Dr. Galloway suggests that one way to resolve the dilemma might be for Congress to write a broad definition of the term "to influence legislation" so as to include indirect as well as direct communication, and then designate the Justice Department to apply the definition to specific cases, under the broad standards laid down in the law. The conflict between disclosure of indirect lobbying costs and the First Amendment guarantees is a real one, and care would have to be taken in drafting a lobbying law to cover grassroots pressure. But it is not an *ignis fatuus;* it could be done.

The Buchanan committee's definition of indirect lobbying was probably too broad. The committee included letter and telegram campaigns, institutional advertising, books and pamphlets on public issues, the salaries of executives, lawyers and publicists and "the operating budgets of all the thousands of organizations throughout the nation whose central purpose is to influence what government does — all of these costs and many more are chargeable to lobbying, whether we like the word or not." But this definition of grassroots lobbying is a bottomless pit.

If a company takes an ad in a national magazine defending

and promoting "free enterprise" or "the profit motive" or "the American way of life," is that lobbying? Warner and Swasey, a machinery manufacturer, has been publishing full-page ads in Newsweek magazine since 1933. Some recent examples have headlines such as these: "Not all the courts and union contracts in the world can repeal the laws of economics" (the message being that profits make jobs); "Whatever happened to the buggy makers — progress for all means growing pains for a few, but is that any reason to penalize growth?" and "It's bad enough to be 'liberal' with the tax money of the hard-working men and women who paid it. But it is unforgivable to be 'liberal' with the future of their country."

This is one kind of advertising which the Buchanan committee defined as indirect lobbying. It is also propaganda. It obviously promotes a point of view. But is it lobbying? Should Warner and Swasey be required to register under the Lobbying Act and report the cost of these ads? No pending legislative matters are mentioned. There are references in some of the ads to taxes, depreciation and the like, but no specific bill or proposal before Congress is discussed, and there is no exhortation to "write your Congressman" in support of or opposition to anything. It is clear enough what political attitude Warner and Swasey would like to see prevail in America, but that is all.

Here is the essence of what is meant by the conflict between disclosure of lobbying costs and the First Amendment's guarantee of free speech. We may feel that Warner and Swasey is propagandizing us, and we may not agree with the sentiments expressed. We may further object to paying part of the cost of being propagandized. (Treasury Department regulations permit the cost of institutional advertising and advertising that presents general views on economic, financial and social issues to be deducted from corporate income taxes as an ordinary expense of doing business.) But if the legal definition of lobbying is expanded to include the general formation of public opinion, practically everything is lobbying, and the definition becomes unmanageable.

In August 1963, some 200,000 people took part in a "march on Washington" to create sentiment in Congress and in the nation for civil rights legislation. An organization manual distributed to the leaders of the march described the demonstration as "a new concept of lobbying." Should all 200,000 marchers have been required to register as lobbyists? The Warner and Swasey ads and the civil rights march *were*, of course, lobbying situations — in the sense that virtually everything that goes on in Washington and in public affairs across the land is lobbying. The bureaucrats in the federal agencies lobby for more funds. The President lobbies for his program. Congressmen lobby for the economic interests of their constituents. Everybody lobbies everybody else. So, too, in this sense, the businessman lobbies for more business; the union lobbies the company for more money; the housewife lobbies for a new washing machine, and the minister lobbies his flock for a new roof on the church. A nation of lobbyists.

All too often the words "lobbyist" and "lobbying" are used widely and indiscriminately to apply to a variety of situations and relationships. But when it comes to drafting a lobbying law, the definition must be far more precise.

By the same token, the conflict between disclosure and free speech is not the insurmountable barrier that some special interest groups would have us believe (Nation's Business, a publication of the U.S. Chamber of Commerce, for instance, fought the McClellan bill bitterly). It is absurd to say, as some do, that a Congress which has written scores of laws compelling private interests to reveal certain information about their financial activities — the Securities and Exchange Act, the Public Utility Holding Company Act, the Taft-Hartley and Landrum-Griffin Acts, to mention only a few — could not write a law requiring the disclosure of grassroots lobbying costs without violating the constitutional rights of anyone.

The McClellan committee's recommendations constitute a productive line of approach. It proposed that spending be disclosed only if the lobbying campaign related to a legislative issue pending before Congress. It required disclosure only if a substantial amount of money — $50,000 or more — was expended, in order "to cover only those large campaigns which, if not the subject of disclosure requirements, might cause the Congress to misjudge public sentiment on pending legislation."

Thus, McClellan's bill would have covered the savings and loan industry's campaign against the interest and dividend withholding proposal, the A.M.A.'s fight against Social Security health care, the drug industry's assault on the Kefauver bill, the effort on behalf of the Dirksen amendment and the oil industry's campaign to enact the Harris-Fulbright bill — all of which involved specific, pending legislation. The proposal did nothing to restrict the expression of opinion — or the spreading of misinformation — in these campaigns. It proposed no curb on free speech. It simply required that Congress and the American people be informed about how much money was being spent to influence major legislative issues, and who was spending it.

While the McClellan bill would not have applied to the Warner and Swasey type of institutional advertisement, it would have covered the cost of ads such as those which appeared in many newspapers during the savings and loan industry's fight against interest and dividend withholding. These broadsides dealt with a specific legislative issue then before Congress. The ad in the Cleveland Plain Dealer, cited previously, described the main feature of the withholding proposal, noted that hearings were in progress and urged readers to communicate with members of Congress. It included the names and addresses of the President, the Senators from Ohio, and the Representatives from the Cleveland area.

If there is ever to be a lobbying law with any meaning at all, it must apply, at a minimum, to clear-cut types of lobbying appeals. That is, it must require that the money spent on grassroots lobbying aimed at specific legislation be reported to Congress and the public, together with the identities of those furnishing the money.

There are gray areas between the institutional ad and the out-and-out lobbying ad. Consider this one: the ad shows a map of the United States with a number of pins stuck in it, and says: "204 leaks in your pocketbook. All those 204 white pins in this map are costing you money. They mark the places where the federal government is in the electric business *indirectly*, through projects such as flood control and conservation. The black pins mark additional government electric power projects now planned or proposed. *There are 421 of them.* Maybe you haven't known how far government has gone into the electric business . . . It affects your pocketbook now. Hidden federal taxes on everything you buy and direct taxes on your wages help pay for it . . . The subject is very important right now because Congress is deciding whether government can take the next big step . . ."

This ad, published by the Southwestern Gas and Electric Company, mentions a legislative issue in general terms, although there is no appeal to the reader to communicate with Congress. Such advertising might or might not have been covered by the McClellan plan, depending on whether the Comptroller General determined that the ad was intended to influence legislation.

Borderline cases of the Southwestern Gas sort could be decided by the agency authorized to administer and enforce the lobbying law — *if* there were such an agency and *if* the lobbying law covered indirect pressure. But at the present time the law does not even cover obvious lobbying appeals such as the savings and loan ads, much less the gray areas.

To avoid conflict with the First Amendment, a strengthened lobbying law probably would have to limit its coverage of grass-roots lobbying to those campaigns that relate to specific legislation. General propaganda and public opinion campaigns undoubtedly are the substrata underlying lobbying, and perhaps we will someday be able to cope with them in a statute, but meanwhile it will be hard enough to write and enact an effective lobbying law.

After an 18-month investigation of the Bobby Baker scandal, the Senate Rules Committee submitted a proposal to tighten the Lobbying Act by authorizing the Comptroller General to enforce it. Under the proposal, this official would be given specific power to check the quarterly lobbying reports for accuracy and completeness, to determine whether individuals and organizations had failed to comply with the registration and financial disclosure requirements of the law and to recommend prosecution for violations. The Senate group made other recommendations bearing indirectly on lobbying. It proposed a rule requiring Senators and all Senate employees earning more than $10,000 a year to submit a list of their financial holdings and business associations to the Comptroller General if their outside holdings were worth more than half their annual salary. The committee recommended also that Senate officers and employees be prohibited from engaging in outside work if it was "inconsistent with the conscientious performance of their official duties."

A stronger resolution offered by Senator Joseph S. Clark, Penn-

sylvania Democrat, was voted down by the committee. Clark
proposed that Senators, Senate employees and their wives or
husbands be required to file annual public reports disclosing all
assets, liabilities and capital gains of $5,000 or more; all sources
of outside income in excess of $100, including gifts, honorariums
(such as speech fees) and expense money, and all financial interests in companies or law firms doing business with or practicing before government agencies. Clark argued that the Rules
Committee's recommendations did not go far enough. He proposed that Senators be required to make public disclosure of
their financial holdings and business connections, rather than
submitting them in the form of confidential reports to the Comptroller General, as the committee suggested. He noted that the
committee proposal did not require disclosure of property held
in the name of a spouse or straw party, and he recommended
closing this loophole by requiring that these holdings be subject
to public disclosure also. Only three of the nine members of the
Rules unit — Senator Claiborne Pell, Rhode Island Democrat;
Senator John Sherman Cooper, Kentucky Republican, and Clark
himself — voted for Clark's resolution.

In testimony before the Joint Committee on Organization of
the Congress in 1965, Congressional Quarterly, the only private group that over the years has maintained a regular surveillance of lobbying reports, urged that the Comptroller General be empowered to administer the Lobbying Act, as well as
retain the required reports on political spending. Neal Peirce,
who testified on behalf of Congressional Quarterly, pointed out
that the lobbying reports are now filed with the Clerk of the
House and the Secretary of the Senate, neither of whom has any
enforcement function. "The full disclosure which is so clearly
in the public's interest," Peirce said, "is not being made today.
Closing the loopholes in the law is one part of the answer. The
second part of the answer is to remove the responsibility for receiving reports and enforcing compliance from the hands of officials who themselves are intimately connected with the political
process." In his testimony for Congressional Quarterly, Peirce
charged that House Clerk Ralph Roberts had hindered public
examination of lobbying and campaign spending reports, especially those for past years. The Comptroller General, Peirce recommended, "should have power to enforce full reporting through

injunctions and fines, and [he] should be charged with making
[the] reports fully and easily available to the public." Popularly known as the federal government's fiscal watchdog, the
Comptroller General heads the General Accounting Office, which
audits the books of government agencies to uncover waste and
financial mismanagement.

Legislation curbing the hidden influence of foreign agents and
lobbyists on United States foreign policy was recommended by
the Senate Foreign Relations Committee in 1965. Headed by
Senator J. William Fulbright, the committee acted after com-
pleting its investigation into the activities of foreign agents,
which has been discussed in a previous chapter. Its proposed
legislation, jointly sponsored by Fulbright and Senator Bourke B.
Hickenlooper of Iowa, ranking Republican on the committee,
would prohibit political contributions by foreign agents on behalf
of their employers, a practice exposed by the committee; clarify
the definitions of those required to register as foreign agents;
give the Attorney General broader power to compel compliance
with the Foreign Agents Registration Act; prohibit contingent-
fee contracts between foreign agents and their employers "based
upon success in political activities to be undertaken by the
agent"; require foreign agents testifying before Congressional
committees to disclose in full the foreign employers they represent, and forbid officials and full-time employees of the United
States government from acting as agents of foreign interests.

When presented with the recommendations by the Rules
Committee and the stronger proposals offered by Senator Clark,
Congress had a perfect record: it approved none of them. Nevertheless, these proposals, when joined to those submitted earlier
by Kennedy and the McClellan committee, add up to a potential
lobbying law that would be vastly more effective than the one
now on the books. Such a law would have the following major
provisions:

(1) It would define a lobbyist as any individual who receives
remuneration for the purpose of influencing legislation or any
organization that receives contributions or dues, any part of
which is used for the purpose of influencing legislation. An individual lobbyist would be a person who, for pay, "engages himself to influence legislation . . . and who . . . devotes *any portion*

of his time to efforts to influence legislation," as Kennedy
phrased it. An organization would be required to register under
the lobbying law if one of its purposes was to influence legislation — not its principal purpose or its main function but simply
one of its purposes.

(2) Individual lobbyists would be required to file quarterly
reports with the Comptroller General listing their total compensation and expenditures for the quarter, together with the
names, addresses and purposes of those who furnished the money.
This would go beyond Kennedy's recommendation that individual lobbyists be required to report only the amount received
for the purpose of lobbying; the new law proposed here would
require lobbyists to disclose their *entire* income and *all* their
expenditures. An exemption would be made for law firms representing clients in non-legislative work, but the burden of proof
would be on the law firm or public relations outfit. It would
have to justify any exclusions to the Comptroller General; such
justification could be carried on privately between the law firm
and the Comptroller General. Otherwise, all lobbying registrations and financial reports would be open for public inspection
and would be reported quarterly to Congress.

(3) Organizations required to register as lobbyists would have
to report all expenditures made for the purpose of influencing
legislation, regardless of amount. They would be required to
report all contributions or dues they received for this purpose,
with the names and addresses of contributors, but not contributions received for non-legislative purposes. The burden of proof
would be on the organization, with the Comptroller General
empowered to gain access to the organization's books, on a private basis, if substantial doubt existed that the group was reporting a correct portion of its contributions and expenditures.
Criminal penalties would be provided for evasions by individual
lobbyists and lobbying organizations, as under the present law.

(4) Contingent-fee lobbying would be prohibited. Political
contributions by lobbyists would not be prohibited, but the
new law would require that all such contributions be reported
by the lobbyist in his quarterly filings with the Comptroller
General and would be a matter of public record.

(5) The term "to influence legislation" would include indirect,
grassroots lobbying campaigns if they related to specific legisla-

tion pending before Congress or clearly likely to come before Congress in the near future. The amount of money spent on these campaigns, the identity of those contributing the money, the identity of those sponsoring and organizing the campaigns, including public relations and advertising firms, the fees paid to these firms, the purposes for which the money was spent — all these things would have to be reported to Congress and through Congress to the public. General propaganda and public opinion campaigns not related to specific legislation would not be covered by the lobbying law, with the Comptroller General empowered to determine what was covered, subject to court appeal.

(6) To guard against deception and misleading information in grassroots lobbying campaigns on specific legislative issues, without abridging the right of free speech, a permanent Joint Congressional Committee on the Legislative Process should be created. This committee would be authorized to receive complaints of deception and misleading information in lobbying campaigns and irregularities in political spending, to hold hearings on these complaints if warranted and to publicize its findings. The committee would be directed to make a continuing study of the lobbying law and the statutes regulating spending. One of its specific tasks would be to study the proper relationship between special interest groups and government and to make legislative recommendations in this field.

(7) The Foreign Agents Registration Act, which originally was directed at a danger that has passed — the activities of Nazi agents and propagandists in the United States — should be scrapped as a separate law and the strengthened provisions recommended by the Foreign Relations Committee should be incorporated in a new lobbying law.

(8) The new law should apply to lobbying in the executive branch — the Defense Department, the space establishment and so on — and to lobbying in the federal regulatory agencies.

By combining the McClellan committee's proposal on grassroots lobbying with the Kennedy approach to the "principal purpose" problem and by designating the Comptroller General as the enforcement officer, as recommended by the Senate Rules Committee, Congress would have the basis for a far stronger and more effective lobbying law. So far as many — possibly

most — legislators were concerned, however, the chief virtue of
the Kennedy, McClellan and Rules Committee proposals was
that everyone knew they had little if any chance of being
enacted into law. Lobbying simply comes too close to the bone
in Congress. It is too intimately involved with "the system"
or "the establishment" for some legislators to contemplate with
equanimity a really effective lobbying law.

But it should not be thought that the national legislature is
congenitally incapable of passing laws dealing with lobbying.
It approved the original Lobbying Act in 1946 (although the
history of that law shows that it was passed hastily and pretty
much as an afterthought), and more recently it enacted another
interesting piece of legislation permitting business firms to claim
their lobbying expenses as a tax deduction.

The House Ways and Means Committee slipped this provision
into the tax bill of 1962 without holding hearings on it, and,
despite opposition by the Kennedy administration, it stayed in
the tax bill and became law. Popularly known as "the lobbying
aid bill" and "the act authorizing the purchase of state legislatures," it permits a taxpayer to deduct the cost of appearing
before or communicating with a legislative body, committee or
individual legislator, as long as it concerns legislation that is of
"direct interest" to the taxpayer's business.

The "direct interest" limitation, Professor David B. Weaver
has pointed out, "is a gesture rather than a serious qualification.
It is hard to conceive of many legislative subjects in which a large
corporate business, say General Motors, will not have some
legitimate interest." [4]

Under this provision, large corporations maintaining staffs of
lobbyists in Washington or hiring attorneys to represent them
in legislative matters can deduct the cost of these services from
their income tax. In effect this means that the individual taxpayer pays about half the salary of the lobbyists for General
Motors, Standard Oil and the rest. But if a taxpayer travels to
Washington or his state capital to testify or lobby on a piece
of legislation which he considers beneficial or harmful to the
public interest — a bill, in other words, which does not affect
his business but about which he feels strongly — he cannot claim
his expenses as a tax deduction.

In the debate on the tax bill, Senators Paul H. Douglas and William Proxmire pointed out that a gambling syndicate could lobby for a law legalizing gambling and then deduct its lobbying expenses, while a minister or other citizen who appeared in opposition to legalized gambling could not claim the same deduction. Under the law, as Douglas and Proxmire emphasized, businessmen and corporations can deduct the dues they pay to a trade association which engages in lobbying, but contributions to organizations such as the League of Women Voters, the American Civil Liberties Union and other *pro bono publico* organizations that testify before legislative committees cannot be deducted.

The antecedents of the lobbying tax deduction go back to 1915, when a Treasury Department ruling held that lobbying expenses were not deductible for tax purposes. Subsequently, in 1918, a Treasury regulation prohibited tax deductions for any expenses involving "lobbying purposes, the promotion or defeat of legislation [and] the exploitation of propaganda." This regulation was upheld by the Supreme Court in the Textile Mills Securities Corporation case of 1941 and again in 1959 in the Cammarano and F. Strauss & Sons cases. In the latter decisions, the court held that the regulation had the force of law because Congress had never changed it. Expenses for indirect, grassroots lobbying were not deductible, either, the court ruled.

The 1959 decisions spread consternation in the business community, which feared that the Internal Revenue Service would now begin to enforce a regulation that hitherto had been only sporadically invoked. The New Orleans Chamber of Commerce protested to Representative Hale Boggs, Louisiana Democrat. He also heard from the Bureau of Governmental Research in New Orleans, whose members feared that their contributions would no longer be deductible.

Boggs introduced a bill that would have permitted tax deductions for grassroots lobbying (including the cost of advertising on legislative issues) as well as direct contact lobbying. This measure was approved by the Ways and Means Committee in 1960 but got no further. In 1962 the committee approved an amended version submitted by Representative John C. Watts, Kentucky Democrat, among whose constituents are the giant Schenley and National Whiskey distillers. The Watts version, which became law, does not cover grassroots pressure; it limits

the tax deduction to the cost of direct lobbying. It is a bad law —
an example of Congressional-lobbying fraternization at its
worst — and it should be repealed. In the constant competition for legislative favor, as Senator Douglas has pointed out,
the tax laws should be neutral. The American taxpayer should
not have to subsidize the operations of any lobbying group.

Congress's friendly helping hand to the business lobbyists in
this and other instances stands in marked contrast to the howls
that go up when the executive branch of government tries some
mass lobbying. In fact, there is a law against the use of public
funds for this purpose, and the legislators sometimes invoke it.
A recent victim was Secretary of Health, Education and Welfare
Anthony J. Celebrezze, who sent a 520-word night letter, costing
a total of $3,562, to all members of the House, urging them
to support an education bill. The Republicans screamed bloody
murder, and Celebrezze, who was new on the job at the time,
said it wouldn't happen again.

A federal law states that no funds appropriated by Congress shall be used to pay for "any personal service, advertisement, telegram, telephone, letter, printed or written matter or
other device" intended to influence the vote of a member of
Congress. It is a perfectly proper statute. The taxpayers' money
should not be used by bureaucrats to influence legislation they
desire or oppose. But by granting a tax deduction for lobbying
by business firms, Congress has created a situation in which
the taxpayers' money *is* being used to influence legislation. And
the use of this money is given to individuals who, unlike the
President of the United States, are not elected by the people.

Although the Kennedy and McClellan lobbying bills were
worthwhile efforts, they suffered from the fundamental flaw
mentioned earlier. They took an after-the-fact approach. They
dealt with effects, not causes. The basic problems in lobbying —
the root causes underlying the sleazy inside deals, the phony
compromises, the special interest favoritism, the denial of the
public welfare — will not be solved by all the after-the-fact
legislation in the world, no matter how well intended. No amount
of tinkering will get at these deep ailments.

The first is the problem of the proper relationship between
organized special interest groups and government. This is a

question of ground rules to insure a fair contest between private and public requirements. A statute that merely requires identification and minimal disclosure does not set ground rules. It does not regulate.

The second is the problem of the corrupt institutions of Congress, which confer a significant and unjustified advantage on the private interest lobbyist. This problem involves the machinery of Congress — the underrepresentation of urban and suburban areas, the disenfranchisement of Negroes, the seniority system, the power of the committee chairmen and other antiquated rules — all the elements that have contributed to the low estate of the legislative branch.

Another problem, one of the most vexatious in American politics, is the financing of political campaigns. The almost abject dependence of many members of Congress on large campaign contributions confers a substantial legislative advantage on well-heeled special interests. The outmoded laws governing political money make virtually every candidate for public office in this country a hypocrite as soon as he seeks the nomination and frequently a cynic by election day.

And finally, there is the way we live now, which is the heart of the matter. The gross materialism of much of American life, the greed and selfishness, the ignorance that feeds on itself, the long neglect of the public sector, only now beginning to be remedied, the pressures for conformity — these, more than laws, really determine the conduct of government in the United States, as they determine all our public actions. Lobbying, as Senator Douglas has observed, "is almost always exclusively concerned with self-interest rather than the broad public interest," and as long as these unworthy strains continue to dominate American life, special interests will exercise an unwarranted influence on government.

The McClellan committee at one point asked a group of political scientists for their suggestions on how to improve the Lobbying Act. Stephen K. Bailey, an authority on Congress and director of the Woodrow Wilson School of Public and International Affairs at Princeton University, replied:

"My own position can be put very simply, and I hope not cynically: [it is] that any statute passed will be violated in spirit or letter — and if the Congress were capable of drafting

a statute which would really control the evils of lobbying, it
would be declared unconstitutional and rightly so.

"I don't mean to be a defeatist on this. It seems to me
that simple registration of those engaged in attempting to influence Congress by direct contact . . . is desirable. But only
the most naive citizen would believe that this gets at more than
the seventh of the iceberg that is above water . . . The real
answer to lobbying is the imposition of moral standards upon
the claims of vested interest. These moral standards can best
be imposed by those in the Congress and in the executive branch
who are conscientiously attempting to find the public interest . . ." [5]

Congress today is in no condition to assert the public morality
and impose it on the claims of vested interest. The outside law
practices and business dealings of some of its members make
this unlikely; the imbalance of political financing increases the
odds against it, and the corrupt institutions of Congress make
it impossible.

The outside business involvements of a number of Senators
and Representatives continue to raise serious questions about
their ability to legislate for the public good, but this is by no
means uniformly true. Some of the most public-spirited members are wealthy men. Moreover, the individual conflicts of
interest seldom determine the outcome of the broad social and
economic issues on which the viability and future of the nation
depend. The personal business interests of Congressmen are
more likely to affect the strictly special interest legislation which
attracts relatively little public attention and which is put
together in an atmosphere of secrecy. Highly technical tax legislation, as pointed out previously, is a prime example of the area
in which personal business affiliations and the need for campaign
funds often operate to influence the outcome. Because Congress
has 535 members and because the broad social and economic
issues generate more concern and more publicity, the likelihood
that the business and financial ties of individual members can
seriously affect this kind of legislation is diminished but not
entirely removed.

When it comes to the big public interest issues, the corruption
of the institutions of Congress and the attitudes of the public
are more important factors. Until Lyndon Johnson brought to

the presidency legislative skills unmatched in this generation and until he gained huge Democratic majorities in the House and Senate, Congress's ancient procedures had been used time and time again to delay or weaken legislation that would advance the general welfare. Again and again, the membership as a whole was denied the right to determine whether or not a proposal was in the public interest and to proceed accordingly. When and if Johnson loses his big majorities, the old pattern is likely to re-assert itself, and new Great Society programs will encounter Congressional iron curtains reminiscent of the Kennedy era. Even now, the *fin de siecle* rules and procedures continue to be used to block the reform of Congress itself.

Public attitudes are the other chief determinant in the legis-lative battles over broad general interest measures. For years, the public sector in the United States — schools, hospitals, equal opportunity for racial minorities, culturally mature treatment of the elderly and the disadvantaged — was starved and neglected. For years, using the terminology of the stock market, there was unrestrained profit-taking in this country at the expense of the general welfare. For years the dominant old men in Congress, reflecting public acquiescence in this imbalance and aided by the private interest lobbyists, set their faces resolutely against in-creased allocations of the nation's resources to the public sector. Time and time again, Congress's decisions rejected greater pro-tection for the public — protection against dangerous drugs, against inequitable tax treatment, against inadequate educa-tion and hospital care, against misleading advertising, against unsafe automobiles and gimcracky appliances, against racial dis-crimination, against, in general, the shoddiness and meretricious-ness of wide areas of American life and values.

With Kennedy's New Frontier and now under Johnson's Great Society, a start has been made toward bringing the public and private sectors into balance. But it is only a start. Despite the self-satisfied podsnappery that regards the pace of social progress as satisfactorily rapid, the hard fact is that the United States remains the most conservative large nation on earth. The coun-try is booming and the rate of economic growth is rising, but the rate of social progress and maturation is slow. The middle class huddles in its suburban uteri, hypnotized by the jibbering figures on the television screen, only occasionally and not lastingly disturbed by the riots in the slums, seemingly heedless of the educational shortcomings of its own double-shift schools, comfortably affluent, placidly unaware.

One result is that large corporations, pre-eminent in the economy and dominant in the public mind, still are virtually certain to get pretty much what they want from government when they really want it. The lobbyists for these companies enjoy a built-in advantage at the outset of any legislative struggle in which their corporation is seriously engaged, any contest in which it believes its vital interests are at stake. The steel industry, blocked from a general price increase, raises prices selectively to achieve the same end result. The Du Pont-General Motors stock bill, the A.T. AND T. Telstar bill, the 27½ percent oil depletion allowance and the scores of other tax loopholes and advantages are examples of the institutionalized advantage that business enjoys in lobbying, the built-in advantage. With depreciation allowances and tax reductions, the government even bribes business to do what it should do voluntarily — invest in industrial expansion and in the future of its talisman, the free enterprise system.

Victories — many of them — have indeed been won in the latter-day struggle to equalize the public and private sectors. But much remains to be done. And in a world whose distinguishing modern characteristic is social upheaval, time is not the friend of America that it once was. The private interest lobbyists, the lobbyists of the status quo, have suffered many setbacks in recent years, but they have not fled the field. Defeated on Medicare, the U.S. Chamber of Commerce attacks on another front. It mounts a new offensive, this time against President Johnson's plan to rebuild the nation's cities. The cost would be "prohibitive," says the Chamber. "The federal government hasn't the money and it hasn't the talents and it has no business building cities in the first place," says Chamber president Robert P. Gerholz. The wheel turns and the same old spokes come up.

Most key issues — education, hospital care, urban redevelopment, civil rights — involve in one way or another a more equitable distribution of national resources. All involve the "greatest good for the greatest number" definition of the public interest. All are guarantees of a better future. There is little dispute that special interest groups are valuable and necessary components of the national life — for one thing, they serve as outlets for legislative desires that, if frustrated, might lead to the kind of political fragmentation and splinterism that plagued France before de Gaulle. But the need cited by Stephen Bailey remains: to impose moral standards upon the claims of vested interest. The claims of privilege still impede the general welfare. A proper balance between government and special interest, between the public and private sector, remains to be devised.

An effective lobbying law, one covering grassroots as well as direct pressure and providing for rigorous enforcement, would be only the first step.

It would have to be followed by an overhaul of the laws dealing with campaign financing in order to give Congress a measure of independence from the tyranny of money. In 1962 President Kennedy's Commission on Campaign Costs, headed by Alexander Heard, warned against a situation in which candidates for major offices are "dependent on individuals or organizations with special interests" for their political survival. The commission proposed a trial system of tax credits and deductions to encourage small and medium-size campaign contributions and thus broaden the base of participation in the election process. But the likelihood is remote that Congress will act to correct the imbalance in campaign financing.

Reform of Congress itself would be the next fundamental step. Senator Clark has drawn up a "Bill of Rights" for Congress, under which a majority of the members of a committee could call meetings, terminate discussion after a reasonable period and call up bills for action. He proposes that committee chairmen be elected by secret ballot at the beginning of the session, that chairmen be barred from serving in that capacity after the age of 70 and that committees be required to report out the President's legislative proposals by July 4 of each year so that Congress as a whole will have time to act on them.

Some of these ideas may, on examination, prove unsound. But they provide a starting point, and the longer Congress delays considering them, the greater its disservice to representative government.

The reforms proposed by Clark, and others suggested by Sena-

tor Clifford P. Case, are central to the question of lobbying. By
restoring democratic procedures to the national legislature, they
would help define a fair and proper relationship between organized special interests and government. While the details of
this relationship are always difficult, the basic principle is simple:
the legislative machinery should be neutral as between interests.
Ideally, there should be no biases, conservative or liberal, built
into the procedures of Congress. If the biases were removed,
the first ground rule for a fair contest between private and public
interests would be established. Legislation could be considered
on its merits by the entire legislature.

Reform of the laws on campaign financing and an overhaul
of Congress's procedures would begin to get at the basic causes
of lobbying abuses, in a way that no amount of tinkering with
the present Lobbying Act ever could.

Lastly, there is the fundamental question of the public's attitude, which, as Lincoln pointed out, makes all legislation possible
or impossible to achieve. The American people must do better
than they have in understanding the vital matter of causal connection. The cause and effect relationship between the defeat
of school bond issues and juvenile delinquency, between slums
and higher taxes for police protection, the destructive cycle of
political apathy, bad government, political alienation and worse
government, between racial despair and racial strife, between
suburban affluence and intellectual stagnation — these are the
causal connections.

So, too, with lobbying. When the cause-effect relationships are
not understood, the lobbyists for special interests operate in a
vacuum. They get what they want by default. The extent to
which the citizen ignores his responsibility to be concerned about
the conduct of public affairs is the extent to which the lobbyist
prevails — and no more. And when the lobbyist prevails, the
people pay. They were paying a billion dollars more in taxes than
they should because of the campaign against interest and dividend withholding. They pay the 6,000 percent markups on pre-
scription drugs. They pay for the foreign aid to two-bit dictators.
They pay a billion and a half dollars a year in extra taxes because
of the various mineral depletion deductions, more than five billion
a year because of the lower capital gains rate and billions more
for the other tax gimmicks and preferences which the lobbyists

have such a large hand in arranging. They just missed paying $600,000,000 a year in higher gas bills when the Harris-Fulbright natural gas measure, pushed through Congress by lobbyists, was vetoed. They pay — and pay plenty — for the successful lobbying campaigns against the truth-in-lending and truth-in-packaging bills and other consumer legislation. They pay in human life for the so-far successful lobbying campaign to block regulation of the mail-order traffic in guns. They pay for the black ghettos and disorganized suburbs.

So, as always, it is a race. An old race between the quick and the dead, between ignorance and survival, between concern and apathy. We are all running in this race; we are all dancing this quickstep. Each of us must decide how the race is going. Each of us must judge for himself how well the people of the United States, in the second half of the twentieth century, measure up to the ancient standard of Pericles:

"An Athenian citizen does not neglect the state because he takes care of his own household; and even those of us who are engaged in business have a very fair idea of politics. We alone regard a man who takes no interest in public affairs not as a harmless but as as a useless character; and if few of us are originators, we are all sound judges of policy."

REFERENCES

CHAPTER 1

1. Alexander Heard, *The Costs of Democracy*. Doubleday and Co., New York.

2. Lester W. Milbrath, in *Public Opinion Quarterly* (Spring 1960).

3. General Interim Report of the Select Committee on Lobbying Activities, House of Representatives. Eighty-First Congress, Second Session. Washington, 1950.

4. Richard L. Neuberger, in *Coronet* (August 1956).

5. Paul W. Cherington and Ralph L. Gillen, *The Business Representative in Washington*. Brookings Institution, Washington, D. C.

6. James MacGregor Burns, in *The New York Times Book Review* (Aug. 19, 1962).

7. Robert F. Drinan, S.J., in *America* (June 20, 1953). (Father Drinan's article, "Legal Control of Lobbying," was written before the Supreme Court's decision in U.S. v. Harriss and was based on earlier court decisions. His description of the Lobbying Act as a "judicial shambles" was even more apt after the Harriss ruling.)

CHAPTER 2

1. V. O. Key Jr., *Politics, Parties and Pressure Groups*. Thomas Y. Crowell Co., New York.

2. Arthur F. Bentley, *The Process of Government*. University of Chicago Press.

3. R. M. MacIver, *The Web of Government*. Macmillan Co., New York.

4. E. H. Carr, quoted in *The New Republic* (Aug. 6, 1951).

5. John G. Fuller, *The Money Changers*. Dial Press, New York.

6. Robert J. Lampman, *The Share of Top Wealth-Holders in National Wealth, 1922-56*. Princeton University Press.

7. Gabriel Kolko, *Wealth and Power in America*. Frederick Praeger, New York.

8. Karl Schriftgiesser, *The Lobbyists*. Little, Brown and Co., Boston.

CHAPTER 3

1. Arthur M. Schlesinger Jr., *The Age of Jackson*. Little, Brown and Co., Boston.

2. Gerald W. Johnson, *America's Silver Age*. Harper & Brothers, New York.

3. W. S. McKechnie, *Magna Carta*. Burt Franklin Publishers, New York.

4. E. Merton Coulter, *Georgia, A Short History*. University of North Carolina Press, Chapel Hill, N.C.

5. David Loth, *Public Plunder, A History of Graft in America*. J. B. Lippincott, Philadelphia.

6. Schriftgiesser, *op. cit.*

7. Glyndon G. Van Deusen, *Thurlow Weed: Wizard of the Lobby*. Little, Brown and Co., Boston.

8. Beverly Smith, in *The Saturday Evening Post* (Dec. 23, 1950).

9. Meade Minnigerode, *Certain Rich Men*. G. P. Putnam's Sons, New York.

10. Margaret Leech, *Reveille in Washington.* Harper & Brothers, New York.
11. Kenneth G. Crawford, *The Pressure Boys: The Inside Story of Lobbying in America.* Julian Messner, Inc., New York.

CHAPTER 4

1. Daniel M. Berman, *A Bill Become a Law: The Civil Rights Act of 1960.* Macmillan Co., New York.
2. Sam Zagoria, in *The New York Times Magazine* (Sept. 8, 1963).
3. Douglass Cater and Walter Pincus, in *The Reporter* (April 13, 1961).
4. Murray Kempton, in *The New Republic* (Aug. 3, 1963).
5. Philip M. Stern, *The Great Treasury Raid.* Random House, New York.

CHAPTER 5

1. Sherman Adams, *Firsthand Report.* Harper & Brothers, New York.
2. George B. Galloway, *The Legislative Process in Congress.* Thomas Y. Crowell Co., New York.
3. E. H. Carr, *op. cit.*
4. *Washington Report,* published by the United States Chamber of Commerce (Vol. 1, No. 23, June 8, 1962).
5. *Congressional Action,* published by the United States Chamber of Commerce (Vol. 6, No. 10, March 26, 1962).
6. *Legislative Handbook for Associations,* published by the Association Service Department of the United States Chamber of Commerce. Washington, D.C.
7. V. O. Key Jr., *op. cit.*

CHAPTER 6

1. Solomon Barkin, quoted in *The Saturday Evening Post* (Dec. 8, 1962).
2. Joseph G. Rayback, *A History of American Labor.* Macmillan Co., New York.
3. Samuel C. Patterson, *The Role of the Labor Lobbyist.* (Paper presented to the American Political Science Association. Washington, D. C. 1962).
4. Sar A. Levitan, in *The Labor Law Journal* (Vol. 10, Oct. 1959).

CHAPTER 7

1. James Bryce, *The American Commonwealth,* Macmillan Co., New York.
2. Report of the Select Committee for Contribution Investigation, United States Senate. Eighty-Fourth Congress, Second Session. Washington, 1956.
3. Lester W. Milbrath, in *The Journal of Politics* (May 1958).
4. Richard E. Neustadt, *Presidential Power: The Politics of Leadership.* John Wiley & Sons, New York.
5. Louis W. Koenig, *The Invisible Presidency.* Rinehart & Co., New York.
6. Bernard Schwartz, *The Professor and the Commissions.* Alfred A. Knopf, New York.
7. Hearings Before the Special Subcommittee on Legislative Oversight, Committee on Interstate and Foreign Commerce, House of Representatives. Eighty-Sixth Congress, Second Session. Washington, 1960.
8. Report of the Special Subcommittee on Legislative Oversight. Eighty-Sixth Congress, Second Session. Washington, 1961.

CHAPTER 8

1. Merriman Smith, *The Good New Days.* Bobbs-Merrill Co., New York.
2. Lester W. Milbrath, in *Public Opinion Quarterly, op. cit.*
3. Report of the Special Committee to Investigate Political Activities, Lobbying and Campaign Contributions, United States Senate. Eighty-Fifth Congress, First Session. Washington, 1957.
4. Report of the Subcommittee on Antitrust and Monopoly, Committee on the Judiciary, United States Senate. Eighty-Seventh Congress, First Session. Washington, 1961.
5. Robert G. Sherrill, in *The Nation* (Mar. 7, 1966).
6. Hearings Before the Subcommittee to Investigate Juvenile Delinquency, Committee on the Judiciary, United States Senate. Eighty-Ninth Congress, First Session. Washington, 1965.
7. *Here's the Issue,* published by the United States Chamber of Commerce (Vol. 1, No. 2, March 19, 1962).
8. Michael J. O'Neill, in *The Reporter* (April 26, 1962).

CHAPTER 9

1. Robert Engler, in *The New Republic* (Sept. 5, 1955).
2. Regulation of Lobbying Act. 60 Stat. 839 (1946), 2 U.S.C. 261-70 (1958).
3. National Association of Manufacturers and Kenneth R. Miller v. J. Howard McGrath. United States District Court for the District of Columbia. Mar. 17, 1952.
4. United States v. Robert M. Harriss, Ralph W. Moore, Tom Linder and the National Farm Committee. 347 U.S. 612 (1954).
5. Stanley Kelley Jr., *Professional Public Relations and Political Power.* Johns Hopkins Press, Baltimore. (For more complete accounts of the American Medical Association's long campaign against "socialized medicine," the reader is referred to this and another book, *The Doctor Business, by* Richard Carter, published by Doubleday and Co., New York. Both are excellent treatments of subjects closely related to lobbying and both are highly recommended.)
6. Robert Engler, in *The New Republic* (Sept. 19, 1955).
7. Report of the Special Committee to Investigate Political Activities, Lobbying and Campaign Contributions, *op. cit.*

CHAPTER 10

1. Senator John F. Kennedy, in *The New York Times* (Feb. 19, 1956).
2. Belle Zeller, in *The Annals of the American Academy of Political and Social Science* (September 1958).
3. George B. Galloway, in a reply to a questionnaire on the operation of the Lobbying Act, in hearings before the Special Subcommittee to Investigate Political Activities, Lobbying and Campaign Contributions. Eighty-Fourth Congress, Second Session. Washington, 1956.
4. David B. Weaver, in *The George Washington Law Review,* George Washington University (June 1963).
5. Stephen K. Bailey, in a letter to Senator John L. McClellan, in hearings before the Special Subcommittee to Investigate Political Activities, Lobbying and Campaign Contributions, *op. cit.*

Opposition to the nuclear test ban treaty—an ad in the Washington Post, August 13, 1963.

AN OPEN LETTER TO President Kennedy

Why are we arming on such a scale?

MR. PRESIDENT:

We see a disturbing contradiction in the policies by which our nation is seeking security.

Recognizing that a major nuclear war would yield no victor and would threaten to destroy mankind, our government has affirmed the goal of general disarmament; yet it pursues an armament policy that guarantees, in our opinion, continuing failure of disarmament negotiations.

Important disclosures by your Administration support this interpretation. Recently Assistant Defense Secretary Gilpatric has stated that "We have a second strike capability at least as extensive as what Russia could deliver by striking first." This means that we have several times the Soviet striking power. The alleged "missile gap" did not materialize—except in reverse. This news increases our immediate sense of security, but how does it affect our hopes for long-term security through general disarmament?

The persistent obstacle has concerned inspection. The United States insists on unlimited inspection at an early stage; the U.S.S.R. rejects it until a late stage. Why?

It is easy to consider the Russians entirely responsible for this impasse, and to question the possibility of negotiating with them. But the recently revealed profound imbalance of nuclear power in our favor suggests that the problem is more complex. Since the Russians cannot disable our retaliatory capacity they cannot accomplish an effective first strike against us. Neither, however, can the United States successfully attack first so long as the exact locations of the Soviet bases are unknown. To protect its limited force the U.S.S.R. maintains geographical secrecy, strenuously resisting our efforts at reconnaissance. The United States cannot maintain secrecy over its territory. Instead, relying on our greater industrial capacity, we have developed an enormous nuclear force.

In this weapons imbalance we see a reasonable explanation for the disarmament deadlock. The Soviet plan would deny the U.S. adequate safeguards against hidden weapons; our plan would deny the U.S.S.R. the secrecy essential to its deterrent force. We find encouragement in this explanation. Disarmament negotiations may become fruitful if a better balance in armaments can eliminate the Soviet need for secrecy.

But can the United States reduce its overwhelming nuclear superiority without weakening its security? Recent technological developments make this course feasible. We have begun to make weapons that are virtually invulnerable: Polaris missiles in submarines and Minuteman missiles buried underground.

With these new weapons, the United States no longer need rely on vast numerical superiority for its defense by deterrence. Our defense force is adequate if it contains enough of these weapons to threaten retaliatory destruction of major Soviet cities.

Yet we see under way a vastly larger program than is required for deterrence. According to the Department of Defense, by 1965 the U.S. intends to have 800 Minutemen, over 200 Atlas and Titan missiles, 950 intercontinental bombers, and about 650 missiles on 41 Polaris submarines. In addition, we have about 1300 planes able to deliver nuclear bombs from overseas bases and carriers. To try to comprehend the meaning of these figures, we may recall that one bomber or missile can deliver more explosive force than was released in all of World War II.

Why is the United States developing this fantastic force?

From recent statements of Defense Secretary McNamara we fear that the reason may be a radical shift, from a primarily defensive policy to the nuclear strategy called "counterforce." This would have us strive for a force so large and discriminating that we could (1) destroy most Soviet military installations, and (2) retain enough reserve power to threaten destruction of their cities. This policy is claimed to allow us to resort to nuclear war, in defense of our most vital interests, without destruction of cities on either side.

On the surface this strategy may seem more humane than a deterrent strategy, which threatens bombing of civilian populations. But can anyone who remembers the bombings of World War II imagine that cities would be spared in any major nuclear war? MR. PRESIDENT, this new strategy might seem to offer temporary solutions to some great problems you face:

¶ It might keep our NATO allies from building nuclear forces by assuring them that we are conspicuously prepared to defend them.

¶ It might even make the Russians more cooperative for a while.

But surely these short-term advantages would soon be swept away in an evil flood of later consequences.

¶ Would not this strategy provoke the very thing it aims to prevent? Would not the U.S.S.R. be driven to maximize its capacity to destroy our cities with the weapons that survived attack?

¶ Would not the policy become bankrupt when the Russians developed enough invulnerable weapons?

¶ Does not this policy perpetuate an unlimited arms race, increasing the likelihood of accidental war in a tense and frightened world?

¶ Worst of all, does not this policy block all progress toward disarmament? Believing that we aim at overwhelming nuclear superiority, has the U.S.S.R. any choice but to maintain secrecy and view our disarmament proposals with extreme suspicion?

We therefore urge that you:

1. Substantially reduce the scale of our nuclear arms program to fit a purely deterrent strategy.
2. Renounce—publicly and firmly—the strategic use of nuclear weapons except in response to a nuclear attack on us or our allies.
3. Revise our disarmament proposals to allow, by a disproportionate weapons reduction, a closer approach to equality before the U.S.S.R. would have to abandon its secrecy.

Let us not drift—or deliberately march—into an aggressive posture.

Let us instead pursue the policies that should follow from your own eloquent statement: *"Today every inhabitant of this planet must contemplate the day when this planet may no longer be habitable. Every man, woman, and child lives under a nuclear sword of Damocles hanging by the slenderest of threads capable of being cut at any moment by accident or miscalculation or by madness. . . . The risk inherent in disarmament pales in comparison to the risks inherent in an unlimited arms race."* United Nations, September, 1961.

NUCLEAR POLICY LETTER COMMITTEE, P. O. BOX 273, LEXINGTON, MASSACHUSETTS

BOSTON UNIVERSITY
Joseph Ablow, *Fine and Applied Arts*
Archie A. Abrams, *Medicine*
Paul Kurt Ackermann, *Modern Languages*
Gerald Barnes, *Sociology*
Chester C. Bennett, *Psychology*
Morton Berman, *English*
Saul Bernstein, *Social Work*
Robert S. Cohen, *Physics*
Rose A. Godbout, *Nursing*
Elizabeth J. Hall, *Nursing*
Sam Hedrick, *Theology*
A. H. Hegnauer, *Physiology*
Dean Hosken, *Religion*
Paul E. Johnson, *Theology*
Conan Kornetsky, *Pharmacology*
John H. Lavely, *Philosophy*
Fabian J. Lionetti, *Biochemistry*
Earl R. Loew, *Physiology*
Jeane Murphy, *Social Work*
Gottfried E. Noether, *Mathematics*
Frieda Rebelsky, *Psychology*
John Gammons Read, *Education*
L. J. Reyna, *Psychology*
Michael Rice, *Physics*
S. Paul Schilling, *Theology*
Edward Wagenknecht, *English*
Marx W. Wartofsky, *Philosophy*

BRANDEIS UNIVERSITY
Lewis A. Coser, *Sociology*
Herman T. Epstein, *Biology*
David L. Falkoff, *Physics*
G. Fasman, *Biochemistry*
Ray G[illegible], *History*
Nahum N. Glatzer, *History*
Oscar Goldman, *Mathematics*
Lawrence Grossman, *Biochemistry*
Richard Held, *Psychology*
Mary Ellen Jones, *Biochemistry*
Richard M. Jones, *Psychology*
Nathan O. Kaplan, *Biochemistry*
Harold P. Klein, *Biology*
Harold I. Levine, *Mathematics*
Henry Linschitz, *Chemistry*
Ramsay MacMullen, *History*
Norbett L. Mintz, *Psychology*
Richard S. Morgan, *Biochemistry*
Ulric Neisser, *Psychology*
Richard S. Palais, *Mathematics*
Philip Rahv, *English*
Myron Rosenblum, *Chemistry*
Frederic Schick, *Philosophy*
Jerome Schiff, *Biology*
Miriam Schurin, *Biology*
Morris S. Schwartz, *Sociology*
Richard L. Sklar, *Politics*
Philip E. Slater, *Sociology*
Morris Soodak, *Biochemistry*
Maurice R. Stein, *Sociology*
Arnold Strickon, *Anthropology*
Maurice Sussmann, *Biology*
Caldwell Titcomb, *Music*
E. V. Walter, *Sociology*
Kurt H. Wolff, *Sociology*
Harry Zohn, *German*
Edgar Zwilling, *Biology*

HARVARD UNIVERSITY
Benjamin Alexander, *Medicine*
Gordon W. Allport, *Social Relations*
Harold Amos, *Bacteriology*
C. B. Anfinsen, *Biological Chemistry*
Joseph C. Aub, *Medicine*
Elso S. Barghoorn, *Biology*
E. S. Castle, *Biology*
David F. Cavers, *Law*
Stanley Cobb, *Neuropathology*
A. H. Coons, *Bacteriology*
Bernard D. Davis, *Bacteriology*
John T. Edsall, *Biology*
Howard W. Emmons, *Applied Physics*
Frank Ervin, *Psychiatry*
Ned Feder, *Biology*
Jacob Fine, *Surgery*
Roderick Firth, *Philosophy*
A. Stone Freedberg, *Medicine*
Sanford Gifford, *Psychiatry*
Myron P. Gilmore, *History*
Elwood Henneman, *Physiology*
Howard H. Hiatt, *Medicine*
J. R. Hightower, *Far Eastern Languages*
Mahlon B. Hoagland, *Bacteriology*
H. Stuart Hughes, *History*
K. J. Isselbacher, *Medicine*
Herman M. Kalckar, *Biochemistry*
Edwin C. Kemble, *Physics*
Alexander Leaf, *Medicine*
R. P. Levine, *Biology*
Bernard Lown, *Nutrition*
Kirtley F. Mather, *Geology*
Everett I. Mendelsohn, *History of Science*
Matthew Meselson, *Biology*
Paul L. Munson, *Pharmacology*
Leonard K. Nash, *Chemistry*
John R. Pappenheimer, *Physiology*
Charles D. Parsons, *Philosophy*
Talcott Parsons, *Social Relations*
John R. Raper, *Biology*
David Riesman, *Social Sciences*
Raymond Siever, *Geology*
B. F. Skinner, *Psychology*
John P. Spiegel, *Psychiatry*
Norman W. Storer, *Social Relations*
James R. Ware, *Chinese*
Ralph H. Wetmore, *Biology*
Joshua Whatmough, *Linguistics*
Amos N. Wilder, *Divinity*
T. Hastings Wilson, *Physiology*
Paul I. Yakovley, *Neurology*

MASSACHUSETTS INSTITUTE OF TECHNOLOGY
Eugene Bell, *Biology*
John Bossons, *Industrial Management*
Noam Chomsky, *Modern Languages*
John F. Cochran, *Physics*
Charles D. Coryell, *Chemistry*
Murray Eden, *Electrical Engineering*
H. W. Fairbairn, *Geology*
B. T. Feld, *Physics*
Herman Feshbach, *Physics*
Harold Freeman, *Statistics*
Glen E. Gordon, *Chemistry*
Myron J. Gordon, *Industrial Management*
Robert L. Kyhl, *Electrical Engineering*
Cyrus Levinthal, *Biology*
M. Stanley Livingston, *Physics*
Salvador E. Luria, *Biology*
Kevin Lynch, *City Planning*
Boris Magasanik, *Biology*
S. J. Mason, *Electrical Engineering*
Norman A. Phillips, *Meteorology*
Hilary Putnam, *Humanities*
Alexander Rich, *Biology*
Bruno Rossi, *Physics*
William F. Schreiber, *Electrical Engineering*
C. Fayette Taylor, *Mechanical Engineering*
Laszlo Tisza, *Physics*
George W. Whitehead, *Mathematics*
Hurd C. Willett, *Meteorology*
John W. Winchester, *Geology*
George Wolf, *Nutrition*

NORTHEASTERN UNIVERSITY
Alan H. Cromer, *Physics*
Marvin Gettner, *Physics*
Michael J. Glaubman, *Physics*
Donald S. Pitkin, *Sociology*
Eugene J. Saletan, *Physics*

TUFTS UNIVERSITY
Freeland K. Abbott, *History*
Louis S. Chase, *Psychiatry*
John Cornwall, *Economics*
Dorothea J. Crook, *Psychology*
William Dameshek, *Medicine*
Albert S. Dreyer, *Social Studies*
Franklyn D. Holzman, *Economics*
Norman I. Krinsky, *Pharmacology*
Zella Luria, *Psychology*
Walter S. McNutt, *Pharmacology*
Robert L'H. Miller, *Religion*
Thornton B. Roby, *Psychology*
Edwin M. Schur, *Sociology*
Jack Tessman, *Physics*
Samuel S. Turesky, *Periodontology*

WELLESLEY COLLEGE
J. L. Benson, *Art*
Charlotte E. Goodfellow, *Latin*
Edward V. Gulick, *History*
Walter E. Houghton, *English*
Katherine Lever, *English*
W. Warren Wagar, *History*

OTHER INSTITUTIONS
Hudson Hoagland, *Biology, Worcester Foundation*
Sumner M. Rosen, *Economics, Simmons College*
Frank G. Rothman, *Biology, Brown University*
Leila Sussman, *Sociology, University of Massachusetts*
Albert Szent-Gyorgyi, *Biology, Marine Biological Laboratory*
David Todd, *Chemistry, Worcester Polytechnical Institute*

This advertisement was paid for by the signers, who are faculty members of professorial rank in the institutions named. The institutional affiliation is listed for identification only.

A grassroots appeal for nuclear disarmament.

THE COMMITTEE OF ONE MILLION
Against the Admission of Communist China to the United Nations

SUITE 909 • 79 MADISON AVENUE, NEW YORK 16, NEW YORK • MURRAY HILL 5-0190

TO: CITY EDITORS   FOR RELEASE TO ALL PAPERS
EDITORIAL WRITERS   MONDAY, SEPTEMBER 24, 1962
COLUMNISTS
COMMENTATORS

259 CONGRESSMEN URGE DEFENSE OF QUEMOY

OPPOSE "TWO CHINA" POLICY AND ADMISSION OF RED CHINA TO U.N.

New York, New York: 36 Senators and 223 Representatives joined in
issuing a Declaration which called for the defense of Quemoy and Matsu and
opposed any "two China" policy which would seat Red China in the United
Nations. The Declaration was circulated by the Committee Of One Million
(Against the Admission of Communist China to the United Nations) which is
headed by Warren R. Austin, former U.S. Senator and first U.S. Ambassador
to the U.N. and Joseph C. Grew, former U. S. Ambassador to Japan and
Under Secretary of State. The group's Steering Committee include Senators
Paul H. Douglas (D., Ill.) and Kenneth B. Keating (R., N.Y.); Represent-
atives Walter H. Judd (R., Minn.) and Francis E. Walter (D., Penna.);
Charles Edison, former Governor of New Jersey and Secretary of the Navy;
and H. Alexander Smith, former U.S. Senator and Special Assistant to the
Secretary of State.

The Declaration said: "The President of the United States and his Secretary
of State are publicly committed to a sound and firm policy toward Communist
China. This position has the support of the American people and the Congress.
Recently, there has been renewed pressure on the part of some American
publications, organizations and individuals calling for drastic changes in this
line of action through offering various and substantial concessions to Communist
China. We, therefore, believe it appropriate at this time to reemphasize and
to reiterate our support of United States policy toward the Peiping regime.

Opposition to admission of Communist China to the United Nations.

285

A Declaration by Members of
The Congress of the United States of America
In Opposition to any Concessions to Red China

THE President of the United States and his Secretary of State are publicly committed to a sound and firm policy toward Communist China. This position has the support of the American people and the Congress. Recently, there has been renewed pressure on the part of some American publications, organizations and individuals calling for drastic changes in this line of action through offering various and substantial concessions to Communist China. We, therefore, believe it appropriate at this time to reemphasize and to reiterate our support of United States policy toward the Peiping regime.

The undersigned have joined with more than 1,250,000 Americans in endorsing the following Statement:

"We continue to oppose the seating of Communist China in the United Nations, thus upholding international morality and keeping faith with the thousands of American youths who gave their lives fighting Communist aggression in Korea. To seat a Communist China which defies, by word and deed, the principles of the U.N. Charter would be to betray the letter, violate the spirit and subvert the purposes of that Charter. We further continue to oppose United States diplomatic recognition or any other steps which would build the power and prestige of the Chinese Communist regime to the detriment of our friends and allies in Asia and of our national security. Any such action would break faith with our dead and the unfortunate Americans still wrongfully imprisoned by Communist China and would dishearten our friends and allies in Asia whose continued will to resist Communist China's pressures and blandishments is so vital to our own security interests in that part of the world."

In order to make our position even more clear, we herewith elaborate:

● We are opposed to any so-called "two-China" policy in the United Nations. The Republic of China is a member in good standing of both the Security Council and the General Assembly. There is no justifiable reason to change its status. We continue to oppose the admission of the representatives of the Peiping regime into any body or agency of the United Nations. Such admission would make a mockery of the Charter and further strengthen the Communist world against the free world.

● We are opposed to trade relations between the United States and Communist China. Such trade would help an avowed enemy far more than it could possibly benefit ourselves.

● We are opposed to permitting Communist China to occupy any additional free territory by force or threat of force. Our country has troops in Southeast Asia in support of this position. Quemoy and Matsu are free territory and we are opposed to abandoning these strategic islands to Communist Chinese conquest. We cannot believe it to be in the interest of either our national security or our national honor to sacrifice the lives of thousands of free Chinese soldiers — and the civilian population of these islands — to Communist aggression.

In endorsing the above, we earnestly believe we are acting in our national interest and the interest of freedom throughout the world and that this statement represents the thinking of the great majority of the American people.

An advertisement manipulating Congress against itself.

286

An example of foreign lobbying—an appeal in behalf of the rebel regime in Rhodesia.

Opposition to interest and dividend withholding—an ad
in the Erie, Pa., Times-News, April 15, 1962

This advertisement against interest and dividend withholding appeared in a Lima, Ohio, paper.

Dear Saver:

If a proposal now before the United States Senate becomes law, the government will collect its share of your interest and dividends before you have them, reinvest them, or even make their acquaintance.

We believe that we have an obligation to you as a saver at (name of your institution) to acquaint you with the facts of this legislative proposal.

Perhaps you have heard of it. It is the proposed 20% withholding tax on interest and dividends incorporated in H.R. 10650 which has just been approved by the House of Representatives and is now before the United States Senate. This 20% would be skimmed off the earnings from all types of investments: United States savings bonds, corporate stocks and bonds, insurance, mutual funds, and savings in banks, savings and loan associations and credit unions.

Our institution and all others that pay interest or dividends would be required to deduct 20% and send it to the government. You would be required to claim this 20% as tax paid when you file your annual personal income tax return.

We could not be required to withhold the 20% on the earnings of persons over age 65 or under 18, but such people would have to establish the fact of their age with us.

Others who for one reason or another would not have to pay federal income tax in any year would have to file an exemption certificate with us and with every organization that pays them interest or dividends. This certificate would have to be filed each year, else withholding would be necessary.

Some people do not pay their full taxes on interest and dividends. This is the reason for the 20% withholding tax proposal on the interest and dividends of everyone. The government is in effect trying to weed the garden with a bulldozer when it requires withholding on the interest and dividends of everyone in order to make sure that it collects taxes owed by the few who do not report all of their interest and dividends on their personal income tax returns.

The strange thing is that this "bulldozer" approach is not necessary. The government's automatic data processing (ADP) center, now partially in operation, will be completed within another year or two. Electronic brains will then examine every tax return and cross check them against every reported interest and dividend payment. ADP is so accurate, according to Internal Revenue Commissioner Mortimer C. Caplin, that cheating will be very difficult for the "foolish few who try." Unfortunately, under withholding all American savers would lose and would be terribly inconvenienced because the government says a "foolish few" may try to beat data processing.

If you agree that this proposed withholding tax against your savings and investments is unfair, then you can do something about it by writing a letter to your two United States senators. Now is the time to protest and ... to those who are writing the tax law. Your senators

U.S. Savings and Loan League letter that brought a stinging rebuke from President Kennedy.

290

United States Savings and Loan League

...Founded in 1892...

EXECUTIVE COMMITTEE

M.L.DYE, President, SALT LAKE CITY, UTAH   F. B YEILDING, JR, Vice President BIRMINGHAM, ALABAMA
NORMAN STRUNK, Executive Vice President, CHICAGO, ILLINOIS

ARTHUR J. BROCKWAY, NEW HAVEN, CONNECTICUT   WILLIAM E. TAYLOR, CLEVELAND, OHIO   GEORGE S METCALFE, ST LOUIS, MISSOURI
ROLAND LEWAN, MILLBURN, NEW JERSEY   RALPH W. SEDGWICK, VERO BEACH, FLORIDA   LLOYD S. BOWLES, DALLAS, TEXAS
GEORGE L. FUESSLER, ERIE, PENNSYLVANIA   ARTHUR G. SHIREMAN, SOUTH BEND, INDIANA   RICHARD N SHORETT, SEATTLE, WASHINGTON
JULIUS W. ANDERSON, ANDERSON, SOUTH CAROLINA   A. C. STEINHAUER, MADISON, WISCONSIN   ROBERT P SPRAGUE, LOS ANGELES, CALIFORNIA
C. ELWOOD KNAPP, PITTSBURGH, PENNSYLVANIA   HENRY A. BUBB, TOPEKA, KANSAS

EXECUTIVE OFFICES - 221 NORTH LA SALLE STREET, TELEPHONE CENTRAL 6-2234

CHICAGO 1, ILLINOIS

NORMAN STRUNK
Executive Vice President

March 30, 1962

Dear Savings Association Executive:

ACTION NEEDED NOW ON TAX BILL IN SENATE

The savings and loan tax battle now has moved to the United States Senate.

.The time has come for every savings and loan executive, officer and director to write a letter to both his United States senators covering either or both the savings and loan tax law and the proposed withholding on interest and dividends.

The time also has come for associations to address letters to their savers, borrowers, and builder and realtor friends. You will recall that earlier this year we asked every association to "get ready" for such a mailing to savers and others by addressing envelopes, etc. This is the time when these envelopes should be used.

With respect to the change in the savings and loan tax, every savings and loan man should realize that the commercial banks are going to make an all-out fight in the Senate to increase the savings and loan taxes already voted in the bill which has just passed the House of Representatives.

If we do not work effectively, the banker proposals might well prevail in the Senate and we would indeed then be in a precarious situation. Thousands of letters from commercial bankers are on their way to the Senate Office Building. All 100 United States senators must hear from their savings and loan associations and, we hope, will hear from millions of savings and loan savers.

Unlike the House of Representatives, tax bills can freely be amended on the floor of the Senate. Thus, every member of the Senate has a chance to be of help in voting on both the withholding proposal and the taxation of thrift institutions.

With respect to letters to savers, we know that some of our members would prefer to communicate only on the withholding tax proposal. Others we know want to write solely on the proposed change in the savings and loan tax. Some will want to write to their savers on both issues.

The Savings and Loan League kept up a barrage of grassroots appeals against the Kennedy proposal.

291

Congress has acted
~and so have we

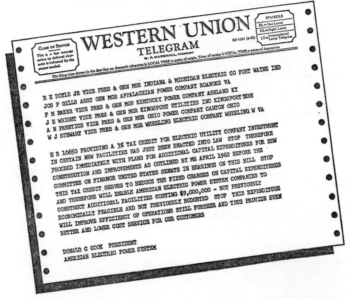

The expenditure of these <u>additional</u> funds will benefit 1,419,000 electric customers in 2371 communities served by the American Electric Power System. It will help strengthen the economy by increasing employment and providing more dollars to purchase goods and services. It will stimulate production and create jobs in the manufacturing and service industries across the nation which supply the products needed in this <u>added construction program</u>.

> In these ways, tax credits for industry can be made a
> powerful stimulating force leading to increased economic strength,
> higher levels of employment and greater national income.

AMERICAN ELECTRIC ⒜ₑₚ POWER SYSTEM

AN INVESTOR OWNED PUBLIC UTILITY   2.BROADWAY, N.Y. HA 2-4800

OPERATING
COMPANIES
OF THE SYSTEM

- APPALACHIAN POWER COMPANY   • INDIANA & MICHIGAN ELECTRIC COMPANY   • KENTUCKY POWER COMPANY
- KINGSPORT UTILITIES, INCORPORATED   • OHIO POWER COMPANY   • WHEELING ELECTRIC COMPANY

Indirect lobbying by business in a full-page advertisement.

292

CONGRESS
COULD EASILY
KILL
THE FEW REMAINING
CHILDREN'S
MAGAZINES

A plea to the House of Representatives for
no further increase in second-class postage rates

CHILDREN'S MAGAZINES are important! They provide good wholesome entertainment. They educate as they entertain and provide essential nourishment for growing young minds. Children's magazines are largely sold by subscription and must use the mails for distribution (unlike, for example, comics, which are mainly delivered to newsstands by truck, freight and express, with only minor reliance on the postal system).

Some, if not all, of the remaining children's magazines, which have struggled so hard to exist, would be killed if second-class postage rates are drastically increased, as now proposed.

Publishing children's magazines is mighty tough these days for a number of reasons: (1) These magazines carry virtually no advertising. (2) Publication of children's magazines is made possible largely from subscription income — and there is a limit to the price parents will pay for magazines for their children.

Children's magazines as a whole now only a little better than break even. In face of rising publishing costs, including postal rate increases, such fine children's magazines as *Children's Activities, Story Parade* and *Walt Disney's Magazine* have recently been forced out of business. This has reduced the number of children's magazines remaining to a mere handful.

Despite an over-all hike of 89% in magazine postage in recent years, the Postal Rate Bill currently reported out by the House Post Office Committee would almost *double* existing postal rates on children's magazines by proposing to increase the minimum cost per copy. The proposed Murray Amendment would *triple* them by the proposed high surcharge.

Children's magazines collectively employ a good many thousand employees and subscription agents who would lose their income from these sources. Printers, engravers, and paper manufacturers would suffer, too.

Biggest losers of all, however, would be America's children!

An example of pressure against a postal rate increase.

293

Americans need jobs-

not a <u>dole</u>, Mr. President.

Grassroots lobbying by coal operators against foreign fuel oil imports—an ad in the Washington Post, August 21, 1962.

"Minimum Freight Rates" Legislation Will Do This, Too!
TELL CONGRESS TO PASS IT!

DON'T let anybody kid you – the American people will save a lot of money when the "Minimum Rates" legislation now before Congress is passed. Fair competition will bring many of today's needlessly high freight charges down–fast. Lower freight charges mean lower prices – for you. Southern Railway's lowered freight rates on grain moving into the South–recently effective after 22 months of frustrating, costly-to-you delay–prove this is true.

We are now moving five-car multiple shipments of grain from Cincinnati, Ohio, to Charlotte, N. C., in our 100-ton "Big John" cars for a price of only $1,809.36 instead of $4,788.00 –the old price. The savings: a whopping $2,978.64 on this one shipment! That's just an example. There are many more like it. Rates with savings

such as this can be made nation-wide. You profit and we profit. Everybody benefits.

Let's look at some frying-pan facts. Food will cost less. A state department of agriculture estimates the savings from lower grain freight rates to be: 1¼¢ on a dozen eggs, 1¢ a pound on chickens. Other agricultural economists back this up and point to equally significant savings on beef, milk, pork, bread and many other market-basket items.

Such savings are fine, as far as they go–but they don't go far enough. The public–that's you–could be saving a lot more. Grain is only one of hundreds of bulk and agricultural products on which railroads can't *lower* freight charges without facing long delays, as in our grain case. Or, all too often, our request to

lower rates is flatly refused. Out-of-date regulation of railroads is responsible for this, and it is costing you and all other consumers of America billions of dollars each year. You pay the freight when you buy anything.

What's the answer? Do *your* part to have Congress pass the "Minimum Rates" bills as they are now written. This will mean reduced freight rates and save you money. It is in *your* interest. Help get it passed. Tell your Senators to vote for S. 1061. Tell your Congressman to vote for H.R. 4700. Do it today.

D.W.Brosnan
PRESIDENT

SOUTHERN RAILWAY SYSTEM
WASHINGTON, D. C.   *SOUTHERN SERVES THE SOUTH*

Another example of grassroots lobbying by business
—a full-page ad on a freight bill.

Postal unions and mail order groups join forces for some cross-lobbying against cuts in the Post Office budget.

A VOTE FOR
UNEMPLOYMENT?

The House of Representatives is scheduled to vote on a bill to increase postal rates. A vote for this bill has the effect of getting many of us fired from our jobs. Our concern is the increase in second class rates.

The Postal Rate Bill will increase the rates that newspapers and magazines pay the Post Office Department by $53,000,000. But it will destroy many magazines and small newspapers which employ members of our skilled trade. In turn, thousands of our craftsmen will be thrown out of work. These jobs will be gone forever because higher and higher postal rates are spelling out the death sentence for some of America's finest publications . . . and these publications are not being replaced.

In the last ten years nearly 100 U. S. magazines alone have stopped publication. When they went out of business thousands of us lost our jobs.

While Congress considers a bill to put us on the street, this country gives billions of tax dollars to Communist countries, some of which they will use to print more propaganda publications. We know these are being shipped into neighbor countries in the Americas. Some of these periodicals will be delivered **free of charge** in the U. S. to our homes — perhaps to the very same persons the pending Postal Rate Bill will throw out of work.

What sort of nonsense is this? During the same period we were giving Comrade Tito of Yugoslavia $2.5 billion, nearly 100 magazines failed. While we were providing Gomulka of Poland with nearly $1 billion, thousands of our families lost their incomes.

In our opinion, this is the worst kind of foolishness. We protest the passage of H.R. 7927.

INTERNATIONAL PRINTING PRESSMEN AND
ASSISTANTS UNION OF NORTH AMERICA
AFL-CIO
ANTHONY J. DeANDRADE, President

Another grassroots appeal by a powerful labor union.

297

RAILROAD "POVERTY" MYTH SHOULD BE EXPOSED

Railroads have been crying "poverty" for a long time. "Poverty" is management's own diagnosis and management would like to write its own prescriptions. The railroads use their alleged plight in an attempt to create a favorable climate for escaping regulation, for smoothing the way for monopolistic mergers and consolidations, for reducing service and eliminating jobs. An example of how the railroads plead "poverty" as an excuse for attacking their employees is seen in a statement made at a recent press conference by J. E. Wolfe, chief spokesman for railroad corporation negotiators. He said, "The nation's railroads, determined to end the featherbedding that is driving them into bankruptcy, have notified the Unions today (July 17) that all the recommendations of the Presidential Railroad Commission will be made effective on August 16, 1962."

FACTS don't show "poverty" or "featherbedding"

INVESTORS ARE REAPING BIG PROFITS

Look at these returns, as of May 21, 1962, on a $100 investment made in 1942 in railroad stocks:

RAILROAD	THEN VALUE OF $100 INVESTMENT		DIVIDENDS PAID ON $100 OF INVESTMENT	TOTAL WORTH OF $100 INVESTMENT
ATLANTIC COAST LINE	$ 488	+	$ 441	= $ 929
BALTIMORE & OHIO	900	+	495	= 1,395
CHESAPEAKE & OHIO	193	+	237	= 430
DELAWARE & HUDSON	567	+	891	= 1,458
GREAT NORTHERN	410	+	418	= 828
ILLINOIS CENTRAL	2,000	+	1,340	= 3,340
LEHIGH VALLEY	200	+	157	= 357
LOUISVILLE & NASHVILLE	207	+	334	= 541
MILWAUKEE ROAD	240	+	340	= 580
NEW YORK CENTRAL	200	+	187	= 387
NICKEL PLATE ROAD	3,500	+	1,757	= 5,257
NORFOLK & WESTERN	269	+	208	= 477
NORTHERN PACIFIC	1,267	+	834	= 2,101
PENNSYLVANIA	83	+	135	= 218
READING	100	+	248	= 348
SANTA FE	625	+	508	= 1,133
SEABOARD	560	+	416	= 976
SOUTHERN PACIFIC	1,300	+	810	= 2,110
SOUTHERN	2,750	+	1,345	= 4,095
UNION PACIFIC	533	+	382	= 915
WESTERN MARYLAND	4,200	+	1,150	= 5,350
WESTERN PACIFIC	250	+	177	= 427

SOURCES: *Moody's Handbook of Widely Held Common Stocks and Monthly Stock Digest, June, 1962, published by Data Digests, Inc.*

GROWTH OF TOTAL CAPITAL SURPLUS AND RETAINED INCOME, 1940-1960, U.S. RAILROADS

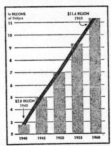

SOURCE: *Annual Transportation Statistics, Interstate Commerce Commission.*

RAILROAD WORKERS LEAD IN OUTPUT

CHICAGO—The ton-mile output of railroad employees is the highest of any form of transportation, as shown in statistics published by RAILWAY AGE, the railroad industry's magazine of news, analysis and interpretation. The average freight-service employee of a railroad out-produces his motor carrier counterpart almost 6 to 1.

TON-MILES PER RAIL EMPLOYEE DOUBLE

Annual revenue ton-miles per rail employee have climbed from 333,000 in 1939 to 727,000 in 1960. —*Annual Report on Transport Statistics for the Year Ended December 31, 1960,* Interstate Commerce Commission.

RAIL MAN-HOUR REVENUE UNITS SOAR

Revenue traffic units per rail man-hour actually worked have risen from 731.9 in 1936 to 1,488.6 in 1960.—ICC, *Transport Statistics in the U.S., Statements M-220, M-300.*

RAILROAD MANPOWER MOST EFFICIENT

A comparison of manpower requirements to move 100,000 tons of freight between New York and San Francisco:

METHOD OF TRANSPORT	MAN-DAYS REQUIRED
HIGHWAY	43,416
AIR (Propeller)	36,708
AIR (Jet)	13,008
WATER	11,158
RAILROAD	3,230

SOURCE: Testimony of James M. Symes, President (now Board Chairman) of the Pennsylvania Railroad Company, before the Sub-Committee on Transportation, House Committee on Armed Services, Hearings on the Adequacy of Transportation in the Event of Mobilization, July, 1959.

CONGRESS SHOULD INVESTIGATE

Is the railroad industry healthy today? Railroad management seems to say "yes" at one time and "no" at another, depending on who's listening. Individual railroad corporation financial statements to their stockholders contradict the "poverty" picture the carriers in association seek to paint as the public image of the industry.

It is essential that the truth be brought to light before the industry is further contracted through mergers, passenger train reductions, freight service curtailments, and wholesale layoffs of employees. The logical way to do this is by Congressional investigation.

There hasn't been a full investigation of the financial structure of the railroad industry since the Truman-Wheeler probe in the 1930's. That investigation revealed that the railroads had evaded the law flagrantly by acquiring control of other railroads through such devices as holding companies.

This year, the President's Transportation Message to Congress pointed up the importance of railroads to the national economy and the country's military security. Railroad workers heartily agree.

Railroad workers now urge Congress to take a new and thorough look into the industry, its public service functions and its financial structure—AND TO EXPOSE ONCE AND FOR ALL THE "POVERTY" MYTH.

RAILWAY LABOR EXECUTIVES' ASSOCIATION

AMERICAN RAILWAY SUPERVISORS' ASSOCIATION • AMERICAN TRAIN DISPATCHERS' ASSOCIATION • BROTHERHOOD OF LOCOMOTIVE ENGINEERS
BROTHERHOOD OF LOCOMOTIVE FIREMEN AND ENGINEMEN • BROTHERHOOD OF MAINTENANCE OF WAY EMPLOYES • BROTHERHOOD OF RAILROAD SIGNALMEN
BROTHERHOOD OF RAILROAD TRAINMEN • BROTHERHOOD RAILWAY CARMEN OF AMERICA
BROTHERHOOD OF RAILWAY AND STEAMSHIP CLERKS, FREIGHT HANDLERS, EXPRESS AND STATION EMPLOYES • BROTHERHOOD OF SLEEPING CAR PORTERS
HOTEL & RESTAURANT EMPLOYEES AND BARTENDERS INTERNATIONAL UNION • INTERNATIONAL ASSOCIATION OF MACHINISTS
INTERNATIONAL BROTHERHOOD OF BOILERMAKERS, IRON SHIP BUILDERS, BLACKSMITHS, FORGERS AND HELPERS • INTERNATIONAL BROTHERHOOD OF ELECTRICAL WORKERS
INTERNATIONAL BROTHERHOOD OF FIREMEN & OILERS • INTERNATIONAL ORGANIZATION MASTERS, MATES & PILOTS OF AMERICA
NATIONAL MARINE ENGINEERS BENEFICIAL ASSOCIATION • ORDER OF RAILWAY CONDUCTORS AND BRAKEMEN • RAILROAD YARDMASTERS OF AMERICA
RAILWAY EMPLOYES' DEPARTMENT, AFL-CIO • SEAFARERS' INTERNATIONAL UNION OF NORTH AMERICA
SHEET METAL WORKERS' INTERNATIONAL ASSOCIATION • SWITCHMEN'S UNION OF NORTH AMERICA • THE ORDER OF RAILROAD TELEGRAPHERS

An example of indirect lobbying by the railroad unions.

Opposition to civil rights legislation—an ad in the
Washington Post of March 9, 1964.

INDEX

ABOUT THE AUTHOR

James Deakin has been a Washington correspondent for the *St. Louis Post-Dispatch* since 1954. He has covered Congress and the federal regulatory agencies and was one of the reporters who broke the story of Sherman Adams' intervention with government agencies on behalf of Boston businessman Bernard Goldfine. He is now the White House correspondent for the *Post-Dispatch*.

His experience in Washington includes coverage of the presidential campaigns of 1956, 1960 and 1964, and many other important stories. As a Congressional reporter, he covered several major lobbying campaigns, including the American Medical Association's battle against Medicare, the savings and loan industry's fight against interest and dividend withholding, the legislative struggle over natural gas regulation, the Bobby Baker hearings and the Fulbright investigation of foreign lobbying.

A native of St. Louis, he attended Washington University, where he received a B.A. degree and later did graduate work in political science. He joined the *Post-Dispatch* staff in 1951 as a reporter. He is a contributor to the *New Republic*.

34